HARPER'S NEW TESTAMENT COMMENTARIES

GENERAL EDITOR: HENRY CHADWICK, D.D.

THE EPISTLE
TO THE HEBREWS

A COMMENTARY ON

THE EPISTLE
TO THE HEBREWS

HUGH MONTEFIORE

HENDRICKSON
PUBLISHERS
PEABODY, MASSACHUSETTS 01961-3473

PREFACE

In writing this Commentary it has been my sole ambition to expound the meaning of the text which was intended by the author when he wrote it. It has been my endeavour to reduce critical problems to simple issues without sacrificing scholarly accuracy. I hope, therefore, that the Commentary may be of some use to those beginning their acquaintance with this Epistle as well as to its seasoned students.

In order not to impede the flow of the Commentary I have not cited other commentators and critics by name except where this is absolutely necessary, and for this reason my own suggestions have not been differentiated from those of my predecessors. A particular theory of authorship and origin is put forward in the Introduction, but the Commentary has been written in such a way that it is hoped to be of use to those who do not hold this particular hypothesis. Greek has been used as sparingly as possible, and in no case should the use of the Greek alphabet in the Commentary confuse a reader who has no knowledge of that language. Textual problems are discussed only when an important variant would make a real difference to the English translation. The *sigla* used are those found in the British and Foreign Bible Society's 2nd edition (1958) of the Greek New Testament.

Anyone who writes a new commentary on a New Testament book is particularly indebted to previous writers. In the case of the Epistle to the Hebrews the debt is very heavy. Particular mention must be made of the encyclopaedic knowledge of Spicq, the Hellenistic erudition of Moffatt, and the insight and acumen of Nairne, Héring, Michel and Käsemann. Special tribute must be paid to the massive common sense and extraordinary spiritual sensitivity of Westcott. Despite the advances of knowledge and learning since Westcott's day, I have found myself returning again and again to ponder his wise comments.

I would like to record my gratitude to the Cambridge group of translators of the new diglot being prepared under the auspices of the British and Foreign Bible Society; for it was in their company that my mind was first sharpened on the critical problems of this Epistle. I must also thank the Society for their kind permission to use the new English diglot translation as a basis for the translation used in this Commentary. (I have often felt bound to diverge from it, but as a basis it has been most useful.) I am also grateful to Professor Henry Chadwick for his patient help and advice, and to Miss Margaret Webb for her swift and accurate typing of the manuscript, and to Cambridge University for having given me nine months' leave of absence, thus enabling me to complete this Commentary before taking up my present work.

In keeping within the British tradition of writing commentaries, I have tried to confine myself entirely to exegesis, and I have not touched on the more difficult problems of hermeneutics. This Epistle presents particularly baffling hermeneutical problems for the twentieth century, since the imagery of cultic sacrifice (with which the Epistle is so concerned) is no longer alive for most people. Nevertheless there are deep spiritual insights in this Epistle, especially in the field of Christology, which have not yet exercised the influence on dogmatics which they deserve to have done.

Such hermeneutical problems, however, lie outside the scope of this Commentary. They are mentioned here only because of the realisation that the task of exegesis, important though it is, must lead on to the more difficult task of hermeneutics, if the New Testament is to be not only a collection of books which interests the scholar, but also one of the ways in which God may speak to men today.

HUGH MONTEFIORE

ABBREVIATIONS

COMMENTARIES

Héring	J. Héring, *L'épître aux Hébreux* (Neuchâtel, 1954).
Michel	O. Michel, *Der Brief an die Hebräer* (Göttingen, 1960).
Moffatt	J. Moffatt, *A Critical and Exegetical Commentary on the Epistle to the Hebrews* (Edinburgh, 1924).
Nairne	A. Nairne, *The Epistle to the Hebrews* (Cambridge, 1917).
Spicq	C. Spicq, *L'épître aux Hébreux* (Paris, 1952).
Westcott	B. F. Westcott, *The Epistle to the Hebrews* (London, 1889).

GENERAL

Antiq.	Antiquities.
Apol.	Apologia.
A.V.	Authorised or King James Version of 1611.
Bell. Jud.	Bellum Judaicum.
Berach.	Tractate Berachoth.
c.	chapter.
CD	fragments of a Zadokite Work ('Damascus Document').
Chag.	Chagigah.
Clem.	Clement.
col.	column.
de Abr.	de Abrahamo.
de Aet. Mundi	de Aeternitate Mundi.
de Agric.	de Agricultura.
de Cherub.	de Cherubim.
de Conf. Ling.	de Confusione Linguarum.
de Congr.	de Congressu quaerendae Eruditionis gratia.
de Dec.	de Decalogo.
de Ebriet.	de Ebrietate.

de Fuga et Inv.	de Fuga et Inventione.
de Migr. Abr.	de Migratione Abrahami.
de Plant.	de Plantatione.
de Prov.	de Providentia.
de Pudic.	de Pudicitia.
de Sacr. Abel. et Cain.	de Sacrificiis Abelis et Caini.
de Somn.	de Somniis.
de Spec. Leg.	de Specialibus Legibus.
de Virt.	de Virtutibus.
de Vita Moys.	de Vita Moysi.
Enchir.	Enchiridion.
Ep.	Epistle.
Epict.	Epictetus.
Ex. R.	Exodus Rabbah.
Gen. R.	Genesis Rabbah.
Hach. Harazim	Hacham Harazim.
Hell.	Hellenica.
H.E.	Historia Ecclesiastica.
in Flacc.	in Flaccum.
J.B.L.	Journal of Biblical Literature.
Jub.	Jubilees.
l.	line.
Leg. ad Gai.	Legatio ad Gaium.
Leg. All.	Legum Allegoriae.
LXX	Septuagint.
Mech.	Mechilta.
Men.	Tractate Menachoth.
M.T.	Massoretic Text.
N.E.B.	New English Bible.
Ned.	Tractate Nedarim.
Paid.	Paidagogos.
Pᵉsiq.	Pᵉsiqta.
1Q Apoc.	Genesis Apocryphon, from Cave 1 of Dead Sea Scrolls.
1QH	Psalms of Thanksgiving from Cave 1.
1Qp Hab	Commentary on Habakkuk from Cave 1.
1QS	Rule of Discipline, exemplar from Cave 1.
1QSa	Adjuncts to Rule of Discipline.
4Q Sl 39	Liturgical Fragments from Cave 4.
4Q Testimonia	Collection of Testimonies from Cave 4.
Quis Rer. Div.	Quis Rerum Divinarum heres sit.

ABBREVIATIONS

Quod Det. Pot.	Quod Deterius Potiori insidiari soleat.
Quod Deus	Quod Deus sit Immutabilis.
Rhet.	Rhetorica.
R.S.V.	Revised Standard Version.
R.V.	Revised Version.
Sanh.	Tractate Sanhedrin.
Strat.	Strategemata.
T. Ash.	Testament of Asher.
T. Dan	Testament of Dan.
T. Levi	Testament of Levi.
v.	verse.
Zeb.	Zebahim.

THE EPISTLE TO THE HEBREWS

INTRODUCTION

THERE was no early attribution of the Epistle to the Hebrews
in the primitive church. The first extant testimony about its
author comes from Clement of Alexandria (Eusebius, *H.E.* 6.
14), who said that Paul wrote the Epistle and that Luke translated it from Hebrew into Greek. As will be noted as the commentary proceeds, there are in the Epistle to the Hebrews many
stylistic, literary and theological points of difference from the
Pauline writings, and it is generally agreed, even by many
Roman Catholic scholars, that Paul could not have written the
Epistle.[1] There is no internal evidence to lend support to
Clement's hypothesis that the Epistle, as we now have it, is a
translation document. But could Luke have written the Epistle?
There are quite a number of points of contact. There are
similarities of style and vocabulary, as well as some correspondences with St. Luke's Gospel, or with the sources which
he used. Luke, like the author to the Hebrews, has an interest
in the Temple, and in the two covenants. But Luke, unlike our
author, is untouched by Alexandrian thought, and he is primarily
interested in facts, and not in the kind of theological speculation
with which this Epistle abounds. Furthermore, it seems incredible that, had he written the Epistle, he would not have introduced somewhere into the Acts of the Apostles a reference to
Christ's high priesthood. He emphasised there the Ascension,
and he stressed the importance of the sufferings of the Christ;
but he did not think of Christ as the high priest of the heavenly
sanctuary. Luke cannot therefore be accepted as a serious
candidate for authorship.

Origen mentions another candidate in the early church,
Clement of Rome (Eusebius, *H.E.* 6. 26). Here again there are

[1] On 24 June 1914 the Pontifical Biblical Commission stated that the
earlier doubts about the Pauline origin of the Epistle were not of such
importance that it was lawful to hesitate about reckoning it among the
genuine Epistles of the Apostle Paul. In 1955, however, the then Secretary
of the Commission stated that decrees concerning the dating and authenticity
of New Testament books were not binding upon Roman scholars (A. Miller,
Benediktinische Monatschrift, XXXI (1955), 49 ff.).

many parallels, even more striking than those which the Lucan writings provide. But Clement cannot be accepted as a likely author. The Epistle to the Hebrews is written by someone with a first-rate mind, an economical style and a great command of language. Clement's Epistle to the Corinthians is written in discursive vein by someone with a second-rate mind and an imitative style. Moreover, if Clement had written this Epistle, it is incredible that its authorship should have remained a mystery at Rome, although the Epistle itself was known there early. Clement of Rome must have known the Epistle, and he made many references to it in his letter to the Corinthians; but he could not have written it.

Tertullian (*de Pudic.* 20) attributed its authorship to Barnabas, the Cypriot Jew of levitical descent who joined with Paul on his early missionary enterprises, and who was responsible for summoning Paul from Tarsus into the limelight of the early church. It is not absolutely impossible that Barnabas could have written the letter; but it is impossible that the Epistle to the Hebrews could have been written by the author of the Epistle of Barnabas. The two Epistles have different conceptions of the meaning of the Old Testament scriptures, and of the relation of the old covenant to the new. It is probable that the Epistle to the Hebrews was attributed to Barnabas because another epistle on the same theme had already been attributed to him. Tertullian's testimony is comparatively late, and it is improbable that he had access to sources about its authorship which were unknown to his predecessors. The attribution to Barnabas (as indeed the earlier attribution to Paul and Luke) was the result of a kind of crude (and unscientific) literary criticism.

The fact seems to be that no one in the early church really knew who had written the Epistle. Modern critics have not been slow to suggest other names. Stephen, Philip, Peter, Silas, Aristion, Prisca and even Jude have been put forward by various scholars. The case for each of these candidates has been often rebutted, and the reader is referred to the relevant literature (cf. for example, Spicq, i, 202 ff.).

A commentator, by reason of his work, is brought closely into touch with the mind of the author of the work on which he is commenting. To study this Epistle is to be brought close to someone with a first-class mind abreast of its subject, who writes with an inner authority and who combines learning, originality and rigorous logic. An Epistle written by such a man would stand on its own. Its author would not wish to pretend that he had not written it, and he would not make references to people who were dead as though they were living. The mention of Timothy in He. xiii. 23 must therefore be genuine, and it may be assumed to refer to the only well-known Timothy in the early church; the one whom Paul took as his associate and fellow-worker, and who appears both in the Acts and in the Pauline Epistles. Thus the letter must have been written early on in the first century A.D.; at least during the lifetime of Timothy.

There is a further indication that the Epistle was written early in the Christian era. The writer has a splendid indifference to the actual circumstances of Jewish sacrifice in the Temple, and to the actual characters of historical high priests. Such indifference is understandable in the early part of the Apostolic Age. It could have been due to ignorance, if the author had not visited Jerusalem and had never seen at first hand the Temple, and had had no contact with the Temple Hierarchy. But after the destruction of the Jewish Temple in A.D. 70, and the consequent cessation of the high priesthood, it is inconceivable that the author of Hebrews should have written with such indifference to what actually happened. The abstract argument of this Epistle demonstrating the superiority of the new covenant with its heavenly sanctuary over the old covenant with its earthly Tent of Meeting, is understandable in the fifties, before the mutterings of Jewish revolt, and before the imminent threat of destruction to the Herodian Temple. But after that Temple had been destroyed, such an argument becomes a mere academic irrelevancy. The best argument for the supersession of the old covenant would have been the destruction of the Temple. It would seem probable, therefore, on internal grounds, that the author, whoever he was, wrote this Epistle early in the Apostolic Age. He must have been a person of great ability and originality. It is almost inconceivable that such a person should have left no mark (other than this Epistle) on the records of the primitive church.

THE EPISTLE TO THE HEBREWS

Our Epistle, while it bears the imprint of an original mind, has a very great deal in common with the theology of the other books of the New Testament. Indeed, it may be dated in the early days of the Apostolic Age, for it is firmly based on the kerygma of the primitive church. The kerygma opens with the proclamation of the fulfilment in Jesus of the promises of the Old Testament; and this is particularly marked in our Epistle, where there are some 37 actual and 70 virtual citations from the books of the old covenant. Our author, who seems to regard the Old Testament as the infallible Word of God (and who therefore never bothers to give the references to his quotations) is not really interested in the original meaning of the passages which he cites, but in their messianic sense. He gives meticulous, word by word, exegesis, pointing to their *teleiosis* or fulfilment under the new covenant. Complete fulfilment however lies in the future. The Epistle consistently manifests a futurist eschatology, according to which the pilgrim People of God have drawn near to the Last Days but have not yet actually entered them.

The death of Jesus and his glorification also receive particular emphasis; and so too the human life of Jesus. Here, indeed, the emphasis is unique among New Testament epistles. Allusions are naturally to be found to some of the events recorded in the synoptic gospels, in particular to those described in St. Luke's Gospel. It is however in the Johannine literature that theological resemblances are most to be found. The Fourth Evangelist, like our author, connects passion and glorification (John xiii. 23 ff.; cf. He. ii. 9); he alludes to Jesus' temptation without giving any details about its circumstances (John xii. 23 ff.; He. ii. 9); he regards the ministry of Jesus as in some sense priestly (cf. John xvii, the 'high priestly prayer'). There are doctrinal similarities in the prologue of St. John's Gospel and the beginning of the Epistle to the Hebrews, especially concerning the relation of the pre-existent Christ to creation. The Fourth Evangelist, like our author, is concerned with a cultus in which worship is offered only in spirit and in truth (John iv. 23), while both authors stress the royalty of Jesus (John xviii. 36; He. vi. 27) and the pre-existence of the Son (John viii. 58; He. i. 5). Nor should it be forgotten that in 1 John ii. 1 f. Jesus is called the 'expiation for our sins' (cf. He. i. 3). But perhaps the most striking simi-

4

larity is the theocentric theology found in the Fourth Gospel and in our Epistle. For the Fourth Evangelist, Jesus is completely dependent on his heavenly Father (cf. John v. 30); and in our Epistle God is the originator of all things under both covenants.

Some similarities may be found too between our Epistle and the First Epistle of St. Peter, notably in the emphasis on the suffering of Jesus (1 Peter ii. 21; cf. He. v. 8), his spotless self-oblation (1 Peter i. 19; cf. He. ix. 14), the importance of his example (1 Peter ii. 21; cf. He. xii. 2), and the spiritual sacrifice of the church (1 Peter ii. 5; cf. He. xiii. 15). It is unnecessary, however, to suppose that there is any other connection between our Epistle and these works, other than their common background in the Hellenistic world.

There is inevitably a large overlap with the theology of Paul, whose writings so faithfully reflect the common tradition of the Apostolic church. For both, God is the final and efficient cause of everything (Ro. ii. 36; He. ii. 10). For both the Law is impotent and has been abrogated by Christ (Ro. iii. 20; He. x. 1 ff.). Both set Sinai and the Heavenly Jerusalem in contrast (Gal. iv. 24 ff.; He. xii. 18 ff.). Both stress the obedience of Christ (Ro. v. 19; He. v. 8). Both regard the death of Jesus as a sacrifice, although Paul does not regard Jesus as a high priest. Both have a similar doctrine of the person of Christ.

Yet there are striking differences. Paul's favourite theological formulae 'in Christ' and 'in Christ Jesus' nowhere appear in our Epistle. Our author does not suppose his readers to be 'in Christ' so much as to be approaching God (He. iv. 16, etc.). Unlike Paul, our author has practically no theology of the Holy Spirit. For Paul, God was the Father of our Lord Jesus Christ; while for our author, God is rather the tremendous almighty omnipotent God who is described in terms not dissimilar from those of the Apocalypse. In our Epistle, Paul's characteristic doctrine of Justification finds no mention, and for him 'faith' has a different nuance from the Apostle's use of the word. For our author the church is not a permanent structure, like a building with foundations, nor does he compare it, as Paul does, to a human body. It is for him rather a household or family, the People of God, wandering upon the face of the earth until their true home in heaven is reached. Perhaps our author's most marked difference from Paul is his theocentric rather than Christocentric theology. For Paul, 'in Christ' is almost the beginning and the end of the matter; but for our author it is the work of God throughout that is most important.

Nevertheless our author has a rich doctrine of the person of Christ. Most of his terms are taken out of common tradition. He emphasises the name Jesus, because he is particularly concerned with the humanity of Jesus. Jesus is a Jew, of the tribe of Judah; but he is also the divine, self-subsistent Son of God; the Christ, the Saviour. He is the leader of our Salvation, the first-born brother in the household of God, of which he is the head. Our author has his own contribution to make in the field of Christology. Perhaps the most important is his outright description of Jesus as God (i. 8). He breaks new ground, too, when he speaks of Jesus as our High Priest (iv. 15), Envoy (iii. 1) and Forerunner (vi. 20).

If the Epistle to the Hebrews finds its place easily in the literature of the New Testament, its relationship to the Jewish literature of the Hellenistic world is not so easy to define, especially so far as Philo is concerned. Philo (whose dates are roughly 25 B.C.–A.D. 45) left behind him many books which happily have been preserved for posterity. He was an educated Jew of Alexandria, whose brother Alexander was the Alabarch and reputedly one of the wealthiest men in the ancient world. Philo, although he regarded the Old Testament as verbally inspired and had a precise knowledge of its contents, expounded it all in an allegorical manner. In this way he was able to explain it to his own way of thinking, which was Hellenistic and 'neoplatonic' rather than Jewish and biblical. By contrast with Philo, our author expounded the Old Testament with meticulous literalness, and he understood it as messianic. He found this messianic meaning, which was for him inherent in the text of the Old Testament, fulfilled in the events of the new covenant.

It would be easy to make a whole series of contrasts between Philo and our author. For the latter, salvation meant escape from the wrath of a righteous God. For Philo, salvation meant the release of the soul from the flesh in order that it might return to its spiritual home in heaven, where it had dwelt before its descent to earth. Our author is concerned with the whole People of God finding their goal in the Heavenly Jerusalem; but Philo is concerned rather with the immortality of the individual soul. For our author, God is the terrible Author of life who speaks with men and whose commands must be obeyed on pain of everlasting doom; but for Philo, God is Pure Being, utterly transcendent, absolutely self-sufficient, who can only communicate with his universe through the mediation of his Logos or Word. Again, our author is concerned with the object of faith, Philo with its psychology. Philo is eloquent about the vision of God: but for our author God is terrifying, too terrifying even to behold. For Philo, God can only be reached through the mediation of the *Logos*, that is, by the ascent of reason to the contemplation of Pure Being; but for our author God is reached through the sacrifice of Jesus Christ. So far as conduct was concerned, our author demanded obedience to commands of God; while Philo wanted the cultivation of those virtues which were highly regarded in the Hellenistic world, considering that divine chastisement and human effort were means of resisting the downward drag of material pleasures. In short, while our author believed that Jesus Christ came to fulfil the promises of the old covenant, Philo believed that Judaism was the true mystery religion, revealed to Moses, the supreme mystagogue, and allegorically described in the pages of the Old Testament.

A comparison between our author and Philo on themes common to both may help to spotlight further their differences. Thus, when our author speaks of 'elementary instruction', he is referring to the primitive Christian catechism (He. v. 13 ff.); but Philo used the same phrase to describe grammar, music, mathematics and rhetoric, all based on sensory observations and therefore earthly and not heavenly disciplines (*de Congr.* 19 ff.). For our author perfection describes the finished sacrifice of Jesus whereby his followers can attain to the fulfilment of what God has promised to them; but for Philo it means rather the possession of all the virtues and in particular freedom from bodily passions (*Leg. All.* 3. 131). For our author Abraham's journey into the unknown is the supreme example of faith in the Old Testament; but for Philo Abraham's greatness consisted in his migration from material bondage and in his marriage with Wisdom (Sarah) which led to his final enjoyment of the mystic vision (*de Migr. Abr.*). For our author Egypt is the place of sin (He. ii. 25), but for Philo Egypt is the place of material bondage (*de Agric.* 89). For our author the antitype of the wilderness tent is heaven itself (ix. 24) but for Philo the antitype consists of the immaterial forms which Moses saw with the eyes of his soul (*de Vita Moys.* 2. 73 f.). As for the furniture of the tabernacle, our author does not allegorise it (He. ix. 5); but for Philo the objects of the cultus symbolise the signs of the zodiac, the four elements, etc. (see commentary on ix. 2 ff.). According to the author of the Epistle to the Hebrews, Jesus, the ascended high priest, exercises his ministry in heaven by intercession (He. vii. 25); while, according to Philo, men rise to God through the priestly ministry of Reason (the *Logos*), which exercises its priesthood in the temple—and for Philo this means in the world (*de Somn.* 1. 215). For our author, the heavenly high priest is fittingly called Melchisadek, King of Salem, for he is King of Righteousness and King of Peace (He. vii. 2); but Philo allegorises these phrases to refer to Reason in as much as it rules with justice over the body and the soul in order to bring peace and joy and happiness (*Leg. All.* 3. 79 f.).

These differences of attitude and outlook between our author and Philo are fundamental. And yet, at the same time, the non-theological similarities between the two writers are equally striking. Many of them will be noticed in the course of the ensuing commentary. Spicq, who has made a full examination of these similarities, finds in our Epistle the ideas and metaphors, the themes and biblical methods, the style, the special vocabulary, the literary forms and the taste of Philo Judaeus (i. pp. 25-91). 'It is even possible that he [our author] had personally known him and been influenced by him [Philo]' (*op. cit.* i. p. 89). Yet the man who wrote the Epistle was not a plagiarist. His Christian convictions had profoundly altered the content and direction of his writing. His philonism has been adapted to interpret the Incarnation in the spirit of a genuine biblicism.[1] After examining the evidence, it is almost impossible

[1] Our author is similar to Philo in his apparent indifference to Rabbinism. According to I. Heinemann, Philo knew nothing of the oral traditions on

to deny the validity of Menegoz's conclusion, cited by Spicq, that our author was 'a philonian converted to Christianity'.

There is only one person who seems to satisfy all the requirements for authorship. He is Apollos. Luther first put his name forward in 1537, but since he did not support this suggestion with arguments, it must be regarded as a lucky guess. Spicq (i. p. 211-219) has collected the many arguments in support of his candidature. A summary of such arguments is given below:

(1) Apollos was of the Jewish race (Acts xviii. 24). It is difficult to believe that anyone but a Jew could have written this Epistle.

(2) Apollos was a native of Alexandria. In view of the connection between the Epistle and the works of Philo Judaeus, noted above, it seems probable that the author of the Epistle to the Hebrews was an Alexandrian.

(3) Apollos was an eloquent man, λόγιος (Acts xviii. 24). The word implies that he was gifted with the learning and the elegance of speech that are associated with eloquence. This would apply well to the author of Hebrews. Its prose is the best Greek in the New Testament. The writer has a feeling, which is unique among New Testament authors, for rhythm, assonance, language, vocabulary and syntax.

(4) Apollos was powerful in the scriptures (Acts xviii. 24). So too was the author of this Epistle. His use of scripture was not, like that of most other New Testament authors, dependent on the common tradition of the early church. In few of his scriptural quotations or arguments does he use or adapt the conventional *testimonia* of the primitive church. His was an original mind, and he was a master of sacred scripture. No other New Testament writing could be the subject of an equal claim to be written by one who was 'mighty in the scriptures'.

(5) Apollos taught 'accurately', according to Luke (Acts xviii. 25). Extreme precision of expression is a mark of Hebrews' style. Again and again *le mot juste* is used. Tenses, words,

which talmudic law was ultimately based (*Philons griechische und jüdische Bildung* [1932]). Not all scholars, however, would agree completely with this judgement (cf. E. R. Goodenough, *An Introduction to Philo Judaeus* [1962 edn.], p. 11).

arguments are all precisely employed. There is nothing vague anywhere in the whole Epistle. Very little weight could be put alone on such a slight correspondence as this; but in view of the other similarities it is perhaps not wholly insignificant.

(6) Apollos taught accurately 'the things concerning Jesus' (Acts xviii. 25). It is noteworthy that in this Epistle the name Jesus is used more than in any other Epistle. Its theme is indeed 'the things concerning Jesus'.

(7) Apollos was instructed in the way of the Lord (Acts xviii. 25). This Epistle contains more historical references to the historical Jesus than any other epistle in the canon. There are references to his birth, baptism and temptations. There is a vivid reference to his agony in Gethsemane, as well as to his death and resurrection. The author of this Epistle seems to have had a greater interest in 'the things concerning the historical Jesus' than the author of any other New Testament epistle.

(8) Apollos was 'full of spiritual fervour' (Acts xviii. 25). (The use of spirit ($\pi\nu\epsilon\hat{\upsilon}\mu\alpha$) in the Greek here does not have a technical meaning.) The Epistle to the Hebrews demands a writer who showed this quality. Its author has no standard of conduct or belief but the highest, and he incites his readers to the pursuit of perfection with a zeal and insistence that is well described as 'spiritual fervour'.

(9) Apollos 'spoke boldly' in the synagogues. Boldness of speech was a common characteristic of the primitive church; but it is perhaps not wholly insignificant that no less than four times does the author of Hebrews use the very word boldness ($\pi\alpha\rho\rho\eta\sigma\iota\alpha$) in his exhortations to his readers.

(10) Apollos was 'very helpful to those who had become believers; for he was indefatigable in confuting the Jews' (Acts xviii. 27 f.). The Epistle to the Hebrews is written to believers,[1] and would have been specially useful in resolving the doubts of Jewish converts to Christianity. The thoroughness of the author's argumentation suggests a certain indefatigableness in his character.

---

[1] The hypothesis of H. Kosmala (*Hebräer, Essener, Christen*, Leiden, 1959), that the Epistle was written to Jews who were not yet Christians, founders in particular on the author's reiterated command to his readers to stand fast to their faith.

(11) Apollos' confutation of the Jews involved 'demonstrating publicly from the scriptures that the Messiah is Jesus' (Acts xviii. 28). Once again, the use of the name Jesus as the subject of Apollos' preaching is to be noted; but even more striking is the statement that the scriptures were used by him to prove that Jesus was Messiah. For the whole argument of the Epistle to the Hebrews is based on scriptural proof; and the scriptures are used to prove that Jesus was Son of God, Messiah, Apostle and High Priest.

(12) Although the Acts of the Apostles contains only a short passage of five verses about Apollos, it is plain that he had made a deep impression on its author. Expressions are used to describe Apollos which have but few parallels elsewhere in the Acts. Moreover Paul writes of Apollos in such a way that he puts him in the same category as himself and Peter (1 Cor. i. 12, iii. 22). Such a category would be appropriate to the person who wrote the Epistle to the Hebrews.

The arguments mentioned above are not original, and in the past they have led many scholars to believe that this Epistle was written by Apollos. They do however fall short of proof. They are compatible with Apollos' authorship of the Epistle, but they do not demonstrate that he must have written it. They fail to shed light on the place from which the Epistle was written, the circumstances and date of its composition, and the destination to which it was sent. Many different places of destination have been put forward, both by those who have held that Apollos wrote the Epistle and by others who have not. Spain, Ravenna, Berea, Ephesus, Colossae and Laodicea, other cities of Galatia, Cyprus, Alexandria, Antioch, Palestine and especially Jerusalem, Jamnia and Caesarea; these have all been put forward. The suggestion was made in the last century[1] that the letter was sent to Corinth after the composition of the Pauline Corinthian correspondence, but this hypothesis has not found much

---

[1] M. Weber, *De numero epistolarum ad Corinthios rectius constituendo*, Wittenberg, 1798–1806; D. Mack, 'Über die ursprünglichen Leser des Briefes an die Hebräer', *Theologische Quartalschrift* (1838), 385–428; Albani, *Zeitschrift für Wissenschaftl. Theologie* (1904), 88–93; H. Appel, *Der Hebräerbrief, ein Schreiben des Apollos an Judenchristen der Korinthischen Gemeinde* (Leipzig, 1918).

support. But it may have been written to the Corinthian church before Paul had sent any letters to the Corinthians at all. Indeed, if there is a literary relationship between this Epistle and Paul's First Epistle to the Corinthians, the Epistle to the Hebrews is almost certainly prior. For it would have been not unnatural for Paul to take up the first four chapters of his Epistle to defend himself against an attack based on a twisting of an earlier letter by Apollos to the Corinthians. But it is hardly conceivable that Apollos (or anyone else), if he was drawing on 1 Corinthians for some of his ideas, would have used only the first four chapters of that letter. Moreover, in these four chapters Paul is explicitly attempting to correct his readers' idea of the relationship of himself and Apollos. This in turn suggests that something that Apollos had said or written had been misunderstood by the Corinthians. A possible reconstruction of events is offered here on the grounds that the Epistle to the Hebrews was written to the church at Corinth by Apollos at Ephesus sometime between A.D. 52 and A.D. 54, while Paul was on his tour of Caesarea, Antioch and the churches of Galatia (Acts xviii. 20-23).[1]

Paul had left Corinth in A.D. 51, probably during the autumn shortly after he had been brought before Gallio (who was pro-consul of Asia from the summer of A.D. 51 until A.D. 52). He journeyed from Corinth to Ephesus, accompanied by Prisca and Aquila, who had settled in Corinth after Claudius' edict banishing all Jews from Rome. Prisca and Aquila seem to have stayed in Ephesus for a few years (and Paul's greetings to them in Ro. xvi. 3 f. may have been sent to them while they were still in Ephesus). They may well have returned to Rome soon after A.D. 54, when Claudius died. After Paul had left Ephesus, Apollos arrived there. He had come from Alexandria. There is no hint from Acts that Apollos had been to Jerusalem, although there was a synagogue of Alexandrians there (Acts vi. 9). It seems improbable on internal grounds that the author of Hebrews had paid a long visit to Jerusalem, because the Epistle

---

[1] After this introduction had been written, Professor C. F. D. Moule very kindly pointed out to me that the same hypothesis had been suggested in a posthumous article by Professor Lo Bue ('The Historical Background of the Epistle to the Hebrews', *J.B.L.* (75) 1958, pp. 52-57). I am glad to find support there for some of the suggestions that follow.

shows almost no signs of Jewish rabbinical learning and its account of sanctuary and priesthood is purely biblical and 'academic'.

It seems likely, from the narrative of Acts, that Paul, when he left Ephesus for Caesarea and Antioch, did not take Silas with him. He probably, like Timothy, stayed behind (cf. Acts xvii. 14). Silas might then have been able to help Apollos in his composition of the closing words of his Epistle just as he had assisted Paul in the composition of 1 and 2 Thessalonians (1 Thess. i. 1; 2 Thess. i. 1) and would later assist Peter in the writing of 1 Peter (1 Peter v. 12). This, as E. G. Selwyn has suggested, would provide the explanation of the striking similarities, between He. xiii. 20 f. and the other three Epistles, which Selwyn lists in his commentary on *The First Epistle of St. Peter* (1946), p. 465.

Apollos had only known the baptism of John. Possibly he had learnt what he knew about Jesus and the Christian Way from the other converts whom Paul later found at Ephesus when he returned there in A.D. 54 (cf. Acts xix. 1-7); but it is equally possible, from the evidence of Acts, that Apollos converted these Ephesians to his own Johannite version of Christianity which he had brought from Alexandria. The fact that there were Twelve of them at Ephesus[1] suggests a headquarters of the movement there, possibly analogous to the Twelve whom Jesus chose. Like them Apollos may be presumed to have been baptised into the name of the Lord Jesus (cf. He. vi. 2), and he would also have had hands laid upon him. The laying on of hands (as part of Christian initiation) is only mentioned in the New Testament in connection with Samaritan converts (Acts viii. 17) and these Ephesian converts (Acts xix. 6). It was probably an additional rite necessary for the release of the Spirit among 'fringe Christians'. In the case of the Ephesian converts, they would have already received the baptism of John, and they needed something more than mere rebaptism in the name of Jesus if they were to share the emotional feelings of assurance which, for Luke, were a manifestation of the Holy Spirit. Herein may be the explanation of the difficult phrase ἐπιθέσεώς τε

[1] Luke elsewhere uses ὡσεί to designate a particular number (cf. Luke iii. 23; ix. 14; xxiii. 44).

χειρῶν in He. vi. 2. The inclusion of laying on of hands in a list of elementary Christian teaching is best explicable in the light of Apollos' own Christian initiation, where this rite would have formed part of his special admission to full Christian membership, as one who had previously known only John's baptism. Furthermore, the usual word for Christian baptism is not βαπτισμός (as here) but βάπτισμα; and the plural form 'doctrine of baptisms' in He. vi. 2 is a strange usage (contrast the 'one baptism' of Eph. iv. 5), unless Apollos is again writing out of his own experience. For he would have received teaching about two baptisms, the baptism of Jesus and the baptism of John (and of the latter Josephus actually uses βαπτισμός in *Antiq.* 18. 5. 2).

Here too may be found the explanation of the difficult phrase in He. x. 22, which occurs in what is generally agreed to be a baptismal context. In the New Testament baptism is described as a form of washing (cf. 1 Cor. vi. 11; Eph. v. 26; Titus iii. 5), but it is explicitly contrasted with bodily washing (1 Peter iii. 21). How then could Apollos in this passage use the phrase 'our bodies washed with pure water'? According to Josephus, the baptism of John was 'a means of purifying the body', which followed after spiritual purification (*Antiq.* 18. 5. 2). (Josephus' interpretation of Johannite baptism is likely to be more accurate than that of the Evangelists, since the latter naturally understood John's baptism in the light of Christian baptism, with which they were familiar.) Apollos had only recently been initiated fully into Christian practice, having previously known only the baptism of John; and this difficult phrase would at least be more understandable if it was Apollos who penned it, rather than someone who had never known Johannite baptism.

Corinth and Ephesus were among the great cities of the ancient world. Direct communication was possible by sea between them. There must have been considerable trade between the two ports. Communication between the Christian churches of the two cities must have been comparatively easy. According to the Western text of Acts xviii. 27, some Corinthians who were living at Ephesus, and who had listened to Apollos, invited him to make the journey with them to their home country; and when he agreed, the Ephesians wrote to the disciples in Corinth to ask them to receive him; and while he was living in Achaea he was very helpful in the synagogues. There is no good reason to doubt the substantial accuracy of this information.

Apollos, then, visited Corinth (Acts xix. 1), and was very well received. A man of his stature could hardly have failed to make a profound impression. Paul later spoke well of his visit (1 Cor. iii. 6-9), and encouraged him to make a second visit (1 Cor. xvi. 12). Apollos then returned from Corinth to Ephesus, where news reached him about difficulties in the Corinthian church.

Up to this point the movements of Apollos have been reconstructed straightforwardly from direct evidence in the New Testament. From this point onwards a reconstruction is offered on the hypothesis that Apollos wrote the Epistle to the Hebrews. It seems that he would have liked to make a visit to Corinth himself, but he could not at the moment (He. xiii. 19). He seems to have hoped to come soon with Timothy (He. xiii. 23), who was well known to the Corinthians because he had joined Paul during Paul's first stay there (Acts xviii. 5). In fact Timothy did not set out for Corinth until Paul sent him after he had returned to Ephesus in A.D. 54 (1 Cor. iv. 17; xvi. 10). The 'release' of Timothy (He. xiii. 23) suggests that he had been imprisoned. Nothing is known of this Ephesian imprisonment, just as nothing is known of a possible imprisonment of Paul when he fought with wild beasts at Ephesus (1 Cor. xv. 32).

Instead of paying a return visit to Corinth, Apollos, it is suggested, wrote a letter, the Epistle now known as 'To the Hebrews'. Apollos obviously took great pains over its composition, and he wrote it after the style of Greek rhetoric. The absence of the conventional opening of New Testament Epistles suggests that it was originally written more as a homily than as a letter. Apollos was noted not for his letters but for his oral preaching and teaching (Acts xviii. 25), so that his prose style might be expected to be rhetorical rather than epistolary. The circumstances in which the Epistle was first penned are unknown. Possibly Apollos may have intended to read his homily in person, but later, in view of a deteriorating situation, he decided not to return to Corinth (cf. 1 Cor. xvi. 12b). The Epistle would have been addressed to the church at Corinth, with particular reference to its Jewish Christian members who were causing trouble. The word 'Hebrews' is actually used by Paul to designate the Corinthian troublemakers, when he borrows his opponents' bravado.[1] 'Are they Hebrews? So am I. Israelites? So am I. Abraham's descendants? So am I.' (2 Cor. xi. 22). It is suggested that these are the Hebrews against whom the 'Epistle to the Hebrews' was especially aimed. The major doctrinal theme of the Epistle is priesthood, and from other New Testament writings emanating from or written to Asia Minor (1 Peter, the Johannine literature, Revelation and the Epistles of Ignatius and Polycarp) it is plain that there was there much Christian speculation on this subject.

But the Epistle is not solely addressed to the Jewish element in the Christian church. Former pagans as well as Jewish Christians may well have had a great interest in the Old Testament scriptures. In any case, the warning about pre-marital and extra-marital sexual relationships (He. xiii. 4; cf. xii. 16) could hardly have been intended for Jewish Christians, but rather for former pagans. The Epistle is written to a mixed Church, predominantly Jewish in origin.

Various attempts have been made to identify the movement within Judaism to which the recipients of this Epistle belonged. The suggestion that our author's readers were ex-Sadducees breaks down because the first chapter of the Epistle shows that Jesus is superior to angels. This could not have been written to former Sadducean priests, since they did not even believe in the existence of angels (cf. Acts xxiii. 8). On the other hand, an almost complete absence throughout the Epistle of the rabbinic method of interpretation makes it impossible to assume that it was written either by a Pharisee or to a Pharisee.

In the last decade it has become fashionable to assume that there was a connection of some sort between the author (or his readers) and the Covenanters at Qumran. This Essene hypothesis has received support from many scholars, and similarities

---

[1] *Hebrews* here means Hebrew Christians and it has none of the associations suggested by M. Black, *The Scrolls and Christian Origins* (1961), pp. 78 ff. The word probably designates Hebrew-speaking Christians when used in Acts vi. 1 and 2 Cor. xi. 22. This in turn suggests that Paul was engaged in Corinth in a struggle with the agents of Palestinian Judaism. This perhaps explains the 'Cephas party' (1 Cor. i. 12; iii. 22).

have been pointed out by O. Michel,[1] Yigael Yadin,[2] R. Spicq,[3] H. Kosmala,[4] R. Schnackenburg,[5] J. Betz,[6] F. F. Bruce,[7] J. Bowman[8] and others. Opinion has differed whether the Epistle was written to Essene converts to Christianity, to Essenes not yet converted to Christianity, or to Christians in danger of lapsing to Essenism. (Some writers suggest that Acts vi. 7 refers to a movement among Essenes to embrace Christianity.) All such theories presuppose a literary and theological relationship between the Epistle to the Hebrews and the Qumran literature. The list of correspondences at first sight seems formidable. Similarities have been suggested concerning methods of exegesis, rituals of initiation, strict disciplinary attitudes towards sin and penitence, the meaning of faith, and identity of moral virtues (especially those mentioned in He. xiii). Correspondences have been pointed out on liturgical matters (especially in the belief in an eschatological high priest, a high doctrine of angels, and a doxological approach to worship). Both sets of writings are said to have similar emphases on exile and sojourn in the desert, migration and pilgrimage. Many identities or close similarities of theological language have been noted. Certain similarities of belief about the fulfilment of the promised new covenant have not escaped the notice of critics.

This is not the place to consider all these alleged correspondences. J. Coppens, in a recent article,[9] has subjected them to critical examination, and the present writer would endorse his conclusions:

> The positive doctrinal contacts between the Epistle to the

[1] *Der Brief an die Hebräer* (10th ed., 1957).
[2] 'The Scrolls and the Epistle to the Hebrews', *Scripta Ierosolymitana*, IV (1958), 36-55.
[3] 'L'Épître aux Hébreux: Apollos, Jean-Baptiste, les Hellénistes et Qumran', *Revue de Qumran*, I (1959), 365-390.
[4] *Hebräer, Essener, Christen* (Leiden, 1959).
[5] 'Die Kirche im Neuen Testament', *Quaestiones Disputatae*, no. 14, (Freiburg, 1961).
[6] *Die Eucharistie in der Zeit der griechischen Väter* (Freiburg, 1961), II. i.
[7] '"To the Hebrews" or "To the Essenes"', *New Testament Studies*, IX (1963), 217-232.
[8] *Hebrews, James, I and II Peter* (London, 1963).
[9] 'Les Affinités qumraniennes de l'épître aux Hébreux', *Nouvelle Revue Théologique*, 84 (1962), 128-141, 257-282.

Hebrews and the Qumran writings are seen to be few and unspecific. . . . In sum, the analogies of the Epistle with the Qumran documents are not such as to make us admit that the author of the Christian writing knew from close at hand the Essene *milieu* or that it had made a marked impression on him. The greatest affinities are found in the hortatory sections. But do these affinities of thought and vocabulary transcend, even there, the common inheritance shared by all Jewish circles? Are they not explained if they are seen to belong to a similar literary environment on which writers who were more or less contemporary were able to draw?[1]

It is possible to make an impressive list of correspondences between most sets of documents emanating from the Jewish milieu of the first century A.D. Indeed, our Epistle seems closer to Philo than to Qumran. More important than similarities are its basic differences, which will be noted in the course of the commentary.

The preservation of the Epistle in spite of its anonymity argues that it must have been sent originally to an important church. Its internal evidence requires a well-known early-founded church of the Diaspora consisting of converted Jews, proselytes and pagans, such as Corinth. Such correspondences as exist between the Epistle and Stephen's speech in Acts may be fully explained by the fact that both bear the marks of the common outlook of Diaspora Judaism (cf. commentary on pp. 137 f.).[2]

Apollos, if he was writing to the Corinthians from Ephesus, naturally would have included the greetings of 'those from Italy' (He. xiii. 24), just as Paul later sent greetings from Aquila and Prisca and the church in their house at Ephesus (1 Cor. xvi. 19). These are the only people in the whole of the New Testament who are described as natives of Italy, and as they had lived for some time at Corinth and had been prominent members there of the Corinthain church, they would naturally have wished to send their salutations to the Corinthian Christians, many of whom they must have known well.

[1] *Op. cit.*, pp. 270 f.
[2] This seems a more probable explanation than the missionary hypothesis advanced by W. Manson, *The Epistle to the Hebrews* (London, 1957).

INTRODUCTION

The situation of the church to which the Epistle to the Hebrews was addressed seems to suit what is known of the Corinthian church. It was a church which had had from its birth difficulties brought about by Jewish opposition, and which was probably regarded with hostility by the Gentile population of the city (although not by the Roman authorities, who were indifferent to it). Paul had a vision there that no one would do him harm (Acts xviii. 10), not that other Corinthian Christians would be unharmed by Jewish opposition. The Gentile resentment was manifested by a general attack on Sosthenes, who held office in the Jewish synagogue (Acts xviii. 16). Gallio the governor was quite unconcerned, just as he refused to intervene in favour of the Jews in matters which he regarded as 'bickering about words and names and the Jewish law' (Acts xviii. 15). It seems that after Apollos had paid his visit, considerable pressure was put on the Jewish Christians to apostatise and relapse into Judaism. Jewish pressure to repudiate Paul's leadership may have been particularly strong, since he is reported to have cursed the Jews at Corinth in words reminiscent of Jesus' trial (Acts xviii. 6). There seems to have been a tendency not merely to repudiate Paul, but also the leaders he had appointed (cf. He. xiii. 24). The readers are asked to remember what happened when they were first converted (He. x. 32 ff.). At Corinth they had suffered abuse and persecution (Acts xviii. 6). It seems too that others besides Paul had been arrested (He. x. 32), and had suffered seizure of their goods, probably at the hands of the Jews. Paul had been made a public spectacle (1 Cor. iv. 9) as well, it would seem, as other members of the church (He. x. 32). Conditions appear to have become worse even than they had been in the early days; for then the Jewish Christians of Corinth had been firm in their faith, and filled with the zeal of the newly converted. But when the Epistle to the Hebrews was written, its readers had degenerated (He. x. 32), and they were in danger of succumbing to Jewish pressure (He. vi. 4 ff.). Meanwhile the pressure against them seems to have increased. Sosthenes, who had held office in the Jewish synagogue and who had had a public beating up by Gentiles (Acts xviii. 17), may have been later converted, and may have preferred to make his home in Ephesus rather than stay in Corinth (1 Cor. i. 1).[1] Nevertheless, despite these difficulties, the Corinthian church had remained generous. Subscriptions had not yet been solicited for the Jerusalem Aid Fund (1 Cor. xvi. 1-4) but both Apollos and Paul congratulated their readers (in almost identical words) on their past and present 'ministry to the saints' (1 Cor. xvi. 15; He. vi. 10). Possibly it is help for the Jerusalem church that was intended here.

Apollos' letter was intended to stir up the enthusiasm of his Christian readers, to show them the superiority of Christianity over the Judaism into which they were in danger of lapsing, and to rally them behind their leaders. He hoped to encourage them to remain steadfast under trial, and to endure persecution even if bloodshed, as he feared, might ensue (He. xii. 4); for the Christian hope was an abiding city beside which the changes and chances of this fleeting world could be seen in proper perspective.

If the hypothesis so far advanced be accepted, then it must be agreed that Apollos' letter both succeeded and failed. It succeeded in so far as nothing more is heard about the view that Jesus was really an angel incognito during his earthly life, if indeed anyone had ever really believed this. (Apollos was concerned to show that Jesus is *superior* to angels, not that he is not an angel.) He succeeded also in raising the morale of the Corinthian Christians. No more is heard of the danger of the Jewish Christians among them lapsing into Judaism. Their deviations took another turn.

It appears that in other ways the Epistle was not successful. Apollos' warning not to be avaricious for money seems to have fallen on deaf ears (He. xiii. 5 f.; cf. 1 Cor. vi. 1-9). Apollos had told his readers that they needed elementary instruction about baptisms (He. vi. 2); but the Corinthians still seem to have needed this when Paul wrote 1 Cor. i. 14-17. Apollos had told his readers that they needed further instruction about the resurrection and eternal judgement (He. vi. 2), but the Corinthians seem to have been extraordinarily perverse about these matters when Paul wrote 1 Cor. xv. 12-32. Again, Apollos had warned his readers about strange foods (He. xiii. 9 f.), without any real

[1] It is possible, of course, that Sosthenes in Acts xviii. 17 is a different person from Sosthenes of 1 Cor. i. 1. The name was not uncommon.

knowledge of what the trouble was about. Paul, on the basis of accurate information about the matter, found it necessary to expound in some detail the Christian attitude to food (1 Cor. viii. 7-13, x. 23-32).

In a special way Apollos' advice failed. His warning about fornication and adultery, so far from being heeded, seems to have been totally ignored, and the position degenerated badly. In what is probably a fragment of Paul's first letter to the Corinthians (to which allusion is made in 1 Cor. v. 9 and which can be found in 2 Cor. vi. 14-vii. 1) Paul echoed the very words and Old Testament citation which Apollos, on this hypothesis, had earlier used. Paul used as one of the 'promises' a citation from 2 Sam. vii. 14 (used in He. i. 5, albeit in a different connection). Paul also urged his readers that we should 'cleanse ourselves from all that can defile flesh or spirit' (cf. He. ix. 14), 'and in the fear of God' (cf. He. xii. 28) 'complete our consecration' (cf. He. x. 14). Paul reminded the Corinthians that they were 'the temple' of the living God (the same image put to a different use in Hebrews *passim*). This warning of Paul, however, seems to have had as little effect on the Corinthians as Apollos had on his readers, and things had gone from bad to worse by the time that Paul wrote 1 Cor. v-vi.

It would seem that Apollos' letter did not merely fail because its contents were unheeded. In one sense it could be said that they were heeded only too well. His letter seems to have been twisted and misrepresented by the dissident Christians of Corinth. It was apparently used against Paul. An 'Apollos party' was formed in Corinth, and in opposition to it there were 'the Paul party' and 'the Cephas party' and 'the Christ party' (1 Cor. i. 12 f.). Apollos himself seems to have had some fear of this when he wrote his Epistle, for he declared that his own conscience was clear (He. xiii. 18). From his command to his readers to obey their leaders (He. xiii. 17), it seems that Apollos already had some inkling of the incipient revolt at Corinth against church authority, and in particular against Paul. He went out of his way to demand the loyalty of his readers, and to demonstrate his own loyalty to those who had founded the Corinthian church. 'Remember those that had the rule over you,' he wrote, 'who spoke to you the word of God' (He. xiii.

7). Paul was later to write: 'Be imitators of me' (1 Cor. iv. 16). Apollos had already been careful to write to his readers about the founding fathers who had first preached at Corinth: 'Considering the outcome of their way of life, imitate their faith' (He. xiii. 7).

When Paul returned to Ephesus from his inland journey via the churches of Galatia (Acts xix. 1), he may be presumed to have met Apollos at Ephesus, who by this time had returned from his visit to Corinth and who had already written them his Epistle. No doubt Paul and he struck up a warm friendship through their fellowship in the Gospel and their common passion for theology and apologetics; for Paul speaks warmly of him (1 Cor. xvi. 12). No doubt Apollos would have put him into the Corinthian picture as far as he knew it. But more news followed, worse news; possibly Sosthenes had arrived (cf. 1 Cor. i. 1); Stephenas, Fortunatus and Achaicus followed (1 Cor. xvi. 17); a letter from Corinth asking for advice had been received; and members of Chloe's household had brought news of schism and factions within the Corinthian church (1 Cor. i. 11). Paul had already written one letter (cf. 1 Cor. v. 9); now he wrote 1 Corinthians.

When Paul wrote the first four chapters of 1 Corinthians, he plainly had a polemical purpose. This purpose may perhaps be best understood against the background of the Epistle to the Hebrews. It seems that his enemies were using this letter to damage his reputation and to repudiate his authority. Paul is, in 1 Cor. i-iv, defending himself against the charge that he is inferior to Apollos. Cephas enters the argument (1 Cor. i. 12, iii. 22) but the real question of the moment concerns only Paul and Apollos (1 Cor. iii. 5, iv. 6).[1] Possibly this is because Apollos was Paul's friend and so he had a real chance of winning over the 'Apollos party'.[2] Paul seems to have been in a difficult position. He had apparently the highest opinion of Apollos, who seems later to have been his friend and companion (Titus iii. 13).[3] He did not write a word against him, yet it would seem that

[1] Peter is mentioned twice and Apollos six times in the first four chapters.
[2] I owe this suggestion to Dr. E. Bammel.
[3] According to P. N. Harrison (*Problem of the Pastoral Epistles* (1921), pp. 115-118) Titus iii. 12-13 is a genuine note written by Paul to Titus between the 'severe letter' and 2 Cor. while Titus was at Corinth.

he alluded to the Epistle that Apollos had written, and to the wrong use that was being made of this letter by the mutinous Corinthians. The following points may be suggested in favour of such a hypothesis:

(1) Apollos had told the Corinthians that the gospel was confirmed for them by those who had first heard it (He. ii. 3), but Paul further congratulated the Corinthians that 'the evidence for the truth of Christ has found confirmation' in them (1 Cor. i. 6). It is perhaps not wholly insignificant that both in Hebrews and in 1 Cor. ἐβεβαιώθη is used. This word is somewhat unusual in the New Testament.

Apollos had expressed the hope that the Corinthians would keep their faith firm to the end (He. iii. 14). His letter in this respect at least was successful. Paul used the same word as he assures the Corinthians that God will keep them firm to the end (1 Cor. i. 8). Perhaps there may be just a trace of contrast here. Apollo was a 'semi-Pelagian', urging his hearers to greater effort. Paul was a 'semi-Augustinian', urging his readers to open their hearts fully to the grace of God.

These correspondences would rightly be regarded as trivial, were it not for the fact that they must be seen in the light of other similarities.

(2) Paul wrote that he 'declared the attested truth of God without display of fine words or wisdom' (1 Cor. ii. 1). The Corinthians may well have claimed that Apollos had used an eloquence which Paul lacked. The style and language of the Epistle has an elegance lacking in Paul's Corinthian correspondence. Paul seems to have answered the charge by saying that he was content to carry conviction by spiritual power (1 Cor. ii. 4).

(3) Apollos regarded 'strong meat' as suitable only for the 'mature' (He. v. 14), and although his readers did not deserve as yet the title of 'mature Christians', nevertheless he determined to go forward with them to fully mature teaching (He. vi. 1). The Corinthians thereupon claimed that they *were* mature. They seem to have told Paul that

they no longer needed his simple doctrine. Paul admitted that when he came first among them, he had determined to know nothing but Christ crucified (1 Cor. ii. 2). But he refused to allow the charge that he was not suitable to lead mature Christians. 'Howbeit we do speak wisdom among the mature', he claims (1 Cor. ii. 6). The same word τέλειος is used. Philo's use of this word shows that it was part of the common linguistic stock of Hellenistic Judaism, but the choice of the same word by Paul in this apologetic passage suggests that he is defending himself against an attack on himself concerning 'mature' Christians.

(4) Paul in his letter next turned to the doctrine of the Holy Spirit (1 Cor. ii. 10-16). In He. v. 13 ff., Apollos wrote about mature men having proper *discrimination*. In 1 Cor. ii. 11 ff. Paul explained that true Christian *discrimination* is a gift of the Holy Spirit. It seems that he was suggesting that this was just what the would-be followers of Apollos at Corinth lacked themselves. Apollos had written that all things are naked and prostrate before God, and that there is no creature that is invisible to him (He. iv. 13). He discerns the thoughts and feelings of the heart (He. iv. 12). Paul underlined that when the Lord comes, the counsels of men's hearts would be disclosed for all to see, and then Paul will be justified (1 Cor. iv. 5).

(5) Paul next claimed that he fed the Corinthians with milk (γάλα) and not with meat (1 Cor. iii. 2). But Apollos had written that his readers needed 'someone to teach them the ABC of God's oracles again: it has come to this, that you need milk (γάλα) instead of solid food' (He. v. 12). It seems as though Paul were defending himself against the charge that he had not given them proper instruction; for he writes: 'For you were not able to bear it; no, not even now can you bear it' (1 Cor. iii. 2). Once again, the use by Philo of γάλα in this connection shows that it was part of the linguistic stock which Apollos and Paul both used, but the context suggests that Paul is deliberately defending himself against attack at this point.

(6) Apollos had written that when the earth drinks in the rain

that falls upon it, it brings forth a useful crop: but if it bears thorns and thistles, it is only fit for burning (He. vi. 7 f.). The Corinthians may have twisted the meaning of this. Whereas Apollos had intended this as a warning to his readers, they seem to have understood it in the sense that it was Apollos who had given them the spiritual rain which would make them bring forth a good crop; Apollos, not Paul. Paul agreed that they were God's field (1 Cor. iii. 9), but replied: 'I planted, Apollos watered; but God gave the increase' (1 Cor. iii. 6). Moreover, Paul insisted that he who planted and he who watered belonged to the same team (1 Cor. iii. 8), so that any attempt of the Corinthians to drive a wedge between himself and Apollos would be fruitless.

(7) Apollos had never claimed that he had laid the foundation of the Corinthian church. He had written to his readers that they ought to be laying over again the foundation (θεμέλιος) of their faith (He. vi. 1), but he did not propose to do this himself, but preferred to push on to mature doctrine (He. vi. 3). The Corinthians thereupon took the opportunity to accuse Paul of giving them only elementary instruction. Paul replied: 'As a wise master builder I laid a foundation (θεμέλιον), and another [i.e. Apollos] builds on it' (1 Cor. iii. 10). Paul goes on to issue a warning. The Corinthians are twisting Apollos' teaching. 'Let each man take heed how he builds on it. For no other foundation can any man lay than that which has been laid, that is, Jesus Christ' (1 Cor. iii. 11). It seems more probable that Paul here is defending himself against a misunderstanding of He. vi. 1 than of Matt. xvi. 18, for Paul is not here defending himself against Petrine claims.

(8) Apollos had written that land which did not bear fruit had a curse hanging over it, and was fit only for burning (He. vi. 8). Paul, however, once again seems to have softened the rigorism of Apollos. The Corinthians were building a false superstructure on Paul's foundation. This did not mean, however, that their doom had been sealed. If the superstructure was sound, it would remain; but if it was unsound, it would be consumed, but the person concerned

would be saved 'but only as through fire' (1 Cor. iii. 13-15).

(9) The Corinthians had put aside Paul's teaching that they were 'a holy temple' unto the Lord. Apollos had taught that the true tabernacle was heaven. How could they then constitute a 'temple'? Why need they then be 'holy'? Paul corrected them by a statement of his position, namely that they (the Corinthians) constitute the real Temple, which is holy because it is inspired by God's spirit (1 Cor. iii. 16 f.; cf. 2 Cor. vi. 16).

(10) Apollos had stressed the importance of faithfulness, and had demonstrated that Jesus was 'faithful' as Son and builder over his household, while Moses had been faithful as servant and member of the household (He. iii. 2-6). The Corinthians accused Paul of being unfaithful as a servant and steward over the household of God at Corinth. This was because he did not stand in the tradition of Moses, and was therefore unacceptable to the 'Hebrews'. Paul agreed that it was required of stewards to be found trustworthy (1 Cor. iv. 1 f.). The same word πιστός is actually used here as in the Epistle to the Hebrews. Paul replied that it was for God, and not for any man, not even for himself, to judge his faithfulness (1 Cor. iv. 4).

(11) Apollos' arguments had been based on strict exegesis of biblical texts. The Corinthian rebels had twisted his arguments and gone beyond scripture. Paul therefore wrote: 'I have applied all this to myself and Apollos for your benefit, brothers, that you may learn by us not to go beyond scripture, that none of you may be puffed up in favour of one over another' (1 Cor. iv. 6). Paul was recalling the Corinthians to the scriptural limits of Apollos' teaching. If ἃ γέγραπται means here simply 'what has been written', Paul may be understood to be warning the Corinthians not to go beyond what Apollos had actually written in his letter.

(12) The Corinthian rebels, in attacking Paul and regarding him as inferior to Apollos, had neglected the respect due to their founding father. Apollos, in his Epistle, had been careful to call his readers 'brothers' (He. iii. 1, 12),

'beloved' (He. vi. 1), never children. Paul, however, wrote to admonish them as 'his beloved children' (1 Cor. iv. 14). Though they had countless guides in Christ, they had only one father. 'I urge you, therefore, be imitators of me' (1 Cor. iv. 16; cf. He. xiii. 7). Paul asked his readers to give up their stupid championship of Apollos (who did not wish for their allegiance) and to return to his allegiance, their founding father.

(13) Those members of the Corinthian church who were in danger of lapsing into Judaism had been habitually absenting themselves from meetings of the church at which, it may be safely assumed, the Christian Eucharist was celebrated (He. x. 25). Apollos warned them about this in the most rigorous terms. As a result, the dissident Corinthians seem to have attended future meetings, but without any real attempt at reformation, with the result that many fell sick and some even died (1 Cor. xi. 30). The Corinthians' behaviour was scandalous. Although they now came together, it was not to eat the Lord's supper (1 Cor. xi. 20). Apollos had warned his readers that their persistent and deliberate absenteeism would result in the terrifying expectation of judgement (He. x. 27), since they had profaned the blood of the covenant. Although the Corinthians now attended the Eucharist, Paul had to warn them that they had come under judgement (1 Cor. xi. 29) since by their behaviour they had desecrated the body and blood of Christ (1 Cor. xi. 27) by which the new covenant had been consecrated (1 Cor. xi. 25). Apollos had said that such behaviour was unforgivable (He. x. 26); but the less rigorous Paul regarded it more lightly as resulting not in condemnation but chastening (1 Cor. xi. 32).

These points of contact between Hebrews and 1 Corinthians are all but one taken from the first four chapters of the latter, and mostly from chapters five, six and thirteen of the Epistle to the Hebrews. Some points are much more telling than others. Some correspondences may be regarded as mere coincidences of expression arising out of the common linguistic stock used by Paul and the author of Hebrews. The hypothesis must be judged by the cumulative strength of so many points of similarity. To these must be added other points of contact, in addition to those previously mentioned, which suggest that Paul had read the Epistle to the Hebrews when he wrote 1 Corinthians, or that he wrote from a similar background of thought.

(a) Paul used the same Old Testament type of the wilderness wanderings as Apollos did in order to warn the Corinthians of the danger of their ways (1 Cor. x. 1-13; cf. He. iii and iv).

(b) Paul used Psalm viii. 6 to show that all things will be (but are not yet) in subjection to the Son (1 Cor. xv. 27). The use of the same text is very similar in He. ii. 8.

(c) Paul wrote of 'the Holy Spirit apportioning to each one individually as he wills' (1 Cor. xii. 11) in words very reminiscent of 'gifts of the Holy Spirit apportioned according to his will' (He. ii. 4).

It may perhaps be noted that, just as the author of Hebrews combined a *Logos* doctrine (He. i. 2 f.) with a futurist eschatology (He. ix. 28), so Paul describes Christ in 1 Cor. i. 24, 30 as the Wisdom of God and as the agent in creation in 1 Cor. viii. 6, and this too is combined with a futurist eschatology (1 Cor. i. 7 f.). Neither, however, actually designates Christ as the *Logos*. This shows that both writers had similar Christologies. If the general hypothesis here put forward finds favour, Apollos rather than Paul may have been the early church's pioneer in the realm of Christology.

These considerations would seem to suggest that the Epistle to the Hebrews was written at Ephesus by Apollos to the church at Corinth, and especially to the Jewish Christian members of it, in A.D. 52–54. Further corroboration of this thesis may be found from a consideration of 1 Clement. Clement cited from 1 Corinthians frequently to drive home his points to his Corinthian readers. The use which Clement made of the Epistle to the Hebrews is even more remarkable, especially as he referred to it at least thirteen times and this is the first time that the Epistle is quoted by the Fathers (as well as the last time for quite a period). Clement may have cited the Epistle to the Hebrews so often because he knew that it had been sent originally to the Corinthians. Before he wrote his letter, he had doubtless informed himself of any early letters which they had in their archives. Members of the Roman Church may have visited Corinth for this purpose: Corinthians had a reputation for hospitality (1 Clem. i), and Clement's Epistle itself was to be despatched by special envoys who were to stay at Corinth (1 Clem. lix).[1]

The connection between our Epistle and 1 Clement has led some scholars to suppose that both these writings have been influenced by the liturgical service in Rome where the authors of both Epistles had worshipped.[2] The reasoning is as follows. 1 Clement bears notable resemblances to the Epistle to the Hebrews. 1 Clement is markedly liturgical, especially in its concluding prayer; and a large proportion of Clement's liturgical expressions echo passages from the Epistle to the Hebrews. The suggestion has been made that both these authors, consciously or unconsciously, drew their thoughts from the liturgical service that they both knew in Rome. This hypothesis must, however, be resisted; and not merely because reasons have already been given to suggest that the Epistle had been written much earlier by Apollos from Ephesus. In the first place, it will be shown in the course of the commentary that the Epistle to the Hebrews is not concerned with the Eucharist, and therefore cannot in that sense be called a liturgical document. In the second place, our Epistle and 1 Clement have opposed views on the offering of the Christian sacrifice. According to our author, there are two kinds of true sacrifice, and two only; the one completed sacrifice of Christ (He. x. 12) and the worshippers' sacrifice of praise and thanksgiving (He. xiii. 15). Clement, on the other hand, has a much broader conception. He spoke of those who presided at the Eucharist as those who 'presented the offerings' (c. xliv). In the Epistle to the Hebrews Jesus is our High Priest who offered himself on Calvary and continually makes intercession for us in heaven. By contrast Christ is, according to 1 Clement, 'the High Priest of all our

---

[1] Professor Lo Bue (*op. cit.*, p. 53) suggested that early knowledge of the Epistle on the part of the Roman community may have been due to the Roman connections of Prisca and Aquila.

[2] Cf. A. Nairne, *The Epistle to the Hebrews* (Cambridge, 1917), p. xxxix.

offerings' (c. xxxvi). It is impossible to believe that both these writings, with their contrasting views of offering and sacrifice, were both derived from the same Roman eucharistic tradition.

If these two writings are not dependent on a common tradition, the similarities between them are such that one must be dependent on the other. Manifestly the Epistle to the Hebrews is earlier than 1 Clement. It follows, then, that Clement used the Epistle to the Hebrews not only as the background of 1 Clement, but also as one of the sources for his eucharistic prayers. It was natural that a letter from the Bishop of Rome should contain many liturgical echoes, since it was written by one who presided at his own Eucharist. The eucharistic rite of Rome, taking shape under Clement, would have influenced that of other churches. Thus, the Epistle to the Hebrews, itself a strictly non-liturgical work, came indirectly to exercise great influence on later liturgies.

Two further questions need to be answered. In the first place, why, it may be asked, did no one seem to know who wrote the Epistle to the Hebrews? The answer to this question may be so obvious as to have escaped detection. The Epistle may not have had Apollos' name on its original autograph. From the seeming muddle of 2 Corinthians, which apparently contains parts of three Pauline letters, it is likely that the Corinthian archives were badly kept. No one had attached Apollos' name to the Epistle. It is probable that Apollos refused to revisit the Corinthian church: he had refused 'absolutely' when Paul wrote 1 Corinthians (1 Cor. xvi. 12). The Epistles could not have been much in use, or 2 Corinthians would never have been allowed to get into its present muddle. The name 'To the Hebrews' could have become attached to it because of its relevance to the attempted *coup* of the Hebrews at Corinth. The generation who knew the name of its author had died out by the time Clement wrote his Epistle in A.D. 95. Until the lucky guess of Luther, the secret was lost.

The second question concerns the remarkable hesitation about the apostolicity of the Epistle in the early church. In particular it was known early in Rome, but Rome seemed most doubtful about its apostolic authorship. Why was its apostolicity most doubted where it was best known? The answer to this seems clear. In the first place, it was known in Rome not to have been written by Paul. Secondly, the doctrine of the Second Repentance had been accepted in Rome by the time that the Shepherd of Hermas had been composed in its present form; probably the doctrine had been accepted even earlier, when the sources which the Shepherd used were originally composed. The objection to the apostolicity of the Epistle to the Hebrews was as much its unbending rigorism as its anonymity. Its apostolicity was doubted partly because its rigorism was suspect. It is significant that in the more rigorous East, its authenticity was earlier accepted.

Whoever wrote the Epistle to the Hebrews had been well schooled in the art of composition. The book has been constructed on a most careful plan. One section leads into the next, and a word at the beginning of a subsection is usually used again at its end. A. Vanhoye,[1] building on an earlier suggestion of Vaganay, has unfolded a most intricate structure, chiasmic in form. His plan carries conviction because the structure he proposes appears to have been worked out by our author as rigorously as the logic of his Epistle. A brief resumé may be given as follows:

[1] *Traduction structurée de l'épître aux Hébreux* (Rome, 1963). Since this introduction was written, Vanhoye has further elaborated his thesis in *La Structure littéraire de l'épître aux Hébreux* (Bruges, 1963).

Since, however, details of authorship, date, destination and structure commonly convince a writer more than his readers, the commentary that follows has been constructed in the hope that it may be of use to those for whom there is as yet no convincing solution to the difficult problems which this Epistle poses.

THE EPISTLE TO THE HEBREWS

1. THE NATURE OF THE SON. i. 1-3a

(1) God, who in the past spoke to the fathers by the prophets in fragmentary and varied fashion, (2) has at the end of this age, spoken to us by the Son, whom he has made rightful owner of all things and through whom he created the universe. (3a) He is the reflection of God's glory and the exact representation of God's being, and he sustains all things by his word of power.

The Epistle opens in sonorous and distinguished prose style but without conventional initial greetings. Possibly the Epistle was originally not composed as a letter but as a homily. The author plunges straight into his theme of the person and function of Jesus, the Son of God; although, characteristically, **God** (the Father) is the subject of the first sentence. **The prophets,** who were the agents of God's word in the old dispensation, included not merely the canonical prophets but also the men of God who preceded them, such as Abraham (Gen. xx. 7), Moses (Deut. xviii. 18), Aaron (Ex. vii. 1) and Elijah (1 Kings xviii. 22). The suggestion has been made that 'angels' should be read here for 'prophets', since in the rest of the chapter there is a contrast between the Son of God and the angels, not the prophets. But there is no textual evidence for this unnecessary change. The author makes a point of contact with his readers by beginning with what was commonly the first point of primitive Christian preaching, namely, that the age of fulfilment had arrived, as foretold by the prophets.

This revelation, however, was only 'partial and piecemeal' (F. F. Bruce). Nevertheless it was real, and the writer immediately follows his doctrinal introduction with a series of testimonies taken from the writings of the old dispensation. Yet it was incomplete because it contained promise, not fulfilment.

33

The brevity of these testimonies, taken from various sources, shows the fragmentary nature of the revelation, and the later argument of the Epistle shows insufficiency of the old dispensation.

This earlier revelation was given to **the fathers,** that is, not necessarily to the forefathers of the recipients of the Epistle (who may not all have been of the Jewish race), but to Israel of the pre-Christian era (cf. xi. 2). This pre-Christian revelation is contrasted with that which is now the common possession of
2 the writer and his readers at **the end of this age** (cf. ix. 26; 1 Peter i. 20; 1 Cor. x. 11). With the entry of the Son into the world, a completely new era has begun, superseding the old order of existence which had all but disappeared (viii. 13), and the writer is close enough to these events to describe this period as 'the end of these days'. The writer's contrast is not between natural and revealed religion or between general and special revelation, but between God's word of promise spoken by the prophets and his final word of fulfilment spoken by his Son. (It is characteristic of biblical thought to conceive of God revealing himself by speech.) The Son, who has been appointed the **rightful owner of all things,** has not been given something which he has previously lacked, nor has he received a lawful inheritance, an idea which would suggest the passing of ownership from the Father to the Son. The universe, since its creation, has always belonged to the Son, for it was through his agency that all forms of created existence came into being (cf. 1 Cor. viii. 6, Col. i. 16, John i. 3). Although the Son was for a short time made inferior to the angels (ii. 7), his subsequent exaltation to the highest honours of heaven did not involve a new status for him, but his re-entry into that which had always been his lawful place (cf. Phil. ii. 6-11).

Having related the Son to mankind and to the universe our
3a author next describes his relationship to the Father. **He is the reflection of God's glory.** The present tense denotes his eternal nature. Light is an image common to most religions in their descriptions of deity, but here it is used not only of God but also of his Son. The Greek word ἀπαύγασμα can mean either reflection or radiance. The majority of the Greek fathers understood it as radiance; but the passive form of the Greek noun,

together with the phrase with which it is coupled in the present context, makes it more probable that reflection is meant here. The two meanings, however, interpenetrate, since the Son's radiance is reflected glory. The glory of God is his divine nature as manifested to men (cf. John i. 14). In the Old Testament the divine glory comprises the radiance, righteousness and power of God. In the New Testament glory tends to be used eschatologically, since God's glory will not be fully revealed until the last day.

Here, however, the word is used to describe God's eternal nature. The glory of God is reflected in the eternal refulgence of the Son. As a son may be said to reflect his father's character, so the Son is the refulgence of his Father's glory, and so **the exact representation of God's being.** This second phrase suggests an engraving, or a stamp upon a coin. Its meaning is hardly to be distinguished from that of image, which Paul uses to relate the pre-existent Son to his Father (Col. i. 15, etc.). The writer does not explain how the Son can be an exact representation of his Father, nor what he means by the phrase: it is enough for him to assert the reality of the Son's representation. The Son does not merely resemble certain aspects of his Father: he is the exact representation of his essence, that is, of what it is that makes God be God.

The Son could exactly represent the Father only if he is himself divine. In virtue of this divine nature the Son **sustains all things.** The Greek participle φέρων could bear the meaning of 'create' instead of 'sustain', but this would only repeat the thought of *v.* 2. More, however, is signified here than merely the passive support of a burden; 'for the Son is not an Atlas sustaining the dead weight of the world' (Westcott). What is here being ascribed to the Son is the providential government of the universe, which is the function of God himself.

The Son governs the universe **by his word of power.** His power is expressed by his utterance of command. Word (λογός) is used in Hebrews to describe revelation (ii. 4; iv. 12), while utterance (ῥῆμα) designates rather divine activity (as here and at xi. 3). Just as the universe was called into existence by the utterance of the Father, so it is sustained by the utterance of his Son.

No previous knowledge of biblical or Hellenistic theology is necessary in order to understand these opening verses of the Epistle, which form, on their own, a clear and comprehensible statement of the person and status of the Son.

Nevertheless the language used has striking parallels elsewhere, especially in writings which emanate from Alexandrian Judaism. Thus for Philo the *Logos* or Word is an impersonal principle of mediation between God and his universe, but personal terms are used by Philo to describe this impersonal principle. The *Logos*, since it stands for the intelligible universe, is the first-born Son (*Quod Deus* 31). He is the image of God (*de Conf. Ling.* 97), and God's agent in his creation of his universe (*de Spec. Leg.* 1. 81). The *Logos* is the image of God, the angel of God, as parhelion to the sun. He is the sun's ray (*de Somn.* 1. 239), the exact representation of the divine power (*Quod. Det. Pot.* 83). This coincidence of usage is remarkable. Further contact with Alexandrian thought is suggested by the place of Wisdom in the wisdom literature. According to Jewish wisdom theology, God formed Wisdom as the beginning of his ways (Prov. viii. 22), so that the first verse of the Bible could be interpreted to mean: 'In Wisdom God created the heaven and the earth'. Wisdom is represented as a pre-existent heavenly figure present with God before the Creation as his 'master craftsman' (Prov. viii. 30), by whom God laid the foundations of the world (Prov. iii. 19). Wisdom is the sustainer and governor of the universe (Wisd. Sol. viii. 1), and she is described in words similar to those used of the Son in Hebrews, as 'a reflection of eternal light and an unspotted mirror of the working of God and an image of his goodness' (Wisd. Sol. vii. 26). Wisdom sits by the throne of God (Wisd. Sol. ix. 4). In this Alexandrian work the person of Wisdom is practically identified with the *Logos* (Wisd. Sol. ix. 2).

The use of hypostatised Wisdom to express the mediator of creation and revelation was not an innovation of our author. Paul too writes of the Son as the agent in creation (1 Cor. viii. 6), the sustainer of the universe (Col. i. 17), and as the image of God (Col. i. 15). For him too the Son is a reflection of the Father's radiance, for he writes of 'the light of the knowledge of the glory of God in the face of Jesus Christ' (2 Cor. iv. 6).

The Fourth Evangelist, writing later, uses ideas, all of which can be paralleled in the wisdom literature, to describe the Son under the form of the *Logos*.

Thus the conjunction of the Messiah concept with the idea of Wisdom is not the invention of our author. On the contrary, the parallels adduced show that he stands in the main stream of New Testament Christology. The introductory verses of the Epistle are written with an assurance which suggests that they contain commonly accepted beliefs, and in any case it is improbable that any epistle would open with controversial or unfamiliar Christological statements (cf. Ro. i. 2-4).

2. THE EXALTATION OF THE SON. i. 3b-4

(3b) When in his own person he had made purification from sins, he took his seat on high at the right hand of Majesty, (4) having become as much superior to the angels as the name which he has by right is more exalted than theirs.

Our author now turns from the Son's eternal being and from his relation to the created universe to summarise the Son's relationship to mankind in sacrificial imagery. The interpretation of Christ's work in terms of sacrifice is found (in varying imagery) in the writings of Paul (Ro. iii. 25; viii. 3; 1 Cor. v. 7; Eph. i. 7, v. 2) and elsewhere in the New Testament (Acts xx. 28; 1 Peter i. 19); and it probably goes back to the words of Jesus himself (cf. Mark x. 45, xiv. 24). The author of Hebrews, however, does not merely use sacrificial imagery: he gives an elaborate explanation of Jesus' death and ascension in terms of the most important of all sacrifices described in the Old Testament, that of the Day of Atonement. The Son is both priest and victim, and in virtue of his completed sacrifice, he has been exalted to take the highest place in heaven, which belongs to him by right.

In the previous verses the pre-existent Son was described; now it is the Son incarnate in the man Jesus. He is the victim

3b **because in his own person he had made purification.** The middle voice of the Greek verb ποιησάμενος renders pleonastic the additional διαυτου found in *p*⁴⁶ D* or διεαυτου found in KL *1739 pm*; while the aorist tense of the participle emphasises that the act of purification has taken place in the past. There is an implicit contrast, to be made explicit later in the Epistle, between the completed act of purification and the annually repeated sacrifice of the levitical high priest (cf. x. 11-14). The writer is not here referring to the effect of the incarnate Son's sacrifice on Christian believers, but to the objective act whereby purification was effected. The phrase translated **purification from sins** might mean purification *of* sins; but the point is not that sins have been purged, but rather that sinners have had their sins purified. This phrase **purification from sins,** found in the New Testament only once outside Hebrews (2 Peter i. 9), is also used only once in the LXX, where it is employed in connection with the high priest's sacrifice on the Day of Atonement (Ex. xxx. 10). Its use here prepares the way for the identification of Jesus with the high priest who ministers in the heavenly tent. Purification from sins means here cleansing from sins generally, not from particular sins. In Hebrews the plural form, **sins,** is more often preferred, because sins are regarded in the Epistle primarily as defilements which prevent access to God and which need removal by cleansing; whereas Paul in general prefers to speak of sin in the singular, as a kind of evil virus which infects the whole personality and which needs to be overcome. It has been suggested that **purification from sins** includes the sins of angels as well as of men, but since there is nowhere else in this Epistle any reference to fallen angels, it is probable that only human sins are here intended.

The completed act of purification leads to the heavenly session of the Son. He did not merely sit down, but solemnly **took his seat on high.** The right-hand seat was the seat of honour (1 Kings ii. 19). It was the prerogative of Davidic kings to sit in the presence of God (cf. 2 Sam. vii. 18), and originally the words of Psalm cx. 1 were addressed to a Davidic king: Sit thou at my right hand, until I make thy enemies my footstool. Our author, however, is not interested in Davidic descent. He regards this verse as a promise directly fulfilled in the exaltation of Jesus. This *testimonium* is cited in i. 13 and x. 12, and alluded to in viii. 1 and xii. 2, as well as many times elsewhere in the New Testament. Psalm cx seems to have exercised a decisive influence on the writer of this Epistle, for not only is the heavenly session of the Son there foretold, but also the Lord is identified with a priest of the rank of Melchisedek (v. 6). He is **at the right hand of Majesty** because Majesty was a periphrasis for God whose name was sometimes avoided for reasons of reverence (cf. the use of Glory in ix. 5).

The Son was exalted to heaven in his glorified humanity. While the Son eternally exists in his essential nature, the glorified Jesus is described, in a phrase which denotes change, as **having become superior to the angels.** This superiority is 4 one not of degree, but of kind. The word 'superior' is recurrent in the Epistle, being used thirteen times. Usually it contrasts the new dispensation with the old, or the life of heaven with the hardships of this world; but here (and in vi. 9 and vii. 7) no such difference is intended. The superiority of the Son could, of course, be shown by setting gospel against law, for the law was given through angels (ii. 2; cf. Gal. iii. 19; Acts vii. 53), while Jesus supersedes the law and so fulfils its promise (vii. 19). But at this stage of the argument this contrast is not expressed. The superiority of the Son to the angels has still to be defined. As yet it is merely asserted to be in the same proportion **as the name which he has by right is more exalted than theirs.** According to Jewish thought, a person's name revealed his essential nature, and it could express his rank and dignity. The name which Jesus has by right must be the name of the Son, as the succeeding verses establish. According to Paul, the name that is above every name is not the Son, but the Lord (Phil. ii. 11). The name of Son, however, unlike that of Lord, has not been given in virtue of exaltation into heaven, but it is his from eternity, and the perfect tense of the Greek verb κεκληρονόμηκεν indicates that it is a name which he has not only been given but keeps.

The sudden introduction of angels at this point has been given various explanations. (*a*) It has been suggested that an undue deference to angels is being attacked, similar to that which Paul denounces in Col. ii. 18. Angels were regarded as intercessors for mankind (1 Enoch xv. 2), and mediators between God and men (1 Enoch ix. 3). Michael was merciful and long suffering (1 Enoch xl. 9) and intercession to God was offered by Gabriel (1 Enoch xl. 6) and all the angels (1 Enoch civ. 1). It is known from Essene documents and from descriptions of their tenets that these sectarians held a very high angelology (for references, cf. T. H. Gaster, *The Scriptures of the Dead Sea Sect* (1957), pp. 316 f.). The suggestion has been made that this Epistle was addressed to Essene converts to Christianity, and other points of contact in the Epistle with Essene beliefs have been adduced.[1]

(b) Again, it has been suggested that in the circles to whom the Epistle was addressed the Son has been equated with one of the 'principalities and powers', the spiritual forces which ruled the universe (cf. 1 Cor. xv. 24; Eph. iii. 10; Col. ii. 15, etc.). It is clear from the Epistles of Paul that belief in these supernatural forces was widespread in the primitive Hellenistic church, and that this conviction exercised great influence on the minds of the early Christians. On the other hand it might be that the Christian faith of those to whom this Epistle was sent had been distorted by other contemporary beliefs which are unknown to us.

(c) A third explanation suggests that the references to angels are unrelated to the context of the Epistle. The *testimonia* which follow from this point onwards are all Old Testament statements which prove that God is addressing someone who is with him in Heaven. Since angels were commonly believed to wait upon the throne of God in heaven (Is. vi. 2) or to be counsellors together with God (Psalm lxxxix. 7), this heavenly being must be presumed to be an angel unless the writer can prove that he is superior to angels; and this he proceeds to do.

This theory fails to take account of two important points. Firstly, the Epistle is written in a definite situation to which reference is made often in the course of the Epistle. Its recipients are in danger of falling away from Christianity into Judaism (cf. vi. 6; x. 26; xiii. 9), and the references to angels, coming as they do in such a prominent place at the beginning of the Epistle, may be presumed to have a bearing on the dangerous

[1] See Introduction, pp. 16 ff.

situation of its recipients. Secondly, such effort is expended by the writer of this letter to show the Son's superiority to angels that he cannot be concerned only with making an 'academic' point. Strictly speaking, one single text would be sufficient to prove this superiority. Our author was not one to prolong his argument unnecessarily, especially at the beginning of the Epistle, before he has begun to expound his main theme. If, however, he was trying not just to make an academic point, but to alter the convictions of the recipients of his Epistle, it is understandable that he hammered home his point with a succession of texts.

The Epistle is written to a Christian church the members of which were in danger of lapsing into Judaism. Here lies the key to the understanding of this problem. Jews who did not accept Christianity regarded Jesus as the false prophet (Sanh. 43a). Jews who became Christians tended to hold an Ebionite view of Christ; that is, they would regard him as the Prophet, or the Messiah, but they would insist that he was a mere man, thus denying his divinity. The recipients of this Epistle, however, were Christians in danger of lapsing into Judaism. Why should they deny their past religious experience as Christians? They would naturally wish still to revere Jesus as more than human, while denying his divinity. Thus they inclined to the belief that he was neither God nor man but an angel.

It was not only the Essenes who held a high doctrine of angels in the first century A.D. A study of apocalyptic literature and rabbinic material shows how widespread among Jews of all classes (with the exception of Sadducees, who disbelieved in their existence) was the conviction that angels played a vital role in the divine dispensation. According to T. Dan. vi. 2, Michael is mediator between God and man. If Satan could change himself into an angel of light (2 Cor. xi. 14), why could not an angel of light change himself into the appearance of a man? If Philo the Jew could frequently write of the *Logos* as an angel, it would have been comparatively easy for a Christian of the Diaspora to think of the Incarnate Word as an angel. In a remarkable passage Philo had written: 'If there be any as yet unfit to be called a Son of God, let him press to take his place under God's First-Born, the Word, who holds the eldership among the angels, an archangel as it were. And many names are his, for his is called "the Beginning" and the Name of God and His Word and Man after his image and "he that sees", that is Israel' (*de Conf. Ling.* 146).

To regard Jesus' ministry as the manifestation of an angel was to make the best of two worlds. On the one hand the unity of God was preserved, for an angel is not divine. On the other hand, there would have been no need to question the reality of past Christian experience, for the Christian's experience of the risen Lord could be interpreted as a real spiritual experience of a very high order—the experience of an angel.

In order to combat this false belief the author of our Epistle has to prove two contrary points: first, that the Son is superior to angels, and therefore divine; and secondly, that the Son was made lower than the angels during his incarnation and became what an angel could never be, a real man of flesh and blood with human passions and weaknesses. This second point is strongly asserted in the main body of the Epistle (ii. 17; iv. 15). The first point is proved by *testimonia* in the succeeding verses.

3. SON SUPERIOR TO ANGELS. i. 5-14

(5) For to which of the angels did God ever say, 'Thou art my Son, today I have begotten thee'? And again, 'I will be a father to him and he will be a son to me'? (6) And again, when he brings the first-born into the world, he says, 'And let all God's angels worship him'. (7) Of the angels he says, 'He who makes his angels winds and his ministers a flame of fire'; (8) but of the Son, 'Thy throne, O God, is for ever and ever, and the sceptre of uprightness is the sceptre of his kingdom. (9) Thou hast loved right and hated wrong, therefore, O God, thy God has anointed thee with the oil of exultation above thy fellows.' (10) Again, 'Thou, O Lord, in the beginning didst lay the foundation of the earth, and the heavens are the works of thy hands; (11) they will perish, but thou remainest; they will all grow old like a garment, (12) thou wilt

42

roll them up like a cloak and like a garment they will be changed; but thou art the same, thy years will not come to an end'. (13) But of which of the angels has he ever said, 'Take thy seat at my right hand until I make thy enemies a footstool for thy feet'? (14) Are they not all ministering spirits sent out on service for those who are to inherit salvation?

Our author next shows the superiority of the Son over the angels by proving it from a list of seven quotations from the Old Testament, five of which are taken from the Psalms and the other two from 2 Samuel and Deuteronomy. These are introduced without explanation, apart from a brief introduction to the third quotation. If our author had done his own research into the Old Testament, some explanation of his selection would have been likely. These *testimonia* seem to have been taken from an existing catena of Old Testament proof texts. They may have possibly existed in the form of a testimony book.

The theory that a testimony book was already in existence in the primitive church for apologetic and missionary use against the Jews has been held by some scholars, and the evidence for it has been based not only on the New Testament but also on the third-century *Testimonia* of Cyprian (plainly an enlargement of an earlier work); and the messianic testimonies found at Qumran (4Q Testimonia) have added some weight to the theory. A more probable explanation, however, can be given for the presence of many testimonies cited in the New Testament. They are sometimes collected into groups of passages, sometimes joined together in different combinations of individual quotations, and sometimes represent a text different from either the Massoretic text or the LXX. There are good reasons for holding that 'the selection and presentation of *testimonia* was not a static achievement, but a process, and one which continued well through the New Testament period and beyond' (C. H. Dodd, *According to the Scriptures* (1952), p. 108). In the course of this development it is possible to detect both 'shift of application and modification of text' (B. Lindars, *New Testament Apologetic* (1961), p. 17).

The list of seven *testimonia* here cited by our author was

unlikely to have been originally devised in order to show the superiority of the Son to the angels, because, although our author uses them here for this purpose, it does not seem, from the evidence of the rest of the New Testament, that this was a matter of dispute elsewhere. The selection of the seven *testimonia* seems ill-adapted for this purpose, since only one of them in the LXX contains the actual word angels. These citations were therefore selected for a purpose different from that which they serve in this Epistle (cf. F. C. Synge, *Hebrews and the Scriptures* (1959), p. 3). The primary purpose of this collection was originally to prove from the Old Testament scriptures the eternal existence and divine nature of God the Son, his incarnation, baptism, resurrection and ascension. The author of Hebrews, however, utilises them here to prove that the Son is superior to the angels.

5 The first citation is from Psalm ii. 7: **Thou art my Son; today I have begotten thee.** This verse of Psalm ii seems to have been interpreted in Jewish tradition as having a messianic interpretation (cf. 1QSa 2. 11). It is cited elsewhere in the New Testament with modified text and different application. Here, however, the LXX text is exactly cited. In the primitive kerygma of the early church the text was applied not as here to the generation of the Son but to the resurrection of Jesus (cf. Ro. i. 4), and it is found with this interpretation in Luke's free composition of Acts xiii. 33 f. Later the verse seems to have been conflated with Is. xlii. 1 to form the words of the Divine Voice at Jesus' Baptism (Mark i. 11 and parallels). This natural step in Christological development was eased by the overlapping meaning of υἱός in Psalm ii. 7 and παῖς in Is. xlii. 1. A further shift is seen in Luke ix. 35, where the verse has left its mark on the account of Jesus' transfiguration. It was never used of the conception or birth of Jesus, for this would have suggested pagan legends of divine paternity, which would have been distasteful to Christian sensibilities. In this Epistle the verse is cited not as a general messianic proof, nor with reference to Jesus' baptism, transfiguration or resurrection, but in order to prove the eternal generation of the Son. Our author has a logical mind, and he starts at the beginning. Angels existed before the creation of the world, and so did the Son. Angels

could collectively be called the 'sons of God' (cf. Gen. vi. 2), but they were created and not begotten; and no angel was individually called Son of God. There is no point in attempting to identify a moment in time which corresponds to **today** in 'today have I begotten thee'; nor is it probable that our author understood it to mean 'eternally' (cf. Philo, *de Fuga et Inv.* 57). He found the word in the *testimonium*, and its interpretation 'was not a question present to his mind' (Moffatt).

The second quotation consists of an accurate citation of 2 Sam. vii. 14 (LXX): **I will be a father to him and he shall be a son to me.** In its original setting this verse is preceded by Nathan's prophecy to David that he will build a house for God, and it is followed by the promise that the throne of David will be established for ever. David was not born by divine paternity, but it is promised that he will be adopted to divine sonship. This text is among those found in the fragmentary collection of messianic texts in Cave 4 of the Dead Sea caves, and the Rabbis recognised in it a messianic promise. This probably explains its original Christian use. Elsewhere in the New Testament it recurs with modified text and altered application. In 2 Cor. vi. 18 it is linked to Is. lii. 11 and modified so as to describe the status of those who have separated themselves from the world; while in Rev. xxi. 7 it is assimilated to Psalm lxxxviii. 26 (LXX) and used eschatologically so as to refer to final inheritance of those who persevere. It was originally included in this catena of *testimonia* because it proves the eternal and continuing status of the Son of God; but our author makes use of it to prove that the Son enjoys a relationship with the Father superior to that of the angels. He employs it to describe the status of the Son, not that of God the Father. Nowhere else in this Epistle is God described as the Father of Christ.

The third quotation, taken from the LXX of Deut. xxxii. 43 (the words are not found in the Hebrew text), has an introductory clause: **Again when he brings the first-born into 6 the world.** This introduction makes it clear that the quotation itself, **Let all God's angels worship him,** is intended to refer to the birth of Jesus. The quotation must have been originally chosen to prove his divine birth. Otherwise it would be a singularly strange verse to select, since in its original Deutero-nomic context it is God, not the Son, whom the angels are commanded to worship. (Apart from one manuscript, the LXX text of Deut. xxxii. 43a does not contain the words 'the angels of God' but 'the sons of God'. Our author, however, gives the correct meaning of the phrase, which is borrowed either from Deut. xxxii. 43b or from the very similar Psalm xcvii. 7.) In the original catena this verse was used to prove that the incarnate Son was worshipped as divine at his birth. An allusion to the heavenly host described in Luke ii. 13 is probably intended, and this constitutes one of the many points of connection between Hebrews and the Lucan writings (cf. C. P. M. Jones in *Studies in the Gospels*, ed. D. E. Nineham (1955), pp. 113-143).

The author of Hebrews makes use of the verse as a proof text that the Son is so far superior to the angels that they worshipped him. Possibly the word first-born had the same literal meaning as in Luke ii. 7; but the author of Hebrews retained it to show that the Son is superior to the angels, in as much as **the first-born** is consecrated to God and holds a pre-eminent position as heir. This was the sense in which the word had earlier been applied collectively to Israel in Psalm lxxxviii. 27 (LXX). Philo had called the *Logos* the first-born Son (*de Conf. Ling.* 146). In the early church the word was regularly used of Jesus (Ro. viii. 29; Col. i. 15, 18; Rev. i. 5), although in the New Testament it stands alone here as a title of Jesus.

7   The fourth quotation is taken from Psalm civ. 4. **Of the angels he says, 'He who makes his angels winds and his ministers a flame of fire'.** The Hebrew text of the psalm is best understood without any reference to angels at all, but our author in following the LXX version concurs with later Rabbinic interpretation of the verse (cf. 4 Ezra viii. 22). Originally this quotation stood sixth in the catena and was used as a proof text of the Christian Pentecost (Acts ii. 2 f.); but our author has put it here as his fourth *testimonium* in order to form a contrast with the quotation that follows it. He may have had in mind the storm and fire on Mount Sinai (Deut. iv. 11) when the law was given through angels (cf. comment on ii. 2). His primary intention, however, in making use of this verse, is to show that angels are made and not begotten, and that they are as insub-

stantial and mutable as wind and fire, and that they do not give orders but carry them out.

The same could not be said **of the Son;** and a contrast between 8 him and the angels is made by means of Psalm xliv. 6 f. (LXX). Even if the Septuagint version of this royal nuptial psalm should be rendered 'God is thy throne', here the translation should be: **Thy throne, O God, is for ever and ever.** The angels minister to the throne: the Son occupies it. The angels are created and subject to change: but the place of the Son is the eternal throne of God. As for the Son, **the sceptre of uprightness is the sceptre of his kingdom,** and this sceptre is a symbol of his universal authority, even over angels. The angels may be susceptible to sin, but the Son has **loved right and hated wrong.** 9 He is superior to them, for he has been raised above them when he was anointed as God. The Hebrew text of the Psalm is best translated 'God, even thy God, has anointed thee' but our author follows the Septuagint text, and so, by regarding the verse as addressed to the Son, he is able to prove the Son's divinity: **O God, thy God hast anointed thee with the oil of exultation above thy fellows.** The author must have been accustomed to the outright ascription of divinity to the Son, for he shows here not the slightest embarrassment. This is the only place in the New Testament where the Son is described simply as ὁ θεός (contrast John i. 1). In the original catena of quotations this verse proved from scripture both the Baptism of Christ (a title which itself means 'the anointed one') and the heavenly announcement at his baptism of his divine sonship; but here the verse is used to show that the Son's superiority to the angels is based on his divine nature.

The next quotation is taken (with two minor alterations) from Psalm ci. 25-27 (LXX). In the Greek version **O Lord** has 10 been added to the Hebrew **Thou in the beginning didst lay the foundation of the earth.** This facilitated the messianic interpretation that is given here to these verses. In the original Hebrew the words are spoken to God, but since in this Epistle the primitive Christian title of The Lord is ascribed to the Son, our author finds no difficulty in applying them to the Son, who already in *v.* 2 has been described as the agent of creation.

The foundations of the earth and the dome of heaven were

the two most stable elements in the Psalmist's world; yet in comparison with the eternity and unchangeableness of God, they

11 are transitory and evanescent. **They will perish but thou**
12 **remainest. They will all grow old like a garment, thou wilt roll them up like a cloak and like a garment they will be changed; but thou art the same, thy years will not come to an end.** The Psalmist looks forward to a new heaven and a new earth (Is. lxv. 17; Rev. xxi. 1; cf. He. xii. 27, where our author declares that the heavens as well as the earth will be shaken). It will be as though God were to give them a new suit of clothes. These words are regarded as addressed not to the Father but to the Son (cf. Philo, *de Fuga et Inv.* 110, where the cosmos is the mantle of the *Logos*). The unexpressed thought must be that, while angels were spectators at the creation (cf. Job xxxviii. 7) and are subject to change, the Son is the agent of creation and is immutable. But this contrast between the Son and the angels is not made explicit in the quotation; and this suggests that in the original catena it was not employed for this purpose. It was probably used to demonstrate that the resurrection of Jesus had been promised in the scriptures. Its main point is to show that the Son does not grow old and die, but remains the same (cf. Psalm xv. 8-11 (LXX), cited in Acts ii. 25 ff., with the same object). Members of the primitive church would have had little difficulty in interpreting the passage in a Christian sense, for they believed that Jesus was the Lord (Ro. x. 9); but it is difficult to understand how this passage could possibly have been used against Jewish opponents, unless the whole Psalm had already, in its Septuagint version, been regarded by the Jews as messianic. There is, however, no evidence to lend support to this, which suggests that the catena was originally formed for use within the church.

The final quotation in this list of *testimonia* comes from Psalm cix. 1 (LXX), to which an allusion has already been made in *v.* 3. This verse has left its mark elsewhere in the New Testament (Ro. viii. 34; Eph. i. 20; Col. iii. 1; 1 Peter iii. 22; Rev. v. 1). According to Mark xii. 35-37 (and parallels) it was used by Jesus to show that the Messiah has a higher status and dignity than a mere Davidic pedigree. According to Acts ii. 34 the verse was cited by Peter after a *testimonium* concerning the resurrection, to show that Jesus' ascension into heaven and his heavenly session were foretold in scripture. It is used here for the same purpose. The present tense of the imperative κάθου implies that the Lord has not only taken his seat but continues his heavenly session.

Both in the Gospels and in Acts the opening words of the Psalm, 'the Lord said unto my Lord', are inserted to show that the Messiah is the Lord. Here, however, this title and dignity is assumed (cf. ii. 3; vii. 14), and so the quotation starts with the words **Take thy seat at my right hand.** The second half of 13 the verse is cited here: **until I make thy enemies a footstool for thy feet;** but our author offers no comment on this. Like others in the primitive church he seems to have preferred the very similar words of Psalm vii. 6 (LXX) where universal dominion is promised, for in ii. 8 he cites them and comments on them. (In 1 Cor. xv, where Psalm cx is cited in *v.* 25, Psalm viii is preferred two verses later.)

Even if eastern enthronement rituals underlie such passages as 1 Tim. iii. 16, it seems unlikely that they have influenced the selection of Psalm cx. 1 in our catena of *testimonia.* The verse was included in the original catena to prove Christ's ascension and final victory. Our author uses it to prove the superiority of the Son over the angels, for the Son sits in the presence of God in the place of honour, while the angels are sent from the presence on missions of service. They are all without exception **ministering spirits,** incapable of incarna- 14 tion. Our author does not hold the Jewish belief in angels of the Presence sacrificing and interceding for the saints (T. Levi iii. 5), for such a concept would detract from the sacrifice and intercession of Jesus. Nor does our author think of the angels' ministry as the ministry of worship (cf. the angelic liturgy of 4Q Sl 39 1 i 16 ff.).[1] The word λειτουργικά, used of priestly service in the Septuagint, and applied to angels by Philo (*de Virt.* 73), here bears its earlier meaning of discharging a function of social obligation (cf. Ro. xii. 7).

As their Greek name implies, angels are messengers. The Son also was sent and he too came to serve. But his single advent was the cause of salvation (v. 9), while the angels are continually

[1] Published in *Supplement to Vetus Testamentum,* vii (1960), 318-345.

sent not to effect salvation but to help those who are to receive
it. The present tense of the Greek participle ἀποστελλόμενα
implies that angels are perpetually being **sent out on service.**
Their task is concerned not with the natural order, but with the
work of redemption. Their mission is **for those who are to
inherit salvation,** that is, for the people of God. Illustrations
of their work can be found in Acts x. 3 and xii. 8. The absolute
use of **salvation** here, without explanation or qualification,
suggests that, when this Epistle was written, this word had
become a commonly accepted Christian term. Its introduction
here skilfully prepares the way for the exhortation that follows.

Salvation in the New Testament is an eschatological word.
In Pauline usage it can refer either to the baptismal state (Eph.
ii. 8), or to the continuing state of Christians (2 Cor. ii. 15) or
to their final destiny (Ro. xiii. 11). In Hebrews the finished
work of Jesus is the ground of salvation (ii. 10; v. 9), but the
future sense of the word predominates, as here. It loses its
original meaning of wholeness or escape and simply stands for
the Christian hope (cf. ix. 28).

This Epistle was written to encourage its recipients from
lapsing. Its emphasis therefore is on human effort rather than
divine predestination, so that the phrase rendered **those who
are to inherit** denotes future expectation rather than divine
decree. The idea of inheritance, common elsewhere in the N.T.,
is particularly characteristic of this Epistle. It is found frequently
in the O.T. and it is derived from God's promise to Abraham
that his seed will inherit the land (Gen. xvii. 8). Used eschatologically, it does not signify a legal title of ownership held in
succession from an earlier owner. It means the rightful possession by absolute gift of that which has been previously promised
but which has not been gained by personal merit.

4. NEED FOR DILIGENCE. ii. 1-4

**(1) Therefore we must pay all the more attention to what
we have been told, in case we drift away. (2) For if the
word spoken through angels was authoritative, and every**

**transgression and disobedience received just retribution,
(3) how shall we escape if we ignore such great salvation?
It was announced by the Lord, with whom it originated;
it was confirmed to us by those who heard; (4) and God
added his witness with signs and wonders, with various
mighty works and with gifts of the Holy Spirit according
to his will.**

Our writer now turns from theological argument to moral
exhortation, as he frequently does again later in the Epistle.
The logical corollary of the Son's superiority over the angels is
that the Son's message has greater authority. **Therefore**—in 1
view of this superiority—it follows that **we must pay all the
more attention to what we have been told.** Our author
does not place himself in a different category from that of his
readers: he includes himself among them as one who is in need
of this reminder. Furthermore, he does not claim to be an eye-
witness of the gospel, nor is he conscious of introducing any
doctrinal innovation. It is from hearing that faith comes (Ro.
x. 17), and our author, like his readers, has heard the church's
tradition of preaching (cf. 2 Thess. ii. 15) and of teaching (cf.
Ro. vi. 17). The Pastor exhorts Timothy to hold fast what he
has heard from Paul (2 Tim. i. 13), but our author admonishes
his readers slightly differently: they are to **pay attention** to
what they have been told. This is a summons both to the mind
and to the will: it carries overtones of a similar summons under
the old dispensation (Deut. iv. 9) which nevertheless did not
prevent the downfall of those to whom it was addressed. Our
writer reminds his readers of the seriousness of their situation.
The Christian religion is such that to relegate it to the background of life is to invite downfall. Indifference spells disaster.
Our author is not thinking of a particular peril, but the general
danger of finding, in such circumstances, that one has slipped
away, almost without realising it, from Christian faith and
practice. The Greek verb $\pi\alpha\rho\alpha\rho\rho\upsilon\hat{\omega}\mu\epsilon\nu$ in the phrase **in case
we drift away** means literally to 'flow by'. It can be used
of water draining out of a vessel, or metaphorically of a
ring slipping off a finger or something slipping out of the
memory.

Our writer goes on to explain his demand for care and attention. It was a common belief in first-century Judaism that the law was given through angelic mediators, a view which was based on the LXX versions of Deut. xxxiii. 2 and Psalm lxviii. 18. It finds expression in Josephus, *Antiq.* 15. 5. 3, and, more doubtfully, in Jub. 1. 27. From contemporary Judaism the idea naturally passed over into primitive Christian thought (Acts vii. 53). Paul, in Gal. iii. 19, contrasts the law which was given through angels with the fulfilment in Jesus Christ of the promise which God gave to Abraham. Our author, however, does not use the word law in this connection. He prefers the
2 expression **the word spoken through angels,** because he wishes to contrast this with the salvation that was first announced by Jesus. He does not, like Paul, set law against gospel (Ro. v. 20 f.). He prefers to describe the new dispensation as 'better' because it accomplishes that which was entirely beyond the scope and intention of the old dispensation.

Nevertheless the word of the old dispensation **was authoritative:** it was accurate and trustworthy, and its validity was self-authenticating (cf. Philo, *de Vita Moys.* 2. 3, where the law is called 'authoritative and unshaken'). The authority of the law was exercised partly through the infliction of punishment incurred by non-observance; **and every transgression and disobedience received just retribution.** The author, in common with other New Testament writers, does not question the propriety of this recompense.

Offences against law have two aspects: the positive aspect of trespassing on forbidden ground, and the negative aspect of disobeying a lawful command. Thus in Ro. v, Paul refers to Adam's sin both as transgression (*v.* 14) and as disobedience (*v.* 19). Since justice has a retributive element, each offence received a penalty commensurate with the offence. Some instances of retributive justice in the Old Testament are given by our author later in his Epistle (iii. 16; cf. 1 Cor. x. 5-11; 2 Peter ii. 6; Jude 5).

If such penalties were imposed for offences against a law of
3 which angels were mediators, **how,** asks our writer, **shall we escape if we ignore such great salvation?** Our author does not here define just what it is from which his readers might

not be able to escape (cf. Acts xvi. 30; 1 Thess. v. 3), but from
the context it is obvious that he means escape from the nemesis
of retribution. As in i. 14, so here also salvation is used absolutely. It refers primarily to the deliverance from future punishment, promised, under the new covenant, to the people of
God. The deliverance is so great because it is effected by the
Son, who is so much greater than the angels.

This salvation **was announced by the Lord, with whom
it originated.** (The Lord is here used as a commonly accepted
title of Jesus, and must be distinguished from 'Lord', which
our author uses to signify God.) There is here a clear reference
to the historical Jesus (cf. v. 7). Among the many points of
contact between this Epistle and the Lucan writings, it is noteworthy that in St. Luke's Gospel, alone of the synoptic gospels,
does Jesus himself pronounce salvation (Luke xix. 9), and by
Luke alone Jesus is called the Saviour (Luke ii. 11) and described
as bringing salvation (i. 69, 71, 77). Probably our author had
in mind, in writing of salvation being announced by the Lord,
such occasions as that described in Luke iv. 17 ff., when Jesus
claims to fulfil long promised hopes of deliverance and forgiveness. The Greek words here mean literally that salvation
'received its beginning of being spoken by the Lord', in rather
the same sense as when Peter, in Acts x. 37 f., speaks of 'the
saying which was published throughout all Judaea, beginning
from Galilee . . . even Jesus of Nazareth'. The author of
Hebrews may have been familiar with the primitive kerygma
embodied in Acts x.

The good news of this salvation had reached the writer of this
Epistle because **it was confirmed to us by those who heard.**
No claim is made for first-hand knowledge by the author. He
does not, like Paul, insist that he did not receive the gospel
from man, and that he had not been taught it (Gal. i. 12). On
the contrary, the message of Jesus was handed down to the
writer and to his contemporaries by those who were 'eye-
witnesses and ministers of the word' (Luke i. 2). Their authoritative witness confirmed the original message of salvation (cf.
1 Cor. i. 6). **And** to this **God added his witness** in a threefold 4
manner. Firstly, he made attestation **with signs and wonders.**
A sign is a divine intervention manifesting God's nature and

revealing his purpose, and a wonder is an extraordinary event the miraculous nature of which evokes awe and astonishment. In the Old Testament God is said to work signs and wonders (cf. Jer. xxxii. 20), but in the New Testament, unlike the Old Testament, 'wonders' never appear without 'signs' (cf. Acts xiv. 3; Ro. xv. 19).

Secondly, God witnesses this salvation **with various mighty works** (cf. 1 Cor. xii. 10 ff.). Mighty works may be distinguished from wonders and signs in as much as they manifest God's power rather than the miraculous nature or inner meaning of what he does.

Thirdly, God corroborated his witness **with gifts of the Holy Spirit according to his will.** Our author here uses very similar language to that of Paul to signify something rather different. In 1 Cor. xii. 11 Paul writes of 'the same Spirit dividing to everyone even as he wills', but in Hebrews it is God who apportions the Holy Spirit according to his (the Father's) will. (This thought is closely paralleled in Gal. iii. 5.)

In marked contrast to the Pauline corpus, there is practically no mention in Hebrews of the Holy Spirit as the common inheritance of all Christians. In this particular passage, the phrase used concerning the Holy Spirit is so similar to Pauline references that it would seem to be a stock phrase rather than original expression of the writer's thought. While it is improbable that this Epistle is addressed to Jewish Christians who were living in or near Jerusalem, it is possible that this threefold attestation of the Gospel is a reference to the historical event of Whitsunday. However, these three words, signs, wonders and mighty works, are coupled together elsewhere in the New Testament. This suggests that the reference is more general. In Acts ii. 22 they are actually applied (in reverse order) to Jesus; while Paul also uses them as illustrations of the way in which Christ works through him (Ro. xv. 19), and as a proof of his apostolic labours (2 Cor. xii. 12). Possibly our author had himself been brought to the Christian faith by apostolic labours, but lack of evidence renders this a matter for speculation only.

(5) For it was not to angels that he has subjected the world to come, about which we are speaking. (6) One has somewhere solemnly declared: 'What is man, that thou rememberest him, or the son of man, that thou hast regard for him? (7) Thou didst make him for a short while lower than the angels; thou didst crown him with glory and honour; (8) thou didst put all things in subjection under his feet.' By 'subjecting everything' to him, it means that he left nothing that is not subject to him. But in fact we do not yet see all things subjected to men; (9) yet we do see one who was made 'for a short while lower than the angels', Jesus, through the suffering of death now 'crowned with glory and honour', so that, separated from God, he might taste death on behalf of all men. (10) For it was fitting that God, for whom and through whom all things exist, should, in bringing many sons to glory, make the leader of their salvation perfect through sufferings.

After establishing the Son's intrinsic superiority over angels, our author now turns to prove a very different point, the real humanity of the incarnate Son. His reasoning here is rather complex and not fully expressed, and the real point of the argument does not properly emerge until several verses later. In the previous section readers have been warned to take care lest they jeopardise their own salvation. **The world to 5 come** is a way of referring to this salvation **about which** he has just been speaking, and which is described later as 'the age to come' (vi. 5) and 'the city to come' (xiii. 14). This does not mean the Christian life in general, or the Christian's foretaste of eternity, or the world of ultimate reality which breaks through the transience of the physical world. It is a Jewish eschatological phrase which signifies the new world order which will come into being at the end of this age after the completion of 'the days of the Messiah'. The use of the word οἰκουμένη for **world** shows that our author thought of this salvation in corporate and social terms.

According to Jewish theology angels ruled over the nations in this world (cf. Deut. xxxii. 8 (LXX); Dan. x. 13). What of the future world? Paul claimed that then men will rule angels (1 Cor. vi. 2 f.). Our author insists that **it is not to angels that he,** that is God, **has subjected** the future world. This suggests a contrast, and the previous argument might lead to the expectation that, if not to angels, then it is to the eternal Son that dominion will be given. But this is not however the point that is to be made. For Psalm viii. 4-6 is quoted to show that all things are to be subjected to one who has actually been made lower than the angels.

These verses are cited from the LXX with almost complete accuracy, except for an insignificant omission. The quotation
6 is prefaced by the words **One has somewhere solemnly declared.** This seemingly nonchalant introduction in fact follows an Alexandrine formula which can be paralleled in Philonic usage (*de Ebriet.* 61). It emphasises the extreme view of scriptural inspiration held by the writer. God speaks through the words of scripture in solemn oracles, so that the name of the human speaker and the context of his words can be forgotten.

Other New Testament writers besides the author of Hebrews made use of Psalm viii, but (apart from Matt. xxi. 16, where Psalm viii. 3 is employed to describe the children who welcome Jesus) it is used with reference to the subjection of all things to Christ and not in connection with his being made a little lower than the angels. According to Eph. i. 22 and 1 Peter iii. 22 this dominion has been given to Christ at his ascension, but according to 1 Cor. xv. 27 and Phil. iii. 21 it will be given to him at his final appearing. Our author adopts the latter interpretation; for in He. x. 13 (where the Psalm is cited again) it is expressly stated that Christ at his ascension was (and still is) awaiting the subjection of all things to himself.

The Hebrew version of this Psalm does not contain a reference to angels but to *elohim*, that is, to God. It is asserted there that man was created a little inferior to God, to be his viceregent on earth. Man has been given universal dominion and has been enthroned with honour and glory. Man here means primarily Adam of the Genesis myth, but the word extends to all mankind. There was rabbinic speculation that the words of the Psalm were addressed to man by the angels (P^{e}siq. 34a) and the Greek version of the Psalm which our author used renders *elohim* by angels.

In this first citation of Psalm viii Jesus is not mentioned, nor do the words refer to him. **What is man, that thou rememberest him, or the son of man, that thou hast regard for him?** The parallelism of Hebrew poetry shows that the son of man is no more here than a periphrasis for man. Our author probably knew of Jesus' self-designation as the Son of Man, and this may have influenced his choice of this *testimonium*. Jesus took the phrase Son of Man from his bible, and the same pattern of man's exaltation after previous degradation is seen here as in the Son of Man passage in Dan. vii (cf. Psalm lxxx. 17). However this may be, our writer does not here apply 'the Son of Man' in Psalm viii. 4 to Jesus at all.

Whereas the meaning of the Psalm is that man has been made a little inferior to the angels, the citation should here be translated **Thou didst make him for a short while lower than** 7 **the angels.** Our author has introduced a time sequence. If man is for a little while lower than angels, there must have been a time when he was not inferior to them; and if this inferiority lasted for only a brief period, the words which follow must apply to the period after this inferior status: **Thou didst crown him with glory and honour: thou didst put all things in** 8 **subjection under his feet.**

Our author now proceeds to a detailed exegesis of this passage. It plainly seems to refer to man. **By 'subjecting everything' to him, it means that he left nothing that is not subject to him.** This is a generalisation that admits of no exception (other than that made by Paul in 1 Cor. xv. 27, that God does not subject himself to man). But, our author continues, as yet this state of affairs is just not true: it is contrary to the evidence of our eyes. Man 'has not lost his capacity for receiving that for which he was created' (Westcott), but he is far from being the monarch of all he surveys. Universal dominion is his future destiny, not his present possession. **In fact we do not yet see all things subjected to men.** The Greek here has 'subjected to him', which must mean **subjected**

to men, for as yet Jesus has not been mentioned. It is not this but the earlier verse of the Psalm that refers to Jesus. Verse 5 of Psalm viii has an obvious messianic fulfilment, for by the 9 eye of faith **we do see one who was made 'for a short while lower than the angels'.** This is Jesus. His name is mentioned here for the first time in the Epistle. It occurs in an emphatic position in the sentence, stressing the humanity of the Saviour by its juxtaposition with 'lower than the angels', and emphasising his work of salvation by its juxtaposition with what follows.

With Jesus' ascension his inferior status has been left behind, and he is **through the suffering of death now 'crowned with glory and honour'.** He wears the royal diadem, not the victor's wreath; and the glory and honour with which he has been crowned are coincident with his *ascension*, not with his pre-existence, baptism, transfiguration or public ministry; nor even with his death. Furthermore he was not crowned because he had to suffer death, but because he had died suffering. The emphasis is on Jesus' suffering unto death rather than on the fact of death itself.

The outcome of his death and ascension was **that, separated from God, he might taste death on behalf of all men.** This was not the result of Jesus being made a little lower than the angels, but (as the order of words in the Greek suggests) of his coronation in heaven. It is the heavenly session of Christ which completes the finished work of Christ upon the Cross. The phrase **taste of death,** a semitism found elsewhere in the New Testament (cf. Mark ix. 1), refers not to Jesus' sampling the experience of being dead, but to his bitter sensation of dying.

The Greek here could mean that Jesus died on behalf of all creatures (including angels), not just **on behalf of all men;** but if this had been intended a neuter plural with the article would have been expected, and in any case, the argument requires that Jesus, being a man, was all men's representative. Jesus did not die instead of all men, for all men still have to die; but Jesus did die on behalf of all mankind as their representative. He did for man what no other man was qualified to do. His salvation avails for all men, if they are willing to accept it. Universalism is qualified by man's obedience to the message of salvation.

Jesus suffered in desolation, without the comfort and consolation of his heavenly Father (Mark xv. 34); and thus he died **separated from God.** This last phrase could be translated to mean that at Jesus' demise it was his humanity and not his divinity that died (cf. the phrase 'gave up the ghost'); but if this were meant, the phrase would be clumsy Greek and the thought would be the theological development of a later age. The words might also be translated to mean that Jesus died for everyone except God; but this exception is so self-evident that it does not need to be expressed.

Almost all MSS here read χάριτι θεοῦ, but χωρὶς θεοῦ was known both to Origen and Jerome, and accepted by Ambrose, Eusebius and Theodore of Mopsuestia. Despite the lack of manuscript attestation (M *424*ᶜ *1739*), the latter reading is to be preferred on both grounds of intrinsic probability and on the principle of *difficilior lectio potior* (the more difficult reading is to be preferred). Our writer is fond of χωρὶς (used twelve times elsewhere in the Epistle), and the word might either have been corrupted into χάριτι through misunderstanding or substituted for reasons of reverence or orthodoxy. χάριτι θεοῦ on the other hand is a bald phrase, not particularly suited to the context and uncharacteristic of our author. It is hard to see how it could have been corrupted into χωρὶς θεοῦ; while the addition of χωρὶς θεοῦ as a scribal gloss, with the subsequent omission of χάριτι θεοῦ, seems an over-complicated explanation. The suggestion that both χωρὶς and χάριτι are corrupt readings lacks manuscript evidence. Conjectural emendations are hardly ever required in New Testament textual criticism.

The writer has stated the fact of Jesus' death. He now explains why Jesus had to suffer and to die. Since God had created man, **it was fitting that God** should take steps to enable man to 10 reach the goal for which he had been created, for the route to this goal had become blocked by sin. The suffering of Christ was not fortuitous, but part of God's providence (cf. Mark viii. 31). It was appropriate that the action taken to help man should include suffering, since suffering is mankind's common lot. God's action is appropriate too at a profounder level. In as much as God is Creator, he is the final and efficient cause of the universe, **for whom and through whom all things exist.** This phrase, which is found in Stoic writings (but not in Philo), has echoes also in Pauline thought (Ro. xi. 36, 1 Cor. viii. 6a). Our author notes a real correspondence between the work of creation and the work of salvation, without actually explaining wherein this correspondence lies. The costly self-offering of a suffering Saviour is, in a mysterious way, congruous with the generosity of a self-effacing Creator. The very idea of creation suggests self-emptying, self-effacement, self-denial by him in whom lies all the fullness of infinite being.

The Greek text could be translated to mean that it was Christ who brought many sons to glory by his perfect sacrifice; but the argument of the sentence (as well as the order of the words) requires the meaning that it was God himself who took action **in bringing many sons to glory,** since this initiative is appropriate to his activity as Creator. **Glory** here signifies the splendour of ultimate salvation, which awaits the consummation of all things. The use of the aorist participle ἀγαγόντα, **in bringing** men **to glory,** cannot mean that God's redeeming activity has preceded Christ's perfect sacrifice, for until the Last Day the saints of the old dispensation cannot be made perfect (xi. 39). Both the perfecting of Christ's sacrifice and God's gift of future salvation are different aspects of the same work of God, and no reference to succession of time is intended. The elect are described as **sons,** since they have been adopted by God to sonship (Ro. viii. 15; Gal. iv. 5; Eph. i. 5). The Epistle to the Hebrews, in common with Pauline and Johannine literature, contains no doctrine of universal divine fatherhood. God is called the 'Father of spirits' (xii. 9), not the father of all men. Men are regarded as having by their sins alienated themselves from their filial relationship with God. The phrase **many sons** does not contradict the earlier statement that Jesus tasted death on behalf of all men. It underlines the lack of universal response to the gospel.

Jesus is called **the leader of their salvation.** The word ἀρχηγός is found in the Acts (iii. 15; v. 31) and elsewhere in this Epistle (xii. 2). It is used in secular literature to designate the founder and protector of a city; but this meaning is inappropriate here, since it is not Jesus but God who is the founder of the heavenly city (xi. 10). ἀρχηγός can also be used to describe the head of a family or clan (Ex. vi. 14; Nu. x. 4), but here it has the added nuance of a leader who commands by going in front of his men and pioneering the way that leads to salvation (cf. v. 9). The word was used of Heracles, and it is probable that against this kind of Hellenistic background the title of Divine Hero was ascribed to Jesus.

If God was to act appropriately, it followed that he should **make the leader of their salvation perfect through sufferings.** This does not imply that Jesus, before his passion, was morally imperfect; indeed, in iv. 15 this is explicitly denied. It refers rather to the full development of Jesus' human character in response to his intense sufferings. It was his perfectly unified response which completed his work of salvation. The idea of a person's life being perfected by a martyr's death was not unknown to Judaism (4 Macc. vii. 15), and in the Gospels Jesus' death is seen as completing and perfecting his life (Luke xiii. 32; John xix. 30). In the Epistle to the Hebrews the ideas of completion and perfection are frequently in the mind of its writer, not only in connection with Jesus' sacrifice but also with reference to the appropriation of its benefits by Christians. According to our author the stern discipline of suffering schooled Jesus to offer his obedience and faithfulness to the full (v. 7 ff.), so that death rendered him incapable of further sacrifice. Because of this perfect and completed sacrifice, he now exercises his priesthood in heaven as the perfected Son (vii. 28).

6. JESUS' FULL HUMANITY. ii. 11-18

(11) For both he who consecrates and those who are consecrated have a common parent. For this reason he is not ashamed to call them brothers, (12) saying, 'I will proclaim thy name to my brothers, I will sing thy praise in the midst of the congregation'; (13) and again, 'I will keep my trust in him'; and again, 'Here am I and the

children whom God has given me'. (14) Therefore, since the children share in blood and flesh, he himself similarly partook of these also, that through death he might depose him who had power over death, that is, the devil, (15) and release those who throughout their life have been subject to servitude through their fear of death. (16) For it is not, of course, angels whom he helps, but the offspring of Abraham. (17) For this reason it was incumbent upon him to be made like to his brothers in every respect, that he might be a merciful and faithful high priest in relation to God, to expiate the sins of the people. (18) For in that he has suffered and was tempted, he is able to help those who are being tempted.

Our author, having spoken of the redeemed as sons of God, 11 now explains their relationship to the Son of God. **For both he who consecrates and those who are consecrated have a common parent.** Consecration is a sacrificial term which signifies the result rather than the mode of sacrifice. Consecration by Christ means man's sanctification and restoration to God through the removal by Christ of impurity brought by sin. A timeless present tense is used here to describe those who are consecrated, including the saints of the old dispensation as well as Christians of the new dispensation. Jesus is here exercising a divine function since, according to the Old Testament, it is God who consecrates. He and those whom he consecrates **have a common parent.** The phrase ἐξ ἑνός could be rendered 'from a common stock', in which case the thought would be similar to that expressed in Acts xvii. 26. There, however, a doctrine of God's universal fatherhood is asserted; but since our author does not hold this doctrine elsewhere in the Epistle, the phrase probably denotes **a common parent.** This is neither Adam nor Abraham but God. In the previous verse those who are consecrated are called sons of God. Jesus too is the Son of God, but in a special sense. He has a special and unique relationship with his Father.

Yet this does not mean that the Son shrinks from regarding others as his brothers. **For this reason he is not ashamed to call them brothers,** that is, those whom he consecrates. (The

N.E.B. translation 'he does not shrink from calling men his brothers' is erroneous.)

According to the gospels the Risen Lord does call his disciples brothers (Matt. xxviii. 10; John xx. 17), but our author prefers to prove his point by the inspired words of the Old Testament. Accordingly he cites Psalm xxii. 23 (with one slight alteration) in the LXX version. He has no qualms in assigning the words of this messianic psalm to Jesus, and in this he follows the tradition of the early church.

This psalm has left a very deep impression on the writings of the New Testament. Originally it was applied to the passion of Jesus, and the gospel accounts of the distribution of Jesus' clothes at Calvary, the attitude of the onlookers and the taunts which were thrown at him all bear the marks of Psalm xxii's influence. Later in this Epistle Psalm xxii. 5 may have influenced the description of Jesus' agony in the garden of Gethsemane (v. 7). Perhaps John's mention of the seamless robe of Jesus (John xix. 23; cf. Psalm xxii. 18) comes closest to the thought of our author, since the seamless robe suggests that Jesus was wearing a priestly garment (cf. Josephus, *Antiq*. 3. 7. 4).

Psalm xxii starts with a description of a righteous martyr, and goes on to describe the vindication that he receives at God's hands. It is a verse from the latter part of the Psalm that is cited here. Jesus is quoted as **saying, 'I will proclaim thy name** 12 **to my brothers, I will sing thy praise in the midst of the congregation'.** It is possible that this verse was used in the early Church as a *testimonium* of the presence of the risen Lord at its worship. It is cited here to show that Jesus recognises his kinship with members of the Christian family. The same point is made by two further texts. **And again,** he quotes the scrip- 13 tures, **'I will keep my trust in him'.** This comes from Is. viii. 17 (the same words are also found in Is. xii. 2 and 2 Sam. xxii. 3). It is cited to show that Jesus had faith in God (cf. xii. 2, where Jesus is called 'leader of faith'). Faith implies human frailty: it signifies dependence, and Jesus shows his kinship with his brethren by declaring his faith in God. These words from Isaiah are put into the mouth of Jesus by our author, again following the tradition of the early church. For Is. viii, like

Psalm xxii, is used elsewhere in the New Testament. Is. viii. 8, with its prophecy of Immanuel, is alluded to in Matt. i. 23 and may have influenced Ro. viii. 31. Is. viii. 12 f., with an exhortation to courage, is quoted in 1 Peter iii. 14 f. Is. viii. 14, about the rock of offence and the stone of stumbling, is used in 1 Peter ii. 8. This chapter of Isaiah was a well-known quarry in which were found prophesies which Jesus had fulfilled; and different parts of the chapter were used with very different applications.

Our author also cites Is. viii. 18. Despite his apparent indifference to biblical contexts, he must have been aware that he was not introducing a new quotation, but continuing the next verse of his earlier quotation. When he writes **And again,** he does not intend to introduce a fresh quotation, but to make a new point (cf. x. 30). **'Here am I and the children whom God has given me'** is a text which is used to show Jesus' kinship with his followers. The Son of God is regarded as the speaker; and in his keeping are placed the children of God. The Son and the children are both members of the same family.

These three different proofs are given to show that Jesus asserts his kinship with other members of God's family; firstly, he calls them brothers, secondly, he shares with them the human attitude of faith in God, and thirdly, he speaks of them as children of God. It is improbable that our writer took these quotations from a florilegium. They come from sections of the Old Testament in frequent use in the early church, and probably our author has himself selected these verses from these well-known sections of the bible to suit his own particular argument.

Now that the kinship of Jesus with men has been established, it remains to be shown that this kinship implies for Jesus a complete humanity, so that the Incarnation was a genuine 14 assumption of human nature in its entirety. **Therefore, since the children share in blood and flesh, he himself similarly partook of these also.** The usual order of words here is inverted, so that blood is mentioned before flesh, probably because of the importance of blood for the writer's argument later in the Epistle (ix. 12 ff.; x. 19). Flesh and blood (a common Jewish collocation) signify the frailty and dependence of men compared with the power and immutability of God (cf. Matt.

xvi. 17). Flesh and blood form a constant and essential characteristic of human life (cf. Polyaenus, *Strat*. 3. 11. 1). They
bind men together in the solidarities of human existence. The
Son of God, by an act of condescension, himself assumed
complete humanity. His flesh and blood were similar to and
as real as his brothers'.

But flesh and blood inevitably entail decay and corruption.
Man cannot avoid death. Expectation of life was short in the
ancient world, while Christians faced the possibility of persecution and martyrdom at almost any time. Fear of death is natural.
It is partly fear of the unknown, partly fear of the suffering
associated with death, but mostly the paralysing fear of non-
being which clutches at the human heart. In addition to fear of
death, there was widespread fear of the punishment that might
follow death (cf. Matt. x. 28). Our writer himself later gives an
awful warning of the terrible consequences of apostasy (cf. x.
26). This fear of death and of punishment after death was not
of course confined to Jews and Christians. Stoic writers protested against the terrors of death (Epict. 3. 26. 28), and
Lucretius the Epicurean wrote his great poem in an attempt to
liberate men from its superstitious terrors.

To this whole question our author now turns. Usually he
writes about the work of Christ in the imagery of a sacrifice
for sins. Here, however, he varies the imagery, and, with
death in mind, he thinks in terms of conquest and liberation,
explaining that the purpose behind the Incarnation was **that
through death he might depose him who had power
over death, that is, the devil.** The Rabbis wrote of the
Angel of Death wielding the power of death (Mech. 72a on
Ex. xx. 20), and in Alexandrine circles it was held that God
did not make death (Wisd. Sol. i. 13). Man was made for
incorruption (Wisd. Sol. ii. 23), and it was through the devil
that death entered the world (Wisd. Sol. ii. 24). And so the devil
had power over death.

It is not explained here how Jesus broke the devil's power by
dying, just as Paul does not explain how Jesus conquered sin
by dying to sin (Ro. vi. 10). Probably the underlying thought
is that by death Jesus passed beyond the power of the devil,
and so, in his risen life, was able to crush his power. The idea

of Christ conquering the powers of evil is found elsewhere in the New Testament (John xvi. 11; cf. Col. ii. 15). In one sense the complete annihilation of the devil awaits the last day (Rev. xii. 9), and the last enemy to be destroyed is death (1 Cor. xv. 26). In another sense Jesus can be said to have destroyed death already (2 Tim. i. 10). Here it is said that Jesus has dethroned

15 the devil (not that he has put an end to death). **And** the result of this is that he can **release those who throughout their life have been subject to servitude through their fear of death.** This has not been a temporary bondage but a permanent enslavement. It is not specified exactly who it is that enslaves men in this way, but presumably the devil is meant. The thought is not far removed from Ro. vi. 17 f., where Paul speaks of men being enslaved by sin and liberated by Christ; or Ro. viii. 21, where the Apostle writes of emancipation from 'the bondage of corruption'. The Gospels provide many illustrations of Jesus, both during his incarnate ministry and as risen Lord, commanding men to 'fear not'; and a striking instance of the liberation of men by Jesus from the fear of death can be found in Rev. i. 18: 'Fear not: I am the First and the Last and the Living One, and I was dead and behold I am living for ever and ever, and I hold the keys of death and Hades'.

The next verse emphasises the nature of Jesus' beneficiaries.

16 **For it is not, of course, angels whom he helps, but the offspring of Abraham.** Before moving to another subject, our author has a final fling at the notion that Jesus was an angel. If he had been an angel, he argues, then Jesus might have helped angels; but since it is men whom he helps, therefore he could not have been an angel. (The fallen angels are apparently unaffected by Jesus' sacrifice.) The Greek fathers understood this passage to refer to the assumption of human nature by the eternal Son. The Greek verb $\epsilon\pi\iota\lambda\alpha\mu\beta\acute{\alpha}\nu\epsilon\tau\alpha\iota$ means literally to 'take hold of', hence, according to the patristic interpretation of the passage, 'to assume', but the meaning 'help' is demanded here not merely by an allusion to Is. xli. 8, but also by the introductory conjunction, which connects this sentence with what precedes and not with what follows.

The use here of the phrase **the offspring of Abraham** emphasises the continuity of the new dispensation with the old, stressing that 'salvation is from the Jews' (John iv. 22); but it does not conflict with the universalism of the Epistle. For our author would have agreed with Paul that **the offspring of Abraham** are not synonymous with Israel (Ro. ix. 6), and that anyone who belongs to Christ is an offspring of Abraham (Gal. iii. 29).

The next verse sums up the whole of the consequent argument of this Epistle. **For this reason it was incumbent upon** 17 **him to be made like to his brothers in every respect, that he might be a merciful and faithful high priest in relation to God, to expiate the sins of the people.** He did not merely resemble man in some facets of human nature. His similarity was absolute (cf. Ro. viii. 3; Phil. ii. 7). If God wished to save mankind, he had no choice but to be fully incarnate, for, as Gregory of Nazianzus later remarked, 'what is not assumed is not healed' (*Ep.* 101. 7). Unless he was fully human, he could not be the representative of men; and it was in this representative capacity that he became **a merciful and faithful high priest in relation to God.**

Here for the first of many times in this Epistle Jesus is called a high priest. The task of any priest is to reconcile, and this is the role of a high priest *par excellence*. Jesus is not only leader and consecrator: he is mediator as well. In as much as he is **merciful and faithful,** he is in strong contrast to the Jewish high priests of the Roman era. He is here called merciful not because he is forgiving (for it is God who forgives) but because he is compassionate. Philo said that a high priest should not show human affections (*de Spec. Leg.* 1. 115); but our author disagreed with him. Jesus is merciful in his relationship to men, and faithful in his relationship to God. He is not faithful because he is merciful: the two epithets describe different facets of his character. Nor is he called faithful because he is in principle trustworthy, but because he was in fact found faithful despite temptation. This point is further explained in the next chapter.

The work of a high priest, elaborated in *cc.* v, vi and vii, is to represent men **in relation to God.** His function is on the Godward side (cf. Ex. xviii. 19), **to expiate the sins of the people.** In New Testament thought (unlike Article 2 of the 39 Articles),

God is never reconciled to men, but men to God. This reconciliation is described here under the imagery of sacrifice. The
present tense of the infinitive, ἱλάσκεσθαι 'to expiate', simply
describes Jesus' priestly function: it does not imply perpetual
and continuing expiation. Propitiation is different from expiation. It has a personal object, and means the appeasement of
someone's wrath. To expiate, however, is to make amends for
sins, and the verb takes as its object the sin to be amended.
Propitiation is not a biblical concept, but expiation is the motive
underlying atonement sacrifice. Expiation is what the high
priest was believed to achieve on the Day of Atonement, when
he expiated the sins of the people. The Greek word λαός used
here for people (from which the English word laity is derived)
is employed in the New Testament to signify the 'people of
God', the whole family whom God has adopted and in which
Jesus is Son among brothers.

In the last verse of this section, the writer once more drives
home the absolute necessity of Jesus' complete humanity, if he
18 is to be of help to men. **For in that he has suffered and was
tempted, he is able to help those who are being tempted.**
Jesus' sufferings were, presumably, those which are caused by
human weakness; that is, by human fear, human grief, and
human pain caused through the infliction of physical injury.
The Greek could be translated to mean: 'being tempted in as
much as he suffered'; but this does not give such good sense,
for Jesus' temptations were not confined to his sufferings (cf.
Luke iv. 13), nor should we suppose that suffering was for him
the only cause or occasion of temptation (cf. Luke xxii. 28). Our
author does not regard temptation as necessarily the first step
on the road to ruin (contrast James 1. 14). He seems to think of
it rather as part of God's providence. He might even say, against
James, that a man is tempted by God, for temptation need be
no more than the conflict between obedience to God and inevitable human frailty.

The fact that Jesus was tempted without giving way means
that he is more, not less, **able to help those who are being
tempted.** A man who has not given way to temptation has
thereby borne its whole brunt, and he knows its full and continuing force better than a person who has succumbed. His

experience as well as his example can assist the weaker brethren. This help that Jesus gives to the tempted is, however, not to be equated with his priestly act of expiation. Expiation is something completed in the past: the help that Jesus gives is one of its continuing effects. Our author mentions this help at this point partly because a word of exhortation to his faltering flock is never far from his thoughts, and partly because his mind, perhaps unconsciously, has retained the collocation of help and expiation found in Psalm lxxix. 9.

7. SON NOT SERVANT. iii. 1-6

(1) Therefore, consecrated brothers, who share a heavenly calling, think on Jesus, the Envoy and High Priest of the faith which we profess; (2) think on him as faithful to him who appointed him, as also Moses was faithful in God's household. (3) He is counted worthy of more glory than Moses, to the extent that the founder of a household has more honour than the household. (4) For every household is founded by someone, and the founder of all things is God. (5) Moses then was faithful as a servant in all God's household, as a testimony to the words which were later to be spoken. (6) But Christ was faithful as a Son over God's household. We are his household, if we hold on to our boldness and the boast of our hope.

The preceding section ends with the description of Jesus as a merciful and faithful high priest. The writer now turns to explain in what capacity Jesus can be called faithful (just as later, in v. 1-10, he elaborates his conception of Jesus as a merciful high priest). He takes this opportunity of reminding his readers of Jesus' example, doubtless in the hope that this will strengthen their resolve: **Therefore think on Jesus, the** 1 **Envoy and High Priest of the faith which we profess.** The reiterated use of the name of Jesus in this Epistle, without the addition of Christ, draws attention to his real humanity. Our author has already pointed out to his readers that they can see

Jesus with the eye of faith (ii. 9): now he instructs them to meditate on him, considering attentively his role and function. He is **the Envoy,** because he is sent by God. The Greek word ἀπόστολος, translated **Envoy,** is the ecclesiastical term for 'apostle'; but it is used here with its primary meaning rather than in a technical Christian sense. By derivation it signifies 'one who is sent'. The word is not applied to Jesus elsewhere in the New Testament (this usage first reappears in Justin, *Apol.* 1. 12), but in the Johannine literature God is frequently said to have sent his Son into the world (cf. John iii. 17, etc.).

Angels, of course, were also sent by God (cf. He. i. 14); but the mission of the Son is unique. It must be understood in close connection with his priestly work. Jesus is both **Envoy and High Priest.** Both these offices are unique. The former refers primarily to the Incarnation, for the Son was sent into the world; while the latter applies mostly to his death, when as high priest he made expiation for sins. But the life of Jesus cannot be sundered from his death. His whole life was a self-offering, and his mission did not end before his death. Moreover in Rabbinic tradition a priest was a *shaliach* of God (Yoma, 19a-b), and the high priest was the *shaliach* of the Jewish Community on the Day of Atonement (Yoma, 1. 5). A *shaliach* (a Hebrew term which simply means 'one who is sent') was used by the Rabbis to designate an authorised representative of a community with plenipotentiary powers. Thus Jesus might be described in Rabbinic terms as a *shaliach* who represented his people before God, and this was precisely his priestly work.

Jesus is both **Envoy and High Priest** of our confession, that is, **of the faith we profess.** There is a certain self-consciousness here in the use of the second person plural. It is Christians (and not Jews) who believe on Jesus in their hearts, and so confess him with their lips (cf. Ro. x. 9). The reference is not to confession before unbelievers (cf. 1 Tim. vi. 12) but to open acknowledgement of faith (cf. 2 Cor. ix. 13). The author addresses his readers as **consecrated brothers who share a heavenly calling.** Both **consecrated** and **brothers** are used frequently in the New Testament to designate Christians, but (with the possible exception of 1 Thess. v. 27) they are not used elsewhere in combination. **Consecrated** here picks up the use

of the similar phrase 'those who are consecrated' in ii. 11. It
refers to those who are chosen to be set aside for divine use. It
implies a corporate destiny of holiness rather than the present
realisation of sanctity. **Brothers** on the other hand denotes the
close kinship which exists between Christians in virtue of their
common faith. The word was taken over by Christians from the
Old Testament, where brother is used to describe a co-religion-
ist. Christian brothers are related in that they **share a heavenly
calling.** Their bond of unity lies not in themselves, but in the
calling which they share. According to the New Testament,
there is only one vocation, to be a Christian. This is a heavenly
calling, not primarily in the sense that God calls from heaven,
but in as much as Christians are called to heaven. The emphasis
here on the heavenly nature of this calling contrasts with
Israel's call to an earthly inheritance.

Our author bids his readers to consider how Jesus' faithfulness is of a higher order than that of Moses. The stress on Jesus'
full humanity makes it necessary to prove that he is superior
to Moses, since Moses was admitted to be superior to all other
men. Philo, rhapsodising on Moses, even calls him a high priest
by divine providence (*de Vita Moys.* 2. 3); but there is no
reason to suppose that our writer has this particular extrava-
gance in mind. It is noteworthy that our author never attempts
in any way to denigrate Moses. He might, for example, have
pointed out that Moses' faithfulness was imperfect (Nu. xx.
7-13). But he casts no aspersions on him whatever. Such is not
his way. He accepts the excellence of the old dispensation, and
he proves that the new is 'better'. Jesus and Moses had this
in common: Jesus was **faithful to him who appointed him,** 2
as also Moses was faithful in God's household. There is a
reference here to Nu. xii. 8, where Moses, having been vindicated
against Aaron and Miriam, is described as the Lord's friend
to whom he spoke face to face. It is required of stewards that
they are faithful (1 Cor. iv. 1 f.). Moses is the Servant of God,
faithful in his household. The Rabbis later deduced from this
passage that Moses was even higher than the angels (Sifre 103).
Our author points out that Jesus too was **faithful to him who
appointed him.** This might be translated 'faithful to him who
created him', and the early Fathers took the phrase to be a

reference to God's creation of Jesus' human nature. (The eternal Son himself, being begotten, was not created.) This, however, gives an awkward sense, and suggests later Christological developments of the patristic age. It is better to understand the phrase as a reference to God's appointment of Jesus as Envoy and High Priest.

3   Jesus, however, is far superior to Moses. **He is counted worthy of more glory than Moses, to the extent that the founder of a household has more honour than the house-**
4   **hold. For every household is founded by someone, and the founder of all things is God.** This constitutes the first of two points of comparison which the writer draws out of his midrash on Nu. xii. 7 f. Honour is the response of men to the God-given splendour which radiates from the persons of Jesus and Moses. Moses' glory as he came down from Sinai is described in Ex. xxxiv. 29-35, and Paul contrasts this fading glory with the overflowing splendour of the new dispensation (2 Cor. iii. 5-11). Our author, however, differs from Paul in that he does not depreciate the glory of Moses, but he claims that Jesus' was greater. Moses was part of God's household, but Jesus was its founder; and it was a commonplace of ancient thought that an architect is greater than his construction (cf. Justin, *Apol.* i. 20; Philo, *de Plant.* 68). Our writer adds that, of course, God is the universal architect. Jesus' founding of the household of God was done to the glory of God, who is Creator of all things. Some scholars, however, understand this passage to mean that it was God who founded his household, not Jesus; but this is incorrect, since our author wished to contrast Moses not with God, but with Jesus. After all, Jesus did found the church. Our writer, however, does not regard the household of God as being founded during the new dispensation. It is continuous with the old, since Moses was faithful within it. Jesus was its founder, not in the sense of temporal priority but as its ground and *raison d'être*.

5   A second point of superiority is now adduced. **Moses then was faithful as a servant in all God's household, as a testimony to the words which were later to be spoken.**
6   **But Christ was faithful as a Son over God's household.** Moses is often called the Servant of God (Ex. xiv. 31; Nu. xii.

7; Deut. iii. 24; etc.). This is an honourable name, applied also
to other great figures of the Old Testament (cf. Dan. vi. 20). It
signifies the free offering of personal service rather than the
social condition of servitude. The value of Moses' service lay
in his **testimony to the words which were later to be
spoken.** These words are not those which Moses himself was
later to speak, nor yet the words of the prophets, but rather 'the
message which was announced by the Lord with whom it originated' (ii. 3). The status of Moses as servant is contrasted with
the status of **Christ** as Son (and the use of the word Christ
points to the superiority of the Messiah over his forerunners).
Our author is here making a very different point from that of
Paul in Gal. iv. 7, where the Christian's status as a son is
contrasted with his former status as a slave under the old dispensation. For our author the nature of God's household has
not been changed by the advent of Christ, nor has the status of
its members been altered. He is simply pointing out the
difference in a household of a son and a servant, however
honoured the servant may be.

The writer uses this point to encourage his readers. **We are
his household, if we hold on to our boldness and the
boast of our hope** (cf. iv. 16; x. 19, 35). Apart from $p^{13, 46}$ B
(*1022*) sa eth Lcf Ambr, the manuscripts add here the words
'firm to the end'; but these are awkward grammatically, and
they constitute a gloss taken from *v.* 14. There is a certain self-
consciousness in the phrase **We are his household.** Jews, as
such, no longer belong to the household of God. Even Christians
are not guaranteed permanent membership of the household,
unless they retain their **boldness.** παρρησία, translated boldness, does not here mean free access to God, but rather the open
acknowledgement of the Christian faith. With boldness is
coupled **the boast of our hope.** This does not mean pride in
our own strength, but an expression of trust in God's purpose
and a reliance on his promises. As the helmsman of a ship holds
on to his course despite difficulties, so the recipients of the
Epistle are exhorted to hold on to their boldness and to the
boast of their hope.

The author's use of the expression 'household of God'
illustrates his conception of the relationship between Christ

and his Church. Paul's anatomical imagery of the Body or his
nuptial analogy of the Bride are not used in this Epistle in this
connection. Our writer does not conceive of Christians as 'in
Christ' (see further on iii. 14). He thinks rather of Christ as the
founder and head of the Christian family. This concept is
essentially corporate, for the ties of the family are very close,
and its members are knit together by common activity as well as
by natural kinship. In the author's day the 'extended family',
with its large variety of age and its ramifications of relationship,
offered a closer analogy to the Church of God than the present
smaller unit of the Western family, usually comprising only
parents and children. The basic difference between our author's
image and that of the Body is that Christ is conceived of as *with*
his family rather than *in* them. Yet there was no innovation in
describing the people of God as a house. This image is found
elsewhere in the New Testament (Eph. ii. 21 f.; 1 Tim. iii. 15;
1 Peter iv. 17), and in the Old Testament the phrase 'the house
of Israel' is very frequently used (cf. the Essene phrase, 'a
holy house for Israel', in 1QS 8. 5 ff.).

8. WARNING FROM THE WILDERNESS. iii. 7-19

**(7) Therefore, as the Holy Spirit is saying: 'Today if you
hear his voice, (8) do not harden your hearts as in the
Exasperation, on the Day of Testing in the wilderness,
(9) where your fathers tested and tried (10) and saw my
deeds for forty years. Therefore I was revolted by this
generation, and I said, They are always deliberately
going astray. They did not know my ways, (11) so I vowed
in my anger, They shall never enter my rest.' (12)
Beware, brothers, lest there shall be in any of you an evil
unbelieving heart, which results in apostasy from the
living God; (13) but rather encourage each other day by
day as long as it is called Today, in order that not one of
you may be hardened in heart by the deceitfulness of
sin, (14) (for we are now partners with Christ, if indeed
we hold firm to the end the confidence which we had at**

the start), (15) as in the saying, 'Today if you hear his voice, do not harden your hearts, as in the Exasperation.' (16) And who heard and caused exasperation? Was it not all those who came out of Egypt under Moses? (17) And with whom was he revolted for forty years? Was it not with those who sinned, and whose corpses fell in the wilderness? (18) And to whom did he swear that they should not enter his rest, if not to those who were disobedient? (19) So we see that, because of unbelief, they were unable to enter.

Our author turns from promise to threat. The faithfulness of Moses makes him think of the unbelief of those whom Moses led into the wilderness. The one thought leads naturally to the other. Our author's mind turns to an Old Testament text, and he cites (with a few alterations) *vv.* 7b-11 of Psalm xcv, a psalm used in synagogue worship for the Sabbath (and later appropriated to the daily worship of the Western church). **Therefore, 7 as the Holy Spirit is saying: Today if you hear his voice, do not harden your hearts, as in the Exasperation, on the 8 Day of Testing in the wilderness.** Paul regarded the biblical accounts of uprisings in the wilderness as 'types' recorded as a warning to Christians (1 Cor. x. 11). Our author, however, regards these words of scripture as directly addressed to the recipients of his Epistle. His readers are faced with exactly the same danger of divine retribution as that which faced the Israelites in the wilderness and the Old Testament readers of this Psalm. In his view the same words are addressed by God to his Christian readers as to the Jews of old. So the readers are warned that **the Holy Spirit is saying** to them now: **Do not harden your hearts.** *The* Holy Spirit (in contrast to Holy Spirit) is habitually used in this Epistle for God's inspiration of the scriptures; but the phrase here emphasises the divine authority of God's command more than the mode of scriptural inspiration.

The emphatic **Today,** placed before **If you hear his voice,** stresses the urgency of God's warning. The phrase **Do not harden your hearts** suggests that it was within the power of his readers to obey. According to the New Testament, God blinds the eyes of Jewish unbelievers (Mark iv. 12; John xii.

40; Acts xxviii. 26; Ro. xi. 8), but he does not harden the hearts of Christian believers.

Psalm xcv refers to the rebellion in the wilderness of Sin, in Rephidim (Ex. xvii. 1 ff.) or Kadesh (Nu. xx. 1 ff.), where the people rebelled against Moses for lack of water. Because God had been put to the test there, the places where this happened were known as Massah and Meribah, and in the LXX these place-names, instead of being transliterated, were translated, as 9 here, by **Exasperation** and **Testing**. This was **where your** 10 **fathers tested and tried and saw my deeds for forty years. Therefore I was revolted by this generation.** (The words of the psalm are regarded as spoken directly by God.) Here our author has in two ways subtly altered the wording of the LXX version. In the first place he writes that God was revolted not by 'that generation' but **this generation,** thereby bringing closer to hand the threat of divine wrath. In the second place the writer has increased the period of the fathers' provocation, and decreased the length of God's anger. According to our text, the fathers' provocation lasted for forty years, but according to the LXX, the fathers' behaviour caused God to be indignant with them for this period of forty years. These forty years were taken by Rabbi Eliezer (c. A.D. 100) to designate the years of the Messiah, but this was possible only through a misinterpretation of the Hebrew text (Sanh. 99a); which our author does not adopt in his interpretation of the passage. Nor does he intend any reference (as many commentators have seen) to the forty years' period of 'wrath' from the death of Jesus to the fall of Jerusalem. Our author is throughout his Epistle strangely uninterested in contemporary references.

The citation from Psalm xcv continues: **And I said, They are always deliberately going astray. They did not know** 11 **my ways, so I vowed in my anger, They shall never enter my rest.** A literal translation of the Greek would suggest that they erred 'in their heart', but as the heart was considered to be the *locus* of the will and the seat of the intellect, their error was intentional and deliberate. They were not merely ignorant of the ways of God. True knowledge of God's ways can only come from the experience of obeying them; but they refused them recognition.

As a result, God did not merely condemn them: he fortified his condemnation by means of a vow (cf. vii. 20): **So I vowed in my anger, They shall never enter my rest.** God's anger is not for our author (as some have suggested that it was for Paul) the impersonal operation of God-given laws of cause and effect: it is rather the personal reaction of God when his patience has been exhausted. The Rabbis debated about the fate of the condemned Israelites from this verse. God vowed in his anger, **They shall never enter my rest.** Rabbi Joshua ben Karha (c. A.D. 150) said that these words referred only to future generations. Rabbi Eliezer said that God later withdrew the oath which he had uttered in anger. Rabbi Akiba (ob. A.D. 132), however, understood it to mean that the whole generation of condemned Israelites was excluded from the world to come (Sanh. 110b). This is the sense in which our writer understands the sentence. He regards this condemnation as irrevocable, because he did not believe in a doctrine of Second Repentance.

The next verse is best taken as beginning a new sentence, rather than dependent on 'therefore' right back at the beginning of *v.* 7. **Beware, brothers, lest there shall be in any of you 12 a wicked unbelieving heart, which results in apostasy from the living God.** Our author regards this danger not as a remote possibility, but as a present peril. He is not content with general exhortation, but he is concerned lest a single member of his flock should lapse. Jesus had said that out of the heart evil thoughts proceed (Mark vii. 21), and for our author unbelief (not mere lack of faith) issues too from the heart. For him this is apostasy. To lapse into Judaism is to fall away from the living God, even though Jews still confessed belief in God. Because our writer regards Christ as God, to renounce Christianity in favour of Judaism is apostasy from God (cf. Gal. iv. 9; cf. John v. 23). In the Old Testament the phrase **the living God** is not infrequent, emphasising the power of the Creator in contrast to the emptiness of idols. Here, however, the words point menacingly to the power of divine retribution (cf. x. 31; contrast xii. 22).

There is a change now to a more positive note. **But rather 13 encourage each other day by day, as long as it is called**

Today, in order that not one of you may be hardened in heart by the deceitfulness of sin. Our author has a strong sense of the mutual encouragement which Christians can give each other, both by regular attendance at public worship (x. 25) and, as here, by personal counsel. This mutual encouragement, he urges, should not merely be given on the first day of the week, but **day by day.** It is necessary, **so long as it is called Today;** that is, not just during the whole of a person's earthly existence, or until the Last Day, but so long as God continues to address men through the words of this Psalm.

The voice of God is to be urgently obeyed, and the consequences of disobedience are terrifying. But on the other hand the effect of mutual encouragement should be **that not one of you may be hardened in heart by the deceitfulness of sin.** Once again, our author shows his concern for each individual. Deceitfulness of sin may cause any of them to harden his heart. The Greek word ἀπάτη in this verse could mean pleasure as well as deceit (cf. Mark iv. 19). But it is improbable that the sclerogenic effect of pleasure is intended. Sin is regarded in this passage almost as a person tricking men into its power. It is probably right to see a reference here to the primal sin wherein Adam and Eve were deceived by the serpent (cf. 1 Tim. ii. 14).

The writer explains, in an interjection, that there is a special reason why his readers should not fall under the influence of
14 sin. **For we are now partners with Christ, if indeed we hold firm to the end the confidence which we had at the start.** The perfect tense of the verb γεγόναμεν stresses that partnership with Christ was effected in the past and continues into the present. Most commentators take the phrase to mean that we are 'partakers of Christ' (R.V.) or that 'we share in Christ' (R.S.V.). This Pauline concept, however, is entirely alien to our author, who regards Christ not as the new humanity into whom believers are incorporated by faith-union, but as the head of the Christian family, the Son among his brothers. The use elsewhere in this Epistle of μέτοχος in connection with the Christian calling (iii. 1) and the Holy Spirit (vi. 4) does not determine its meaning in this passage, where it signifies fellow-partner.

This partnership with Christ demands faithfulness: we can only remain **partners if indeed we hold firm to the end the confidence which we had at the start.** It is not uncommon for converts to begin with an initial flush of enthusiasm (cf. x. 32), only to flag, falter and fail to persevere. Our writer regards this not as a distant danger, but as a present possibility (cf. iii. 6). His readers' confidence, instead of developing from its initial impulse (the Greek phrase here means literally 'the beginning of our confidence'), is now in real danger of wavering. The word ὑπόστασις, translated as **confidence** (cf. xi. 1), means literally 'standing under' and thus ground or basis. *Hypostasis* can have the philosophical meaning of existence or essence (cf. i. 3) which later developed as specialised terms in the technical language of patristic Christology. Here it signifies that upon which a man bases his attitude, i.e. his confidence. Our author does not specify precisely what is entailed by keeping confidence **firm to the end.** He is concerned to contrast the end of faith with its beginning, not to identify its termination with death or with the Last Day.

It is possible that the reiteration of Psalm xcv. 8 (LXX) in the next verse should be taken either with the preceding *v.* 14, or with *v.* 16 which follows it. It is best, however, to take it with the earlier *v.* 13 as a recapitulation of the words of Psalm xcv (LXX) cited in that verse. Thus *v.* 14, with its reminder of Christians' partnership with Christ, is best understood as a parenthesis, and the writer resumes his earlier warning, **as in the saying, 'Today if you hear his voice, do not harden** 15 **your hearts, as in the Exasperation'.**

Our author next proceeds to analyse the relationship between rebellion and retribution in a series of rhetorical questions after the manner of a Greek diatribe. **And who heard and caused** 16 **exasperation? Was it not all those who came out of Egypt under Moses?** A different punctuation would give the following very different meaning: 'Some heard and caused exasperation, but not all those who came out of Egypt'. This would not only involve difficult Greek syntax, but it would also be a most misleading way of referring to the 600,000 Israelites who came out of Egypt (Ex. xii. 37), every one of whom died in the wilderness except Joshua and Caleb (Nu. xiv. 38). **And with** 17 whom was he revolted for forty years? Was it not with those who sinned and whose corpses fell in the wilderness? Our author here reverts to the LXX text of Psalm xcv, where it is said that God's disgust lasted throughout the forty years (contrast *v*. 10). His reference to **corpses**, however, is

18 not taken from this Psalm but from Nu. xiv. 29 (LXX). **And to whom did he swear that they should not enter his rest,**

19 **if not to those who were disobedient? So we see that, because of unbelief, they were unable to enter.** Their entry was not a physical but a moral impossibility.

The progression of the author's argument here is relentless. On the part of man heedlessness leads to sin, sin leads to disobedience, and disobedience leads to unbelief. The response of God to this is firstly exasperation, secondly disgust, then the sentence of death and finally a vow of perpetual exclusion from his rest.

9. THE REST AND THE PEOPLE OF GOD. iv. 1-11

(1) We should therefore be on guard, for fear that any of you, while the promise of entering his rest still remains open, thinks that he has missed the opportunity of reaching it. (2) For indeed we have heard the good news, just as they did too; but the message which they heard did not benefit them, because for the hearers it was not blended with faith. (3) We who have believed are entering that rest, as he has said, 'So I vowed in my anger, They shall never enter my rest', even though his works had been finished from the foundation of the world. (4) For he has spoken somewhere about the seventh day as follows, 'And God rested on the seventh day from all his works', (5) and again this saying, 'They shall never enter my rest'. (6) Since then it still remains for some people to enter, and since those who heard the good news in the first place did not enter because of disobedience, (7) again he appoints a particular day, 'Today', speaking by David so long afterwards, as has been quoted before,

'Today if you hear his voice, do not harden your hearts'. (8) For if Joshua had given them rest, God would not later be speaking about another day. (9) So there still remains a sabbath rest for the people of God. (10) For he who has entered his rest has himself rested from his works, as God has rested from his. (11) Let us therefore strive to enter that rest, so that no one may fall through the same kind of disobedience.

The terrible consequences of sin and disobedience have just been pointed out, based on the present warning of Psalm xcv (LXX). Yet this psalm was actually written many hundreds of years before our Epistle. If the Israelites in the wilderness had been permanently excluded from the 'rest' of which God had spoken, how could the readers of this Epistle be sure that the promise which had been forfeited by the Israelites still remained open for them? Our author sees the force of this objection, which might lead his readers to indifference or to despair. **We should therefore be on guard, for fear that any of you, 1 while the promise of entering his rest still remains open, thinks that he has missed the opportunity of reaching it.** Although this is the first mention in the Epistle of a promise, the exclusion of the rebellious Israelites presupposes that there must have been an earlier promise of entry from which they have been excluded. The succeeding verses explain on what grounds this promise of rest remains open.

Stronger language is used here than in iii. 12 about the necessity of guarding against the dangers which beset the Christian life. Most commentators have not, however, seen much difference between the dangers mentioned in the two passages, translating here as follows: 'We should therefore remain in fear lest any of you, by neglecting the promise of entering his rest, might seem (or might be judged) to have failed to reach it'. According to this interpretation the writer, for reasons of pastoral tact, has not wished to commit himself to the definite statement that some of his readers may have by neglect already put themselves beyond the reach of God's promises (cf. vi. 9) but prefers rather to use a moderating expression in the hope of frightening his readers into a deepened discipleship. This rendering is, however, unsuited to the context. For the verses which follow are not concerned with the disaster of having failed to obtain the divine promise, but with the danger of thinking that the promise is no longer operative.

Our author begins his explanation of the continuing nature of God's promise by pointing out the similarities and differences
2 between his readers and the rejected Israelites. **For indeed we have heard the good news, just as they did too; but the message which they heard did not benefit them, because for the hearers it was not blended with faith.** The word εὐηγγελισμένοι, translated **heard the good news,** became a technical term for the preaching of the Christian gospel (and the English word Evangel is transliterated from the same Greek root). In the Old Testament it is used, as here, with its primary meaning of bringing good news (e.g. Is. lii. 7). The rejected Israelites heard the good news of God's promise just as Christians too have heard it. But for the former it was useless. The Greek phrase ὁ λόγος τῆς ἀκοῆς, translated the **message which they heard,** is literally 'the word of hearing'; or, if ἀκοή were to be taken in an active sense, it could bear the meaning of 'the word of preaching' as in 1 Thess. ii. 13. Whether the writer intended to refer to the word spoken or heard, it was equally profitless since **for the hearers it was not blended with faith.**

At this point in the text there are several manuscript variations from the Greek words which are rendered by the last phrase. The most important of these makes this phrase not an explanation of the reasons why the word which they heard was profitless to them, but a description of those who heard the word and failed to profit by it. There is considerable support for the accusative plural συγκεκερασμένους (instead of the nominative singular συγκεκερασμένος). It is found in p¹³, ⁴⁶ A B D*ᵒK M 69 vg bo syʰ sa(3) bo Chr Theodᵐᵒᵖˢ Aug. With this reading the sentence should be rendered: 'The message which they heard did not profit them, since they did not mix with (or were not united with) those who heard in faith'. According to this interpretation, 'those who heard in faith' should be identified with Moses, Joshua and Caleb, and the good news which was heard would have been profitable if the Israelites had been united with their leaders in the solidarity of

faith. Such an idea, however, is uncharacteristic of our author
and it probably rests on a primitive corruption of the text. For
the change from nominative masculine singular to accusative
plural involves the addition of only one letter and is explicable
here by homoioteleuton, while a change the other way round
cannot be so easily explained. Accordingly the reading συγκεκερασμένος is preferable. The good news, spoken and heard,
must be joined with faith if it is to be effective for salvation (cf.
Ro. x. 8 f.).

Christians possess this faith which the rejected Israelites
lacked; **we who have believed are entering that rest, as** 3
**he has said, 'So I vowed in my anger, They shall never
enter my rest'.** At their Christian initiation our author and
his readers had made an act of belief and this has now become
a permanent attitude of faith. Because the Israelites had lacked
that faith they had been rejected; and because our writer and
his readers possess that faith **they are** now **entering that rest.**
Contrary to some commentators, the Greek text means neither
that they are certain to enter, nor that they will enter, but that
they are already in process of entering. The Christian pilgrimage
is not an aimless wandering, like that of the Israelites in the
desert. It is a deliberate, straight course on a well-mapped
route. Every step brings the company of Christians nearer their
destination. At the beginning the pilgrim is given a foretaste
of the future in order to whet his appetite (vi. 4). But in this
Epistle there is no realised eschatology (cf. comment on xii. 22).
The text does not mean that Christians have actually entered,
but that they are entering that rest. Life is a hard pilgrimage,
beset by temptations; but Christians have a leader (ii. 10; xii. 2)
who has already gone before them (vi. 20) and finished the
course (xii. 2), and at the end of the road there is rest and
refreshment in the city of the living God (xii. 28).

God excluded the rebellious Israelites from this rest, **even
though his works had been finished from the foundation
of the world.** This 'rest', like everything else God has made,
was created when the universe came into being. The fear was
groundless that God, since he has excluded the rejected Israelites from his rest, would not allow anyone else to enter. Time is
irrelevant for the fulfilment of God's purposes. That which was

created at the beginning is reserved for the end. The 'rest' is already in being; and so the promise must still stand.

This point, as usual, is proved by means of scriptural texts. Once again the biblical references seem casual (cf. ii. 6), but the apparent vagueness really signifies that a well-known text is
4 being quoted here. **For he has spoken somewhere about the seventh day as follows, 'And God rested on the seventh**
5 **day from all his works', and again this saying, 'They shall never enter my rest'.** The first of these two quotations is taken from Gen. ii. 2. The juxtaposition of these two texts is important for the argument. For it has to be shown that the phrase 'my rest' in Psalm xcv. 11 does not mean 'the rest in Canaan which I promised them'. Did not the successors of the rejected Israelites enter the promised rest when they entered the land of their inheritance? If so, how can it be proved that God's rest still lies in the future? The answer to these questions is provided by Gen. ii. 2. If **God rested on the seventh day from all his works,** the phrase 'my rest' must signify the 'rest' which God enjoyed after creating the universe. He offered to share his 'rest' with mankind. And therefore the promise of entering the 'rest' is still open.

This 'rest' is not a vague promise which was cancelled when it was rejected by those to whom it was originally made. God has renewed it, with a definite time when it is to be accepted.
6 **Since then it still remains for some people to enter, and since those who heard the good news in the first place**
7 **did not enter because of disobedience, again he appoints a particular day, 'Today'.** This naming of a particular day was done years and years after the Israelites had been excluded from God's rest. For this Psalm was, humanly speaking, written by David (the LXX, but not the M.T., ascribes it specifically to him). David lived centuries after the wilderness wanderings. God is believed by our author to be addressing Psalm xcv to him and to his contemporaries; yet, when these words were first spoken, God was **speaking by David so long afterwards,** that is, so long after the events to which Psalm xcv refer, **as** can be seen in the passage which **has been quoted before, 'Today if you hear his voice, do not harden your hearts'.** Thus a second argument is adduced to show that the 'rest' of

Psalm xcv is to be identified with heaven, and not with entry into the promised land; this time an *a posteriori* argument. **If 8 Joshua had given them rest, God would not later,** through a psalm of David, **be speaking about another day.** The Greek form of Joshua is the same as that of Jesus, and the naming of Joshua here designates him as a kind of type of Jesus. Joshua went at the head of the tribes of Israel as their earthly commander, but Jesus is the spiritual commander who pioneered the way for his brothers to their eternal destiny. Jesus accomplished under the new dispensation something better than Joshua could achieve under the old dispensation. Joshua could only lead his people to their earthly inheritance, while Jesus is the leader who opened the way for his people to their abiding and eternal rest.

The final conclusion of this complex biblical exegesis is now reached. **So there still remains a sabbath rest for the people** 9 **of God. For he who has entered his rest has himself rested** 10 **from his works, as God has rested from his.** God stopped work on the seventh day, and the promise of his rest is still offered to men; not however to anyone, but to the people of God. This sabbath rest of God after the creation of the universe was the model on which God instituted the Jewish sabbath. This was a 'rest'; and the same word for 'rest' which is used in Psalm xcv (LXX) is employed to describe the sabbath in Ex. xxxiv. 21, xxxv. 2 (LXX). The sabbath had as its object the hallowing of life (cf. Ex. xxxi. 14), and it was venerated as a 'delight' (cf. Is. lviii. 13); not merely an afterglow of the delights of Paradise, but also an anticipation of the delights of Heaven. 'The Sabbath is the image of the world to come' (Gen. R. 17 (12a)). Our author's conception of heaven as a sabbath rest is therefore in accordance with Jewish thought, although the actual word σαββατισμός is not found elsewhere in the bible.

The use by our author of the imagery of the wilderness wanderings and of the idea of 'rest', however superficial some of his arguments from the biblical texts may seem, reflects some of his deepest convictions and expresses some of his fundamental attitudes towards the Christian life. For him life is a struggle, fittingly concluded by a sabbath rest. He does not think of the people of God as inhabiting city dwellings built upon firm foundations, but rather as living like nomads in tents, looking forward to the city that is to come. In this transient world there is no ultimate security, no final achievement, no objective fulfilment. The vision of the end gives encouragement to brave the inevitable hardships of the Christian pilgrimage. Travellers are heartened by the knowledge that their leader who has gone before them and who has made their journey possible has himself shared the human weaknesses with which pilgrims are beset. Our author conceives his task to be not primarily instruction but rather encouragement of God's people (and warning against defaulters who may 'fall out') on their forward march across the wilderness of life. 'Stiffen your drooping hands and straighten your failing knees and make straight paths for your feet', they are ordered (xii. 12); and our author gives moral admonitions which might be termed 'a highway code' to keep them moving in a body direct towards their goal.

There is nothing novel in the use of this imagery. The type of the Exodus was formative for Judaism, and also exercised great influence on early Christian thinking (cf. H. Sahlin, in *The Root of the Vine*, ed. A. Fridrichsen (1953), pp. 81 ff.). Although our author has his own characteristic method of arguing his points, he is using an accepted theme of primitive Christian catechesis (cf. 1 Cor. x). Moreover the Jewish scriptures contain many references both to the 'rest' which God will give to his people after their wanderings, and to the 'rest' which God gives to individuals to meet their need for peace and repose. Jesus himself is reported to have promised, in words reminiscent of Ecclus. li. 27, that he will give rest to the weary (Matt. xi. 28). Our author takes up the twin themes of present journeying and final rest, and blends them with the concept of Jesus as high priest. It was not until later that speculation in gnostic circles arose about the nature of this rest (cf. Gospel of Truth, f. xxii.[r] l. 1; Gospel of Thomas, logia 50, 51, 60, 90).

The author's last word on the subject of God's rest consists
11 of an exhortation, with an appeal to effort and enthusiasm. **Let us therefore strive to enter that rest, so that no one may fall through the same kind of disobedience.** The Greek word translated **kind** normally means 'example'. Here, how-

ever our author is warning his readers against following the
example of others, not against giving an example themselves;
and so it is best to take ὑπόδειγμα as signifying what the cognate
word παράδειγμα usually means. The warning is not about
falling into disobedience, but falling, like the rejected Israelites,
through disobedience.

10. THE SWORD OF GOD. iv. 12-14

**(12) For the word of God is alive and active, sharper than
any two-edged sword, penetrating to the dividing point
of soul and spirit, and joints and marrow, and discerning
the feelings and intents of the heart. (13) No created
thing is invisible to him, but everything is naked and
prostrate before the eyes of him to whom we must render
account. (14) Since then we have a great high priest who
has passed through the heavens, Jesus, the Son of God,
let us hold fast to what we profess.**

The previous exhortation is followed by an even sterner
warning which is concerned with the uselessness of merely
outward acceptance and obedience. God penetrates beneath the
surface. Nothing can be hidden from him whose presence is
all-pervasive and whose eyes are omnipresent. **For the word of 12
God is alive and active.** This 'word' does not signify the
person of the eternal Son, for he is never, in this Epistle,
explicitly identified with the *Logos*. It means rather God
speaking to his people, both in the old dispensation and in the
new; God speaking by prophesy, by scripture, by any mode
which he chooses to use (cf. Ro. ix. 6; 1 Cor. xiv. 36; 2 Tim. ii.
9, etc.). The 'word' here has nothing to do with Hellenistic
concepts of the rational element in creation: it signifies God's
power communicating itself to and challenging men.

Our author is doubtless aware of Alexandrine speculations
about the *Logos*, and to some extent he borrows his language
from these sources. The background of his thought, however,
is fundamentally biblical, although it is often expressed in

Alexandrine language. Here, for example, **the word of God** does not need Philo's *Logos* for its explanation (any more than it needs the Memra of the Targums). It is rather a development of the Old Testament conception of the Word of the Lord. This word **is alive.** It is not dead speech expressed in empty words; on the contrary it has within itself the dynamism and power associated with life. And so it is **active:** 'it will not return to me void, but it shall accomplish that which I please' (Is. lv. 11). It is **sharper than a two-edged sword.** This particular comparison is found in different forms elsewhere in the New Testament (Eph. vi. 17; Rev. xix. 15), and it presumably stems from the similarity of shape (and on some occasions of function) between a tongue and a dagger. The use of this image is found in Greek secular literature (Sophocles, *Ajax* 584) as well as frequently in Philo (e.g. *Quis Rer. Div.* 130-132). It is also used in the Old Testament (Prov. v. 4; cf. Gospel of Truth, f. xiii.[r] l. 2).

The imagery of a sword is used here to indicate the power of God's word to pierce through a man, **penetrating to the dividing point of soul and spirit, and joints and marrow.** In this Epistle the word ψυχή (comparatively rare in the New Testament) often means life. Here, however, it refers to the animated organism into which God has breathed his spirit so that it has become a living being. The word of God can penetrate to the very ground of a man's being and can distinguish between divine agency and that upon which it works; almost, it could be said, between grace and nature. The reference to joints and marrow helps to complete the picture of the power of God's word to penetrate to the centre of a man's personality. The phrase is not meant to be a metaphorical way of referring to the inmost juncture of the soul and spirit, nor does the passage mean that God's word divides the soul and spirit from the bones and marrow. It is rather that there is no aspect of human personality to the centre of which God's word cannot pierce. No man can keep his secrets to himself, for the word of God is active in **discerning the feelings and intents of the heart.** The heart is the centre of human personality, and so God's word penetrates there (cf. 1 Sam. xvi. 7; 1 Chron. xxviii. 9; Psalm cxxxix. 1; Jer. xx. 12). It judges and sifts a man's thoughts, both those that are coloured by the affections (**feelings**) and those which stir the will (**intents**).

Some remarkable parallels to this passage about the penetrative power of God's word can be found in Philo (e.g. *Quis Rer. Div.* 130 ff.). For Philo, however, the *Logos* is the principle of differentiation in the universe, but for our author it represents the dynamic activity of the omnipresent God. Perhaps the closest parallel to this passage in the New Testament is found in Simeon's words to Mary: 'A sword shall pierce through thine own soul, and the thoughts of many hearts shall be revealed' (Luke ii. 35).

Because God's word is pervasive throughout the universe, it penetrates to the core of human personality. **No created thing 13 is invisible to him, but everything is naked and prostrate before the eyes of him to whom we must render account.** The reference here is neither to God's word, nor to the Son, but to God himself. It was a commonplace of Jewish thought that God sees everything (Prov. xv. 3; cf. 1 Enoch ix. 5; Philo, *de Cherub.* 16). The word τετραχηλισμένα, translated **prostrate**, means literally 'gripped by the neck'. The early fathers thought that it was synonymous here with **naked**, and later commentators have tried to show that this meaning, unevidenced elsewhere, can be explained either because animals for sacrifice were hung up by the bare neck (or laid out with bared neck), or because wrestlers were said to down their opponents by pushing back their necks, thus exposing their faces. Some even think that there is a reference here to the complaint that Jews were 'a stiff-necked people' (Ex. xxxii. 9). In fact the only attested meanings of the verb are 'to grip by the neck' or (metaphorically) 'to prostrate'. The latter gives perfectly good sense here (cf. 1 Cor. xiv. 25), and should be retained. 'Naked and prostrate' is a mild and unobjectionable hysteroproteron. There is also a second disputed translation in this verse. The phrase **before whom we must render account** could be translated 'with whom we have to do' (R.V.), taking *logos* here to mean speech. This however would give a particularly jejune meaning, to which ii. 6 does not provide a real parallel; while to **render account** fits in with the sense of the passage.

By means of a brief summary the argument is now resumed

14 at the point where it was left in ii. 18. **Since then we have a great high priest who has passed through the heavens, Jesus, the Son of God, let us hold fast to what we profess.** Jesus has already been described as high priest (ii. 17). The expression **great high priest** is probably little more than pleonastic usage (cf. Philo, *de Somn.* 1. 219), as the Hebrew phrase for high priest means, literally, 'great priest'. The use of the phrase does however suggest that Jesus is greater than the levitical high priests. They have only passed through the veil of the tent; but Jesus has actually passed through the heavens to the throne of God himself (cf. Eph. iv. 10 ff.). It was popularly supposed that there were seven heavens (cf. 2 Enoch iii-xx; Chag. 12) and that God dwelt far above them. The earlier declaration that Jesus has taken his seat on the right hand of God (i. 3, 13) presupposes that he **has passed through the heavens** and the reader is prepared for the coming exposition of the high priestly work of Jesus. The juxtaposition of **Jesus** and **Son of God** stresses both the humanity of Jesus and the divinity of the Son. The hortatory words, **Let us hold fast to what we profess,** briefly summarise the preceding two chapters (cf. especially iii. 1, 6, 14).

11. THE COMPASSION OF CHRIST. iv. 15-16

(15) For we do not have a high priest who is unable to sympathise with our weaknesses, but one who in every respect has been tempted similarly to us, yet without sin. (16) Let us therefore confidently approach the throne of grace, that we may receive mercy and find grace to help in time of need.

In iii. 17 Jesus was described as a merciful and faithful high priest. It has been explained how Jesus' faithfulness was of a higher order than that of Moses. It has not, however, been fully explained in what sense Jesus can be called a compassionate 15 high priest (cf. iii. 17). A return is now made to this point. **For we do not have a high priest who is unable to sympathise**

**with our weaknesses, but one who in every respect has
been tempted similarly to us, yet without sin.** The objection is here anticipated that one so exalted cannot properly
sympathise with human frailties. For these weaknesses, inherent
in humanity, not only concern the physical side of human
life (Gal. iv. 13), but also the intellectual (Ro. vi. 19), religious
(Ro. viii. 26) and moral (1 Cor. viii. 9) spheres of human
existence. Jesus is not said to **sympathise** with these weaknesses in the sense that contemplation of them arouses in him
feelings of pity and compassion. He sympathises because he has,
through common experience, a real kinship with those who suffer.

His temptations had not been confined to certain compart-
ments of his life (e.g. to those particular temptations which are
specially mentioned in the gospels), but they covered the whole
range of human experience. **In every respect he has been
tempted similarly to us, yet without sin.** Here there is
ambiguity in the Greek, an ambiguity which is for once best
left in the English translation. The Greek can have two meanings; either that Jesus' temptations were exactly the same as
ours, except that he never succumbed to them and so he never
sinned; or that Jesus' temptations were exactly the same as ours,
except for those temptations which are the result of previous
sins. Probably our author did not clearly distinguish between
the two. The conviction of Jesus' sinlessness is deeply em-
bedded in the New Testament (2 Cor. v. 21; 1 Peter ii. 22; 1
John iii. 5; cf. John viii. 46). The gospel records portray one
who neither sinned nor had consciousness of guilt. No doubt
the account of the Suffering Servant in Is. liii and the analogy
of an unspotted and flawless sacrificial offering helped to give
expression to the doctrine of Jesus' sinlessness; but the doctrine
itself was based on the impression which Jesus made on his
disciples and which he has always made on his followers. Some
theologians have explained that the absence of original sin
rendered Jesus invulnerable to sin. This, however, would seem
to suggest that since he lacked common human frailties he was
not fully incarnate. These speculations would not have occurred
to our author. He is clear that temptation itself is not a sin: on
the contrary, temptation consists of the tension between a
desire to give deliberate consent to sin and a determination of

steadfast obedience to God. But the question is not raised how a perfect character could develop without human errors and mistakes and without reaction against authority, or how these could be avoided during the complex of attitudes and emotions associated with adolescence. Probably by sin our author means conscious and deliberate disobedience, and in this sense he can truthfully say that Jesus was tempted, **yet without sin.** Philo, too, suggests that the *Logos* as high priest should be sinless (*de Spec. Leg.* 1. 230); but then Philo's *Logos* had no experience of the frailties inherent in adult existence.

Precisely because Christians have a compassionate high priest, they have grounds for confident assurance (cf. iii. 6; x. 19, 35) that the barriers between God and man have been removed. And so the Christian way is much better than the Judaism into which his readers are in danger of lapsing. For in Judaism only the priests could approach God, but our writer encourages *all*
16 his readers: **Let us therefore confidently approach the throne of grace, that we may receive mercy and find grace to help in time of need.** The meaning here is not primarily cultic. Our author has in mind not so much approach for worship, as approach to the highest authority who has it in his power to favour the requests that are made to him. **The throne of grace** is where God sits (not where Jesus sits); and from his throne God dispenses to the penitent not justice, but free undeserved pardon. The penitent sinner receives not merely mercy and compassion as a present gift, but also the continuance of divine favour to assist him whenever need arises. In his need the sinner can ask for and **receive mercy** now; and in addition to this request he can also **find,** unasked for, **grace to help in time of** future **need.**

12. APPOINTMENT TO HIGH PRIESTHOOD.
v. 1-4

(1) For every high priest is chosen from among men and is appointed to represent men in relation to God, to offer gifts and sacrifices for sins. (2) He can deal gently with

the ignorant and erring, since he also is beset with weakness, (3) and on this account he is obliged to make sinofferings for himself as well as for the people. (4) No one takes the office for himself, but only when called by God, just as Aaron was.

Our author now turns back to the major doctrinal theme of his Epistle. Starting from the levitical high priesthood, he establishes three necessary qualifications for the office, humanity, compassion and divine appointment; and then he proves that Jesus was high priest by showing that he had these three qualifications. For this proof, no use is made of either rabbinic speculations or rabbinic exegesis of scripture. Here, as elsewhere in the Epistle, the descriptions of Jewish institutions and beliefs are taken straight from the Old Testament. Our author seems uninterested both in the actual holders of the high priestly office and in contemporary Jewish views about the office.

It is biblical teaching that **every high priest is chosen from** 1 **among men and is appointed to represent men in relation to God.** Because a high priest is himself a man, he can act as representative of men. In fact the Jewish priesthood had a smaller range. Aaron and the levitical priesthood were chosen from among the children of Israel to minister to the Israelites (Ex. xxviii. 1; Nu. xviii. 17). Our author, however, speaks in universal terms, for he includes within his generalisation the universal priesthood of Christ. The high priest is described solely in terms of his biblical functions, to **represent** man to God in worship. The contemporary secular role of the high priest as President of the Sanhedrin or as Primate of the Jewish nation is ignored. The high priest's sole function mentioned here is **to offer gifts and sacrifices for sins.** If sacrifice was at the heart of Hebrew religion, oblation was at the heart of sacrifice. No man could stand before God with empty hands. He must offer a gift as an acknowledgement of adoration, gratitude and homage; and, in as much as man is a sinner, sacrifice must also be offered in expiation for sins. The priesthood was instituted so that priests might represent men before God in sacrifice. It is tempting to understand the **gifts** which the high priest offers as signifying meal-offerings, and the sacrifices as

blood **sacrifices;** but the two words can be used interchange-
ably in the LXX, and our author is here using an inclusive
phrase to describe all expiatory sacrifices **for sins** offered by
the high priest, especially those of the Day of Atonement. It is
noteworthy that, according to the LXX, on this occasion only,
sacrifices are made **for sins;** on all other occasions they are
made 'for sin'.

Having established that a high priest is a man from among
men, our writer next points to the weakness of human nature.

2 **He can deal gently with the weak and erring, since he
also is beset with weakness.** The word μετριοπαθεῖν, translated **deal gently with,** means literally to 'moderate feelings
towards'; a very Philonic virtue, mid-way between insensitivity
and hypersensitivity. Here, however, the word must be understood in its secondary meaning which is associated with magna-
nimity. Our author is concerned not with matters of tempera-
ment, but with a sympathetic attitude made possible by shared
experience. **The ignorant and erring** form a single class of
unwitting sinners. Their sins alone can be expiated through
sacrifice. He who sins 'with a high hand' (Nu. xv. 30 f.) can
never be forgiven. To be **beset with weakness** is a remarkable
understatement about the high priesthood during the Roman
era; but our author is concerned only with general biblical
principles, not with known weaknesses of actual high priests.
According to Lev. iv. 3-12, ix. 7, xvi. 6, 11, a high priest, since

3 he suffers from human frailty, **is obliged** first **to make sin-
offerings for himself** on the Day of Atonement by offering a
young bullock, **as well as** later **for the people** by the sacrifice
of a goat.

The third point that the writer makes about high priesthood
is that the office (literally, the honour) is a divine appointment.

4 **No one takes the office for himself, but only when called
by God, just as Aaron was.** Aaron's call by God is described
in Ex. xxviii. 1. To assume office without a divine call could be
disastrous. Korah and his company were destroyed precisely
because they had arrogated to themselves the office of burning
incense to the Lord without his call (Nu. xvi. 32 f.). Our author
is again showing a splendid indifference to the actual circumstances of his day under which high priests were elected to their

office. Before the Exile belief in the divine appointment was not thought incompatible with the hereditary office of high priest. After the Exile, however, the civil power soon assumed the right in selecting the high priest, and the office ceased to be for a life tenure. The appointment was often made in disgraceful circumstances. For example, the appointment in A.D. 67 of Phannias, the last high priest, was made in a way very hard indeed to square with the belief in divine appointment to the office (Josephus, *Bell. Jud.* 4. 3. 8).

13. JESUS AS HIGH PRIEST. v. 5-10

(5) So also the Christ did not take upon himself the glory of becoming high priest, but was appointed by One who said to him, 'Thou art my Son, today I have begotten thee'; (6) just as elsewhere he also says, 'Thou art a priest for ever in the rank of Melchisedek'. (7) In the days of his earthly life he offered prayers and supplications, with loud cries and tears, to him who was able to save him from death, and being heard was set free from fear. (8) Although he was Son, he learned obedience from what he suffered, (9) and having been made perfect he became the cause of eternal salvation for all who obey him, (10) being named by God high priest in the rank of Melchisedek.

Why did the author ever think of describing Jesus as a high priest? It may have been suggested to him by reflection on the tradition, which goes right back to the words of Jesus himself, that his death was a sacrifice; and he may have asked himself by whom this sacrifice had been offered. He may further have been influenced to think of Jesus as the high priest of the heavenly tent by the sayings of Jesus found in the New Testament in various forms, that he would build a temple not made with hands (Mark xiv. 58; xv. 29; Matt. xxvi. 61; John ii. 19). Perhaps, too, the messianic interpretation of Psalm cx, attributed to Jesus himself, may have set

95

him thinking about the implications of verse 4 of that psalm with its reference to the Melchisedekian priesthood. It is conceivable, too, that the traditions underlying the so-called High Priestly Prayer of John xvii, if our author knew them, may have encouraged him to persevere in thinking along these lines. Much had been written in Judaism about the heavenly temple, but there is no reference in earlier or contemporary Jewish literature to our author's doctrine of the Messiah's Melchisedekian priesthood, nor can the attribution of high priesthood to Christ be found in the other writings of the primitive Church. The Epistle to the Hebrews confronts us with a rare instance of fresh creative thinking by an individual of the early Christian church. His argument is grounded in detailed knowledge of the scriptures, sustained by the logical thinking of a forceful and rigorous intellect, and expressed with the elegance and precision of a cultured Hellenist.

After establishing representative capacity, human sympathy and divine appointment as three necessary qualifications for the high priesthood, our author next shows how Jesus fulfilled them. Characteristically he takes the three in inverse order. The divine appointment of Jesus' high priesthood is proved
5 from two biblical texts. **So also the Christ did not take upon himself the glory of becoming high priest, but was appointed by One who said to him, 'Thou art my Son,**
6 **today I have begotten thee'; just as elsewhere he also says, 'Thou art a priest for ever in the rank of Melchisedek.'** The first quotation is from Psalm ii. 7 (already cited in i. 5 in another connection) and the second is from Psalm cx. 4. (In i. 13, Psalm cx. 1 was cited.) The words of both Psalms are assumed here, as in the earlier quotations, to be addressed by God to his Son. Our author has to establish, in connection with Jesus' high priesthood, that he is Son of God, for only a high priest who is Son of God can have his rightful place at God's right hand. Only the Son can fittingly minister in the heavenly sanctuary, and only the intercession of the Son can have full efficacy with God.

Jesus is the Son of God, begotten in eternity (cf. i. 5). (This passage does not imply the everlasting begetting of the Son by the Father, which is a development of later Christology.) Our author wrote that there was **One who said to him 'Thou art my Son'**, because he believed that at a particular 'moment' in eternity the Son was begotten. He also wrote that **elsewhere he also says, 'Thou art a priest for ever'**, for this declaration of Psalm cx. 4 has continuing and indeed everlasting force. Jesus' high priesthood must have begun at the moment of the Incarnation (cf. x. 5), since before that the Son did not have the human experience prerequisite for the office; but the appointment itself is everlasting. He has been made **a priest for ever,** so that he can have no successor to himself. His priesthood is **in the rank of Melchisedek.** This type of priesthood as yet receives only a bare mention: it is to be the subject of extended treatment in chapter vii. The author of Psalm cx, in his reference to the priesthood of Melchisedek, was probably thinking of some Hasmonean prince who would combine in his person both royal and priestly office. If Psalm cx. 4 is regarded as addressed by the Father to the Son, then Jesus' appointment to the office of king and priest may be regarded as proven, just as Psalm ii. 7 proves that he really is the Son of God.

Next, our author proves the human sufferings (and hence the human sympathy) of Jesus by a reference to an incident **in the 7 days of his earthly life** (literally, in the days of his flesh, where flesh indicates the frailty and transitoriness of human existence). There is a reference here to Jesus' agony in the garden, when **he offered prayers and supplications, with loud cries and tears, to him who was able to save him from death.** The word προσενέγκας, translated **offered,** is an allusion to the sacrificial cultus. Here it implies that Christ's agony in Gethsemane was a representative act, summing up and representing before God all the entreaties of men in their hour of desperate need. **Prayers and supplications** formed a common collocation of words, the former emphasising the need which evokes the petition, the latter stressing the suppliant attitude of the petitioner. The plural forms suggest the long duration of the agony. The Gospels do not actually record that Jesus' prayers were accompanied by **loud cries and tears.** These details may have been suggested by Psalm xxii, and the Jews are said to have put great value on tears which accompany prayer. On the whole, however, it seems more probable that this small detail was either found by our author in the source of his description of Christ's agony in Gethsemane, or added by him to darken the picture of Christ's sufferings. This historical incident had evidently made a very deep impression upon our author, so that he writes here with great feeling.

The fact that Jesus prayed for himself demonstrates his real humanity, for deity has no need to make supplication. The nature of Jesus' prayer underlines his natural human fear of death: 'Take this cup from me' (Mark xiv. 36). All things are possible to God, even delivery from death; and so his prayer was made to **him who was able to save him from death.** This was not a prayer to be brought by safe conduct through death into a new life. It was a natural human prayer for delivery from the cup of suffering and for escape from imminent death. At the same time it was accompanied by complete submission to the divine will: 'But not what I will, but what thou willest'.

The petition was not granted; but **being heard** he **was set free from fear** (literally, being heard from his (godly) fear). Most commentators have understood this to mean 'being heard for his godly fear' (R.V.). The word εὐλάβεια means first prudence, then timidity, thence reverence and godly fear, and finally almost 'religion'. There is a double reason why the traditional translation should be rejected. In the first place, if 'being heard' means no more than it actually says, it must be objected that God hears all who pray in godly fear. In the second place, if 'being heard' means 'having his prayer granted', it is denied by the facts. For Jesus' prayer to be saved from death was not granted; and he died. These difficulties have led to desperate attempts to make sense of the passage. It has been suggested that the word translated **fear** is really a periphrasis for God, or even the name of an angel; that there has been a primitive (and totally unevidenced) corruption of the text, which originally ran 'and being not heard . . .'. It has even been suggested that the author intended 'from his fear' to be taken with the preceding clause, in spite of the difficult structure of the sentence, so that Jesus 'offered prayers and supplications arising out of his fear', leaving 'and being heard' as an awkward pendant; or that 'from his fear' should be taken with the following clause, so that 'because of his fear Jesus learned

from what he suffered'. None of these explanations are satis-
factory.

The best solution is to take the phrase as a pregnant construction; **and being heard (was set free) from fear.** It is true
that the phrase is cryptic and that Jesus' liberation from fear is
only indirectly relevant to the main point of the sentence, which
is that Jesus learnt obedience from his sufferings. Yet this meaning is grammatically possible: it agrees with the order of the
Greek words; and it does correspond to what actually happened.
Jesus' prayer to be saved from death was not granted; but his
fear of death was removed, and the Gospels portray him submitting himself to the events of Holy Week, devoid of terror or
anxiety from this point onwards. If Jesus was to release those
who through fear of death had been in lifelong servitude (ii. 15),
he himself had to be triumphant over his own fear of death.

Moreover, there is a real connection between the refusal to
grant his petition and his learning of obedience. It is precisely
because his prayer was not granted that **although he was Son,** 8
he learned obedience from what he suffered. He learnt
that prayer can meet with an answer very different from that
which is requested. He learnt, too, to submit himself to the
very conditions from which he had asked to be freed. Suffering
is the lot of humanity. It is to be expected by all who are sons
of God the Father; but scarcely by him who is himself the Son
of God. The coupling of learning and obedience (which make
an aphoristic jingle in Greek) was a commonplace in the
Hellenistic world, and it is also found in biblical writings; but
the attribution of learning through suffering to the Son of God
was a daring paradox for Hellenistic thought, where it was
axiomatic that God is impassible.

Our author is, of course, speaking here of the Son not as
eternally divine but as fully and completely incarnate. He does
not say that the Son learnt to obey through sufferings, nor that
he learnt obedience as one who had not known its meaning
before. Rather, he took his obedience 'up to death' (Phil. ii. 8),
to the point beyond which it could be taken no further.
The greater the test, the more profound obedience it evoked.
Thus the Son learnt full obedience in the only way possible in
an incarnate life, through submission to the will of God in a

situation of ultimate concern and under pressure of emotional shock and physical distress.

This is the sense in which the Son can properly be described 9 as **having been made perfect.** It is inherent in humanity to develop. Not to change is either subhuman (in the sense of arrested development) or superhuman (in the sense of transcendence of human limitations). 'As Jesus grew up, he advanced in wisdom and in favour with God and men' (Luke ii. 52). Perfection of human character is not a static quality of excellence: it consists in a perfect (or absolutely appropriate) response to each of life's changing circumstances. Since death marks the end of life, a person whose life has been marked throughout by obedience and who ends it with a perfectly unified response may be described as having been made perfect at his death (cf. ii. 10). As our writer explains later, it is by Jesus' perfect offering of his obedience that Christians have been sanctified (x. 5 ff.). Here, however, he looks to the future. Paul contrasted the disastrous effects of Adam's fall with the overflowing benefits of Christ's obedience and he saw the latter as the ground of his future hope of righteousness. Similarly our author sees the perfect obedience of Christ in his sufferings as the reason why **he became the cause of eternal salvation for all who obey him.** In ii. 10 Jesus has already been called 'the leader of salvation'. The phrase 'cause of salvation' was not uncommon in the Hellenistic world (cf. Philo, *de Agric.* 96); but the phrase **cause of eternal salvation** is unique. It appropriately expresses the uniqueness of Christ's work. **Eternal** could mean unending, or pertaining to the timelessness of eternity. It is used here, as customarily in this Epistle, to denote that which belongs to 'the world to come'. The phrase **all who obey him** indicates both the universality of Christ's work **(all),** as well as the limiting conditions attached to its benefits **(who obey him).** It is not fortuitous that Christ's obedience after his unanswered prayer for safety is mentioned in the same sentence as the salvation promised to Christians who obey him. Our writer sees a profound connection between these two. 'Christ, who asked to be saved from death, by his death obtains the salvation of men. Having learnt to obey, he saves those who obey.' (Spicq.)

Our author is now about to embark on a lengthy exhortation
and thus to break off his doctrinal exposition until vi. 20. So
he pauses here to give a short summary of the doctrine which
still has to be expounded: **being named by God high priest** 10
in the rank of Melchisedek. Strictly speaking, Psalm cx is
addressed not to a high priest but to a priest in the rank of
Melchisedek; but in as much as the addressee sits at God's
right hand (Psalm cx. 1) and holds royal as well as sacerdotal
privileges, he may be appropriately described in terms of high
priesthood.

14. FOOD FOR ADULTS. v. 11 - vi. 3

**(11) About him we have much to say that is difficult to
explain, since you have become dull of hearing. (12)
Indeed, although you ought to be teachers by this time,
you again need someone to teach you the ABC of the
oracles of God, and you have come to need milk, not
solid food. (13) For anyone who lives on milk is without
experience of discourse between right and wrong, for he
is an infant. (14) But solid food is for mature men, who,
in virtue of their condition, have had their perceptions
trained to distinguish between good and evil. (vi. 1)
Therefore let us leave elementary Christian doctrine and
advance towards maturity, not laying again a foundation
of renunciation of dead works and of faith towards God,
(2) instruction concerning water rites and the laying on
of hands, and resurrection from the dead and eternal
judgement. (3) And indeed advance we shall, if God
permits.**

The last section ended with a reference to Melchisedek, to
whom a return is made in vi. 20, after the end of a long
exhortation which begins at this point. In view of the previous
verse it is probably **about him** (i.e. Melchisedek) rather than 11
about the whole subject under discussion, that our author
writes: **we have much to say that is difficult to explain**

(cf. xiii. 22). The difficulty is one which confronts our author, not his readers. It is difficult for him to find words with which to describe Melchisedek's relationship to Christ **since,** he tells his readers, **you have become dull of hearing.** The recipients of the letter have not become physically deaf but spiritually obtuse. In this use of the metaphor of hearing there is perhaps an undertone of rebuke to his readers for their tendency towards disobedience. Furthermore, the Greek word νωθροί, here translated **dull,** can denote, in the papyri, those who are sick and ill; so that there may well be here the further implication that his readers' spiritual deafness is due to spiritual malaise.

So far from progressing, they have actually gone backwards.
12 **Indeed, although you ought to be teachers by this time, you again need someone to teach you the ABC of the oracles of God.** The suggestion that the readers should have become teachers does not mean that a small specialised group of intelligentsia is being addressed. Anyone who is instructed in his faith may be expected to be able to explain it to others (1 Peter iii. 15; cf. Ro. ii. 21). The phrase, **to be teachers,** like so many phrases in this section, is taken from the language of Greek ethical, and particularly Stoic, philosophy (cf. Epict. *Enchir*. 51). Similar phrases in the writings of Greek philosophers 'prove that it is a general expression for stirring people up to acquaint themselves with what should be familiar' (Moffatt). The meaning here is not that they need to be taught again 'which be the first principles of the oracles of God' (A.V.), for they must have known what these were. Our author's complaint is that they did not believe in these as religious truth. The word στοιχεῖα, translated here as **ABC,** is also used by Paul (Gal. iv. 3, 9; Col. ii. 8. 20), possibly in the same sense, but more probably to signify the elemental spirits of the universe. Here the word denotes the first letters of the alphabet, and a literal translation of the Greek text here would be 'the ABC of the beginning'. **The oracles of God** are not confined to the words of Jesus or to the writings of the prophets or to the words of scripture: they include all that is spoken by God's word (cf. iv. 12).

When our author writes **You have come to need milk, not solid food,** he is using a metaphor common in Greek literature, and employed also by Paul (1 Cor. iii. 1 f.). This metaphor is further elaborated. **For anyone who lives on 13 milk is without experience of discourse between right and wrong, for he is an infant.** The phrase ἄπειρος λόγου δικαιοσύνης means literally 'unacquainted with the word of righteousness'. This has been variously interpreted to mean: (*a*) 'unacquainted with the righteousness of God revealed in Christ'—a Pauline conception, uncharacteristic of our author; (*b*) 'unacquainted with the teaching of righteousness found in scripture as a whole'—a phrase parallel to the previous remark about the oracles of God, but not a particularly appropriate comment about infants; (*c*) 'incapable of accurate self-expression' (construing the phrase 'the word of justice' to mean *le mot juste*); (*d*) (a variant of the previous interpretation) 'incapable of understanding normal adult language', as though the writer should be forced into using baby talk; and finally (*e*) the meaning accepted here, 'without experience of moral truth'. This interpretation is adopted partly because the whole of this section is modelled on the writings of Greek ethical philosophers, but primarily because it provides a precise contrast with the condition of grown men as described in the next verse. **But solid food is for mature men, who, in virtue of their 14 condition, have had their perceptions trained to distinguish between good and evil.** It is not practice or habit as such that enables grown men to have moral discrimination, but rather their state or condition which is the result of previous habit or practice. This is the technical vocabulary of Greek philosophy. Comparisons of language have been made here with Galen, Marcus Aurelius and Sextus Empiricus. Yet, although the vocabulary is pagan, it has been baptised into Christ. In particular, the meaning of the word τέλειοι to describe **mature** Christians (the same word also means perfect) is not controlled by Greek philosophy or Hellenistic mystery religions (where the word was used to describe initiates). The word has become a part of Christian vocabulary. Paul, like our author, contrasts infancy with maturity in the Christian life (Eph. iv. 13 f.; cf. 1 Cor. xiv. 20), and he, too, frequently uses **mature** to describe disciplined and experienced Christians (cf. 1 Cor. ii. 6), which is what the word means here. Our author has a special interest in the whole group of Greek words cognate with the word translated here **mature,** and his call to Christian maturity and perfection, grounded in the perfection of Christ, is the major positive ethical theme of the Epistle.

These four verses of chapter v contain a rebuke to the recipients of the Epistle for their failure to progress in their understanding of Christianity. They had gone backwards, not forwards: they needed to learn again the rudiments of their faith. Yet the writer now seems to ignore all this. Far from returning to elementary matters, he declares that he intends to go on to advanced Christian doctrine. Furthermore, he intends to proceed thus as a direct consequence of their need for elementary

1 instruction. **Therefore let us leave elementary Christian doctrine and advance towards maturity.** Many explanations have been given of this apparent paradox: (*a*) that there was a pause between the composition of chapters v and vi; (*b*) that the author at the end of chapter v had indulged in rhetorical hyperbole; (*c*) that he had in the previous verses intentionally exaggerated in order to bestir his readers; (*d*) that he looked right back to the doctrine of Christ's high priesthood (and not merely to his readers' elementary ignorance) for the reason why they must advance to mature doctrine. The true explanation is simpler and more profound. Apart from apostasy, no retrogression is possible in the Christian life. Failure to progress brings danger of collapse. The only way of recovering lost ground is to forge ahead. Moreover, an intellectual failure to advance towards a mature understanding of the Christian faith results not merely in intellectual but also in moral and spiritual torpor.

The **elementary Christian doctrine** which must be left behind is, literally, 'the word of the beginning of Christ' (cf. v. 12). The **maturity** towards which advance must be made is the perfection of Christian doctrine; and **advance** will not be merely the consequence of personal effort by the readers but, as the Greek implies, the result of being borne along on the flood-tide of the author's argument. He himself was not the wise masterbuilder who had founded his readers' faith (contrast 1 Cor. iii. 10), and if he now mentions elementary teaching, he makes it plain that he is **not laying again a foundation of**

renunciation of dead works and of faith towards God, instruction concerning water rites and the laying on of hands, and resurrection from the dead and eternal judgement. 2 These essential subjects for prebaptismal catechetical instruction receive only a bare mention, since our author wishes to press on.

Jesus himself is reported to have preached 'Repent and believe in the gospel' (Mark i. 15), and repentance became the foundation stone of early Christian preaching and teaching (cf. Acts ii. 38; xvii. 30). Repentance meant much more than feelings of sorrow for past sins, with which it is often equated. It implied rather a radical change of heart, a turning from selfishness and self-concern to a God-centred life. **Renunciation** in particular formed a regular part of catechetical instruction (Ro. xiii. 12; Col. iii. 8). The **dead works** to be renounced include all the activities of anyone who is out of relationship with the living God (cf. ix. 14); these are devoid of the quickening power of grace, and hence sterile and deadening. The complement of renunciation is **faith towards God.** This is not a cold intellectual conviction, but a personal relationship of trust and dependence towards the Father of the Lord Jesus Christ.

This elementary catechesis could also be described as **instruction concerning water rites and the laying on of hands.** διδαχήν, read by only p⁴⁶ B d, probably gives the true reading, so that **instruction** here is in apposition to the 'foundation' of v. 1. (The remaining MSS read διδαχῆς because of a primitive corruption due to homoioteleuton.) 1 Cor. i. 12 ff. illustrates the need of church members for further instruction on baptism, and similarly 1 Cor. xv. 12 shows the need for further teaching on resurrection and eternal judgement. The word βαπτισμῶν, translated here **water rites,** is used again in ix. 10 for ablutions required by the Jewish law (cf. Mark vii. 4). There is, however, no reference in this passage to Old Testament ablutions, nor does **the laying on of hands** refer to the imposition of hands in Jewish sacrifice (cf. Lev. i. 4) or to the ordination of Jewish elders (cf. Nu. xxvii. 18), or to healing (cf. 1Q Apoc. col. xx, l. 29). Our author is not describing dead works to be renounced, but the positive content of elementary Christian instruction. The usual word for Christian baptism is

βάπτισμα not βαπτισμός, and the plural form βαπτισμῶν used
here is unparalleled in the N.T. (contrast 'the one baptism' of
Eph. iv. 5). But if this Epistle emanated from Ephesus, and was
written by one who had known only John's baptism (Acts
xviii. 25), an explanation can be given of our author's usage. If
he had known only the baptism of John (described by Josephus
as βαπτισμός in *Antiq*. 18. 5. 2), he would have been rebaptised
into the name of Jesus, and in these exceptional circumstances
he would also have had hands laid on him (cf. Acts xix. 5 f.).
Such a convert would have had to have instruction on the two
water rites and also on the laying on of hands.

Teaching was also necessary on **the resurrection of the
dead and eternal judgement.** This was not merely futurist
in scope. Such teaching looked backwards to Christ's act of
justification, culminating in his resurrection and ascension; and
backwards too to the Christian's resurrection from his old dead
life when he was justified at his baptism. It also looked inwards
into the present status of Christians as well as forwards to their
eternal destiny.

Our author rerers back to *v.* 1 where he has resolved to
3 advance to mature doctrine. **And indeed advance we shall,
if God permits.** The mention of divine permission is more
than conventional sentiment (cf. 1 Cor. xvi. 7). Our author is
nothing if not in dead earnest. His six articles of primitive
catechesis are here concluded. They must not be regarded as
forming a universally accepted and exhaustive programme of prebaptismal instruction in the primitive church. They probably
represent our author's own personal experience of catechesis.

15. PERIL OF PERMANENT EXCLUSION. vi. 4-8

**(4) For it is impossible, when men have once been
enlightened, and have had a taste of the gift of heaven
and a share in the Holy Spirit, (5) and have tasted too the
goodness of God's word and the powers of the age to
come, (6) and then have fallen away; it is impossible to
bring them back a second time to repentance, since they**

are crucifying the Son of God in their own selves and exposing him to mockery and contempt. (7) For ground, when it has drunk in the rain that often descends upon it and has borne useful vegetation to those for whom it is tilled, receives a blessing from God; (8) but if it produces thorns and thistles, it is judged worthless and a curse hangs over it; and its end is burning.

It is now made clearer why our author is determined not to linger over elementary Christian teaching. There is no point in relearning it, if it has been forgotten. It is out of the question, in his view, for a Christian to start all over again. **For it is 4 impossible when men have once been enlightened, and have had a taste of the gift of heaven and a share in the Holy Spirit, and have tasted too the goodness of God's 5 word and the powers of the age to come, and then have 6 fallen away; it is impossible to bring them back a second time to repentance, since they are crucifying the Son of God in their own selves and exposing him to mockery and contempt.** This rigorist statement may be paralleled elsewhere in this Epistle (x. 26 ff.; xii. 17), and is similar in tone (but not in content) to Essene thought (1QS 2. 13ff.). The primitive church held that apostasy was much more wicked than refusal to accept Christianity. Rejection of Christ might be due to ignorance (cf. Luke xxiii. 34) while an apostate denies him whom once he has known.

The New Testament does not present an absolutely united front to the question of post-baptismal sin; and the problem was not easy to resolve. In principle, post-baptismal sin was impossible, since the old personality had been stripped off at baptism, and a new personality had been put on. In point of fact, however, Christians still sinned (Matt. xviii. 15). This paradox finds clear expression in 1 John, where on the one hand 'whoever is begotten of God does no sin' (1 John iii. 9), and on the other hand Christians have sin, and to deny this is self-deception (1 John i. 8 ff.). One way of resolving this problem was to make a distinction between sin and mortal sin (1 John v. 16). Mortal sin could not be absolved, just as the sin against the Holy Spirit could never be forgiven (Mark iii. 29).

Paul did not take very seriously what has been called 'the momentary failure of a faith imperfectly formed' (W. Telfer, *The Forgiveness of Sins* (1959), p. 24). On the whole he was gentle with converts, gentler than our author (cf. 1 Cor. i. 4 ff.; iii. 15). But he knew that Christian liberty could degenerate into license, and he found it necessary to warn his converts that some sins were incompatible with the Christian life. For these, life-long excommunication was prescribed (1 Cor. v. 11). This was not primarily a punishment but a remedy, imposed in the hope of God's ultimate mercy (1 Cor. v. 5; cf. 1 Tim. i. 20). In the Pastoral Epistles (1 Tim. v. 20), and in the General Epistles (James iv. 2; 1 Peter iv. 15) it is recognised that Christians can still commit sin, but probably little more was meant by sin here than those post-baptismal sins which were caused by oversight, ignorance or the frailty of human nature. The appalling sin of apostasy (and, it must be added, murder or deviations from Christian standards of sexual morality) were in a different category altogether. Just as sins committed 'with a high hand' could not be expiated under the old covenant, so these sins lay right outside the terms of the new covenant. They were regarded as the outcome of a deliberate renunciation of the Christian way of life.

For men who had committed these sins there could be no hope of forgiveness. Christ's death and resurrection had taken place once and for all; and since Christian baptism involved entry into his once-for-all death and resurrection, baptism too must be once-for-all, so that its benefits could be given only once and if renounced could not be restored. Under the pressure of persecution, the church later modified this hard doctrine (cf. 2 Clem. xiii. 1; Hermas 4. 3. 1-6). Our author certainly does not countenance any relaxation. Those who have been baptised **have once been enlightened** (cf. x. 32; 2 Cor. iv. 4, 6). Christian initiation resulted in spiritual illumination (the word later became a technical term for baptism) and a later renunciation indicated a permanent deprivation of spiritual sight.

Baptism is further described in words probably common to the early church (cf. Acts xviii. 26). Those who have been baptised **have had a taste of the gift of heaven and a share in the Holy Spirit.** Personal experience of any kind could be described as 'tasting'; but the word is particularly apposite because 'the enjoyment here described is only partial and inchoative' (Westcott). **The gift** mentioned is not the Eucharist, nor Christian joy nor peace nor suchlike: it is the richness of the whole Christian life, and this gift belongs properly to the world **of heaven.** In terms of objective reality as well as subjective experience it could be described as **a share in the Holy Spirit** (cf. 1 Cor. xii. 13). Here, however, the 'tasting' may possibly include a reference to the milk and honey of the baptismal rites and the 'share in the Holy Spirit' to the imposition of hands.

Those who have been initiated into Christianity **have tasted too the goodness of God's word and the powers of the age to come.** ῥῆμα not λόγος is used here for God's word. The reference is not to the whole message of the gospel, but to some particular utterance, probably the solemn proclamation of God's promises at baptism (cf. 1 Peter iii. 21). **The powers of the age to come** are the present manifestations of the Spirit (cf. 1 Cor. xii. 1 ff.), which break in, from baptism onwards, on those on whom the ends of the world have come (1 Cor. x. 11).

If men have experienced all this, **and then have fallen away** into apostasy, **it is impossible to bring them back a second time to repentance.** The subject of the verb is here unexpressed. Is it God or the preacher who cannot bring such a sinner back to repentance? Or can he not bring himself back? The author does not answer these questions, and probably he never clearly formulated them in this way. Commentators, dismayed by his rigorism, have attempted different moderating interpretations. The passage, it has been said, refers only to the impossibility of the rite of rebaptism, not to the impossibility of repentance; or it is concerned only with the impossibility of ecclesiastical penance in such cases; or it is merely a general rule to which there may be many individual exceptions; or the passage declares what is impossible with men, while with God all things are possible.

Such interpretations go against the plain meaning of the Greek and the whole tenor of the author's argument. By the phrase **fallen away** apostasy is signified. Our author had himself a very strong moral sense and a profound feeling for moral propriety. In his judgement it would have been morally

impossible to bring back apostates **a second time to a repentance** which involved a radical change of heart, **since they are** still **crucifying the Son of God in their own selves and exposing him to mockery and contempt.** The formal expression **Son of God** is used to emphasise the enormity of the offence. Such people are not recrucifying Christ, for that would involve placing him again on the Cross; but they are crucifying him in a new and horrible way. Our author does not mean that they are carrying out this terrible deed for their own advantage (although in fact to their own dreadful loss): they **are** actually **crucifying** Christ **in their own selves.** By their apostasy they are openly denying him to whom they have pledged themselves, and thereby they are **exposing him to mockery and contempt.**

There follows an illustration of this terrible warning, taken from agricultural life. In the gospels many parables of husbandry can be found. Their original object was usually to focus attention on the yield of the harvest. Our author, however, characteristically uses his illustration in order to point out what

7 happens when there is no harvest at all. **For ground, when it has drunk in the rain that often descends upon it and has borne useful vegetation to those for whom it is tilled, receives a blessing from God.** There is perhaps a reminiscence of Genesis ii. 3 here. The ground is not given a special blessing, it participates in the general blessing which God has

8 given to his creation (cf. 1 Cor. iii. 6 f.). **But if it produces thorns and thistles, it is judged worthless and a curse hangs over it; and its end is burning.** There are certainly overtones here of God's curse upon the ground as a result of the sin of Adam and Eve in Gen. iii. 17 ff. There are three separate stages of condemnation: first, the land is rejected; secondly, it is under imminent threat (not in the sense that it has just missed being cursed, but in the sense that a curse overhangs it); and thirdly, the final end of the land (not the end of the curse) is burning (cf. 1 Cor. iii. 15). The details of the analogy should not be overpressed, for the land which our author had in mind would have been burned not to destroy it but in order to assist the growth of new shoots (unless he was thinking of devastation caused by some natural catastrophe).

(9) But in your case, beloved, although we speak like this, we are confident of better things connected with salvation. (10) For God is not unjust, so as to forget your work and the love which you showed for his name by your past service for the saints—and indeed by your present service. (11) Yet we long that each of you should show the same eagerness for the full and final realisation of your hope, (12) so that you may not be sluggish, but imitators of those who through faith and patience inherit the promises.

After the terrifying warning of *vv.* 4-8, there is a marked change of tone. **But in your case, beloved, although we** 9 **speak like this, we are confident of better things connected with salvation.** This is the only occasion when our author shows any warmth towards his readers. He even uses the affectionate term **beloved** (for the first and last time in the letter). He has been able to overcome his fears for his readers. Far from approaching the curse, they are in the neighbourhood of salvation. The ground of this new-found confidence is explained. **For God is not unjust, so as to forget your work** 10 **and the love which you showed for his name by your past service for the saints—and indeed by your present service.** The love which they had shown was not so much love in God's name or for his sake, but simply love for God. This love for God (literally, **for his name**) shows itself in love for neighbour. **Service for the saints** (cf. 1 Cor. xvi. 15) may well mean gifts for the Christians of the Jerusalem church, who were often called 'the saints'. The Jerusalem Aid Fund, however, had probably not yet been formally opened in the church of the recipients of this Epistle (cf. 1 Cor. xvi. 1). There is no doctrine here of the merit of good works. Nor is there any suggestion of a recompense for services rendered, but rather for the love which must issue in good works if it is real love. Love brings its own reward, both now and in the future (cf. Mark ix. 41; 1 Cor. iii. 8). To suggest otherwise would be to deny the righteousness of God. The author's strong sense of moral propriety affects his statements about salvation as much as what he writes about rejection (cf. *v.* 6). God cannot deny his own moral nature.

Despite this warmer tone, a slight note of reservation can be
11 detected. **Yet we long that each of you should show the same eagerness for the full and final realisation of your hope.** There still remains a warmer feeling towards the recipients than in the earlier passages, coupled here with a reiterated concern for the welfare of each single one of them. They had shown eagerness at the beginning: that was to be expected. But it was the continuing of the same unto the end, until it be thoroughly finished, that would yield **the full and final realisation of** their **hope** (cf. x. 22). The writer did not particularly want his readers to be full of subjective feelings of optimism: he was anxious that they should attain to the objec-
12 tive fulfilment of their final destiny, **so that you may not be sluggish, but imitators of those who through faith and patience inherit the promises.** Once again, there is a hint that the future is still dangerous. At present they were dull of hearing (v. 11); soon their enthusiasm might flag. The best means of progress would be to follow the inspiring example of others. Ahead in chapter xi a long list of past heroes will be given; but here the writer seems to point to the example of contemporaries. For our author, faith involves patience, since it means confidence in the unseen God and trust in the unknown future (xi. 1). Faith and confidence provide the means by which God has ordained that the **promises** of future salvation, which are found in the Old Testament, can be won.

17. PROMISE AND OATH. vi. 13-20

(13) For when God made a promise to Abraham, he swore by himself, since he had no one greater to swear by, (14) saying, 'I will indeed bless you, and I will indeed multiply you'; (15) and thus it was that Abraham, after waiting

patiently, obtained the promise. (16) For men swear by one greater than themselves, and an oath provides for them a confirmation which is beyond the reach of all dispute. (17) Wherefore God, wishing to show more fully to the heirs of his promise the unchangeableness of his will, guaranteed it by an oath, (18) in order that through two unchangeable things, in which it is impossible for God to lie, we who have fled for refuge might have strong encouragement to hold fast to the hope that lies before us. (19) This hope we have like an anchor for our life. It is safe and sure; and it enters into the inner sanctuary of the veil, (20) where as forerunner Jesus entered on our behalf, having become high priest for ever in the rank of Melchisedek.

The previous section ended with an exhortation to imitate those who through faith and patience inherit the promises. This suggested to the writer's mind the case of Abraham, than whom there could not be a better example. **For when God made a** 13 **promise to Abraham, he swore by himself, since he had no one greater to swear by, saying, 'I will indeed bless** 14 **you, and I will indeed multiply you'.** This Old Testament quotation, taken (almost exactly) from Gen. xxii. 16 f. (LXX), contains God's oath on the occasion of Abraham's obedient offering of his son in sacrifice. (This is mentioned again in xi. 17.) God's word needs no attestation other than itself and its consequent fulfilment; but 'the interposition of an oath implied delay in the fulfilment of the promise' (Westcott). The Rabbis commented on the singular statement that God **swore by him-self** (Berach. 32. 1; Ex. R. 44); and so did Philo. Philo regarded the idea of a divine oath as an accommodation by the writer to his reader's intelligence (*de Sacr. Abel. et Cain.* 91 ff.) but in commenting on this very verse (Gen. xxii. 16) he suggested that God alone can testify to himself, 'for there is nothing better than he' (*Leg. All.* 3. 203).

God's promise to Abraham had a gradual fulfilment. The first stage was the birth of Isaac, twenty-five years after the call of Abraham (Gen. xii. 4; xxi. 5); and the second stage was the

birth of Esau and Jacob sixty years later (Gen. xxv. 26). The
promise was not, however, finally fulfilled until the coming of
Christ (Gal. iii. 16) and of the Christian descendants of Abraham
(Ro. iv. 13, 16). And so Abraham could not see his promise
fully realised (except in the sense of John viii. 56, that he 'saw
my day'; a phrase based on rabbinic interpretation of Gen.
xxiv. 1); and thus it is true that Abraham, like the rest of the
heroes under the old dispensation, did not himself obtain the
promise (xi. 39). On the other hand, Abraham did see the birth
15 of his own sons and grandchildren, **and thus it was that** in
another sense **Abraham, after waiting patiently, obtained
the promise**—part of it, that is, and only after waiting patiently.
For his first child was not born until he himself was a hundred
years old (Gen. xxi. 5) long after his wife could have been
expected to bear children (cf. Ro. iv. 19; He. xi. 11 f.); and his
grandchildren were not born until he had reached the extraordinary age of one hundred and sixty years (Gen. xxv. 26),
fifteen years before he died (Gen. xxv. 7). Thus Abraham provided a signal example of faith and patience. Moreover, the
promise for which he waited was the occasion of the first divine
oath, and it marks the beginning and indeed the foundation of
the whole of the divine dispensation, both of the old and new
covenant. By his promise and oath God took the initiative; but
Abraham, by his own qualities of faith and patience, obtained
the promise.

The object of an oath is to call God as a witness to the truth
of what is said; in Philo's words, God giving witness in a
disputed matter (*de Spec. Leg.* 2. 10). Jewish laws on oaths were
complex (cf. Mishnah Shebuoth), and Jesus himself had some
hard words to say on the subject (Matt. xxiii. 16 ff.). Our author,
it should be noted, does not share the Essene detestation for all
oaths except the oath of initiation (Josephus, *Bell. Jud.*, 2. 8. 6;
1QS 5. 8; cf. Matt. v. 33 f.; James v. 12). This consideration
adds strength to the view that this Epistle has nothing directly
to do with Qumran.

16   Our author even seems to approve of oaths. **For men swear
by one greater than themselves, and an oath provides
for them a confirmation which is beyond the reach of
all dispute.** An oath has a double function. Positively, it adds

moral and legal force to a statement (for who would dare to call
God as a false witness?). Negatively, it ends controversy among
men by introducing the testimony of God (cf. Philo, *de Somn.*
I. 12). **Wherefore God, wishing to show more fully to the** 17
heirs of his promise the unchangeableness of his will,
guaranteed it by an oath. These **heirs** are not confined to
Abraham's lineal descendants, but all believing Christians are
included among them (Gal. iii. 7). The promise of God, by
itself, was sure and certain; and the addition of an oath helped
to **show more fully** the irrevocable nature of God's promise,
which was to bring universal blessing to mankind through
Abraham's offspring (Gen. xxii. 18).

But which particular oath did our author mean? A suggestion
has been made that there is a reference here to the oath of
Psalm cx. 1: 'The Lord has sworn and will not go back on his
word'. Although verse 4 of this Psalm is alluded to in *v.* 20 below,
the first verse of the Psalm is not quoted until vii. 21. It is
probable, therefore, that the oath to which our author is referring here is the divine oath to Abraham, cited a few verses back
at *v.* 13. The Greek word μεσιτεύειν means literally to act as
mediator (not the meaning here, for God cannot act as his own
mediator), and hence to negotiate, interpose and intercede (none
of which meanings is suitable here); finally to guarantee (cf.
Philo, *de Spec. Leg.* 4. 31), which is the meaning that the verb
has here. God did this **in order that, through two unchange-** 18
able things, in which it is impossible for God to lie, we
who have fled for refuge might have strong encourage-
ment to hold fast to the hope that lies before us. The
promise and the oath are, of course, the **two unchangeable**
things. It is against the moral nature of God to lie (Tit i. 2; cf.
Philo, *de Sacr. Abel. et Cain.* 93). (The anarthrous use of θεός
here shows that the reference is to the divine nature rather than
person.) **We who have fled for refuge** is a phrase which has
been thought to describe the physical circumstances of the
author and his readers as émigrés and exiles from their homeland. This is as improbable as the suggestion that the phrase is a
common description of Christians (cf. 'those who have believed',
iv. 3). Nor is it useful to ask whether the author intended to
signify by the phrase flight from evil or flight towards God,

because he plainly meant both. Philo spoke of eternal life as 'a flight to pure being' (*de Fuga et Inv.* 78), and our author implies that the city of God is the one true city of refuge.

By the combination of promise and oath God gave doubly **strong encouragement** (not exhortation, as the word sometimes means). **To hold fast to** an object is much more deliberate than merely to grasp it, and the use of this word here prepares the way for the metaphorical use of 'anchor' in the text verse. **Hope** is not a feeling of aspiration, but the realisation of final destiny. Our author writes about **the hope that lies before us** as though he were thinking of a ship riding at anchor.

19 **This hope we have like an anchor for our life.** This is not just a sheltered mooring for that most precious part of human personality which is commonly called the soul. On the contrary, it is an anchor which guarantees inner peace and security for the whole of life. This metaphor of an anchor is not used in the bible, but it was common among the maritime peoples of the Hellenistic world (cf. Philo, *de Somn.* 1. 227). It is found as a Christian symbol in the catacombs, and, according to Clement of Alexandria, it could be safely used by Christians as an emblem on a signet ring (*Paid.* 3. 11. 59). According to our author, **it is safe and sure,** a common combination of adjectives in Greek ethical literature (cf. Philo, *Quis Rer. Div.* 314). 'It is undisturbed by outward influences (ἀσφαλής), and it is firm in its inherent character (βέβαιος)' (Westcott).

At this point the writer changes his metaphor violently. He has just been comparing hope to an anchor, strong and immobile: now he regards it as moving and penetrating, for **it enters into the inner sanctuary of the veil.** (It is, of course, hope and not the anchor which is said to enter the sanctuary!) This transposition permits the author to return to the main doctrinal theme of his Epistle, abandoned at v. 10 and interrupted by a lengthy exhortation. Hope signifies our final destiny, and consideration of this leads back to the heavenly temple, where Jesus has already entered. The Tent of Meeting had two veils; an outer covering and the inner veil separating the Holy Place from the Most Holy (cf. Lev. xvi, 2, 12). It is the latter that is referred to here. Into this inner sanctuary Jesus

20 entered **as forerunner.** A forerunner precedes and announces

those who come after; but the word is best understood here in its military sense (cf. ii. 10).[1] Jesus constitutes the advance guard who is already in heaven and who by his entry has assured the consequent entry of all who are his. It is in this representative capacity that he **entered on our behalf.** Already, before he entered, he had **become high priest for ever in the rank of Melchisedek.** Just what this means the author proceeds to explain in the next chapter.

18. THE PERSON OF MELCHISEDEK. vii. 1-3

(1) This Melchisedek was king of Salem, priest of God Most High. He met Abraham returning from the slaughter of the kings and blessed him, (2) and to him Abraham apportioned a tithe of everything. Firstly, his name means 'king of righteousness'; then he is also king of Salem, that is, 'king of peace'. (3) He has no father, no mother, no lineage, no beginning to his days and no end to his life, but being made to resemble the Son of God he remains a priest for all time.

Our author returns to Melchisedek (cf. vi. 20). His argument proceeds by four stages: (i) the scriptural story of Melchisedek (*vv.* 1-3); (ii) Melchisedek's superiority over Abraham and Levi (*vv.* 4-10); (iii) The replacement of the Levitical priesthood by Jesus' priesthood (*vv.* 11-19); (iv) The superiority and the perfection of Jesus' high priesthood (*vv.* 20-28).

Apart from his exegesis of the inner meaning of the name, where he follows Philo (*Leg. All.* 3. 79), our author's exposition of Melchisedek is highly original. Philo only refers to Melchisedek on two other occasions, one of which concerns an allegorical explanation of the bread and wine that Melchisedek brought forth (*Leg. All.* 3. 82), and the other a mystical interpretation of Abraham's gift of tithes (*de Congr.* 99). Melchisedek seems not to have figured at all in contemporary rabbinic speculations.

---

[1] It is possible that our author used this word to show that Jesus, not John the Baptist, is the true forerunner.

Perhaps the polemical use of this Epistle against the Jews contributed to their comparative neglect of him. Already by the end of the first century A.D. the mystery of his origin had been dispelled by the assumption that he was a son of Shem (Ned. 32b). In 1Q Apoc (col. xxii, ll. 14-17) he receives only a bare mention, very different from the favourable midrash on the victory of Abraham which immediately precedes this reference. In Jub. xiii. 25 there is a *lacuna* where a narrative concerning Melchisedek has been lost or excised. Possibly in the circles where the book of Jubilees was read the passage had been removed, because of antipathy to the Hasmonean dynasty. Josephus says that Hyrcanus called himself (like Melchisedek) 'high priest of God Most High' (*Antiq.* 15. 2. 4); and among people such as the Qumran covenanters the name Melchisedek may have become suspect owing to their distrust of those who claimed a priesthood like that of Melchisedek. If so, it seems unlikely that the Epistle had any connection with Qumran.

1 Gen. xiv. 17-20 is cited. **This Melchisedek was king of Salem, priest of God Most High. He met Abraham return-**
2 **ing from the slaughter of the kings and blessed him, and to him Abraham apportioned a tithe of everything.** Melchisedek had gone to meet Abraham when he returned from his successful rout of a coalition of four Canaanite kings against the King of Sodom and his confederates. In ancient cultures kings often served as priests, so that a priest-king need cause no surprise. Our author speaks of him as a high priest: in the Old Testament he is spoken of as a priest, but the distinction is not in his case important because of his unique status as priest. **God Most High** whom he served was the name of an Amorean deity, and this title name continued to be employed down to Hellenistic times. When it is used in the Bible as a name for God 'it is often found on the margin of Judaism' (Héring.)

Our author, however, is not interested in the historical aspects of the tale, only in the scriptural record and its meaning. **Firstly, his name means 'king of righteousness'; then he is also king of Salem, that is, 'king of peace'.** This is the Alexandrine method of exegesis. Philo makes exactly the same points, but for him they prove how the mind can bring order

and peace to the body (*Leg. All.* 3. 80 f.). In ancient times a
person's name had great importance, for a man's personality
was expressed by his name. The exegesis here would not therefore have seemed so forced in our author's day as it might
appear today. Melchisedek actually means 'My King (is)
righteous'. Zedek (righteous) may have once been worshipped
at Jerusalem (cf. Josh. x. 1), with which Salem may be identified
(cf. Josephus, *Antiq.* 7. 3. 2; *Bell. Jud.* 6. 10. 1; but Jerome
equated it with the Salim of John iii. 23). The Hebrew for peace
is *shalom*, hence our author's derivation of the name. (He fails,
however, to make the point that Melchisedek officiated in the
same city where Jesus later sacrificed himself.) The meanings
of the two names Melchisedek and Salem have been introduced
to prove that righteousness and peace are combined in the
Melchisedekian order of priesthood (cf. Is. ix. 6 f.). These
qualities found fulfilment in Christ (1 John ii. 1; Eph. ii. 14).

   Melchisedek was unique. **He has no father, no mother, no** 3
**lineage, no beginning to his days and no end to his life,
but being made to resemble the Son of God he remains a
priest for all time.** The Greek words translated **no father,
no mother** could describe an orphan, a bastard, someone low
born or a pagan deity. Here they suggest a supernatural origin.
Our author makes use of the Alexandrine principle that what is
unmentioned in the Bible can be presumed not to exist (cf.
Philo, *Quod Det. Pot.* 178). Our author is, of course, only
concerned here with the words of the scriptural story, not with
the historical person of Melchisedek himself.

   Melchisedek's lack of lineage is to be contrasted with the
hereditary succession of the levitical priesthood for which
Aaronic descent was required on the father's side (Nu. xvi. 40),
and Israelite nationality on the mother's side (Ezra ii. 61 f.).
Melchisedek appears suddenly in the Genesis narrative, and
just as suddenly he disappears; and so, arguing from silence (cf.
Sanh. 107 b), our author asserts that he has **no beginning to
his days and no end to his life.** This is a negative way of
asserting that he is eternal; stated positively, **being made to
resemble the Son of God, he remains a priest for all time.**
'The resemblance lies in the biblical representation and not
primarily in Melchisedek himself' (Westcott). His priesthood

is permanent, exclusive, unique and therefore eternal; and he thus provides the type of the eternal priesthood of **the Son of God.**

There is one incident in Gen. xiv. 18 which our author does not mention: 'Melchisedek brought forth bread and wine'. He could scarcely have been ignorant of this passage, for he cites very exactly from the LXX at this point, and he knew his bible very well. Presumably he did not mention this incident anywhere in his Epistle because it was not germane to his purpose. Bread and wine were used at the Christian Eucharist. Our author could therefore hardly have had the Eucharist directly in mind when he was writing this Epistle (cf. comment on ix. 20).

19. THE SUPERIORITY OF MELCHISEDEK. vii. 4-10

(4) Consider how great this man is to whom Abraham the patriarch gave a tithe of his best spoils. (5) Those of the descendants of Levi who receive the priestly office are authorised to collect tithes from the people according to the Law, that is, from their fellow-Israelites, although they too are descendants of Abraham. (6) But this man, whose descent is not traced from them, received a tithe from Abraham, and blessed even the man who had received the promises. (7) Unquestionably the lesser is blessed by the greater. (8) Further, in the one case it is mortal men who are receiving tithes, in the other case a man who is affirmed to be still alive. (9) And it might even be said that Levi, who receives tithes, has himself been tithed through Abraham; (10) for he was in his ancestor's loins when Melchisedek met him.

In verses 4-10 four points are made to prove Melchisedek's superiority. (1) Melchisedek received tithes from Abraham. **4 Consider how great this man is to whom Abraham the patriarch gave a tithe of his best spoils.** The spontaneous gift by Abraham of a tenth of his booty shows that he realised his own inferiority to Melchisedek—Abraham, the founder of the Jewish race, the recipient of the promise on which the whole of Judaism was grounded! What a contrast here to the levitical priesthood! **Those of the descendants of Levi who receive** 5 **the priestly office are authorised to collect tithes from the people according to the Law, that is, from their fellow-Israelites, although they too are descendants of Abraham.** Our author does not refer here to all the descendants of Levi, but only to the priests. They alone got the full benefit of the tithes, and the Levites had to pay to them 'a tithe of the tithe' (Nu. xviii. 26 f.). According to Nu. xviii. 21 the tithes were the priests' return for priestly service; but according to Lev. xxvii. 30 they were a holy offering to the Lord, and according to Deut. x. 8 f. they were for the relief of the tribe of Levi, the members of which had no portion in Israel.

The Deuteronomic passage was in our author's mind at this point. Tithes were for the support of priests; but **the Law** only authorised the collection of tithe from fellow-Israelites, that is, from **the people** of God's choice. Thus the levitical priesthood was exercised among kinsfolk, and its superiority was manifested within the extended family of Abraham's descendants. **But this man, whose descent is not traced from them,** 6 **received a tithe from Abraham.** Abraham gave Melchisedek what he would not have had to give to a levitical priest. Melchisedek's superiority over the levitical priests is therefore in a different category from their superiority over the rest of Abraham's descendants.

(2) Melchisedek further showed his superiority by giving Abraham a benediction. He **blessed even the man who had received the promises.** To give a blessing is a mark of authority. In a family, in accordance with the 'natural order of priesthood', fathers bless their children (Gen. xxvii. 23), and in the extended family of a nation a king can bless his people (2 Sam. vi. 18). **Unquestionably the lesser is blessed by** 7 **the greater.** God had promised Abraham that in his offspring all the nations of the world would be blessed (Gen. xxii. 18); and if Melchisedek could bless *him*, then his status must be superior to the levitical order of priesthood.

(3) Melchisedek's priesthood is superior to the levitical

8 priesthood because it is permanent. **Further, in the one case it is mortal men who are receiving tithes, in the other case a man who is affirmed to be still alive.** Levite priests die like other men, but Melchisedek was believed to be immortal. This belief was grounded on Psalm cx. 4: 'a priest for ever in the rank of Melchisedek'. The attribution to Melchisedek of eternal life is an inference from the text, not an explicit affirmation of scripture.

(4) Melchisedek is superior because Levi had actually paid
9 him tithes. **And it might even be said that Levi, who receives tithes, has himself been tithed through Abraham;**
10 **for he was in his ancestor's loins when Melchisedek met him.** The author seemed to have been aware that this statement would appear odd at first sight. Yet to his world, with its strong sense of social solidarity, the idea would not have been so strange as today. It might, however, be objected that Abraham was not a priest when he paid the tithes, and thus his subordination to Melchisedek did not prejudice the priestly prerogatives of his later descendants through Levi. But the patriarch acted in the name of all his future family. The promise given to Abraham was that 'in thee' all the nations of the earth should be blessed (Gen. xii. 3). The children of Abraham are one with him (cf. Paul's use of 'in Adam' and 'in Christ' in 1 Cor. xv. 22).

20. THE REPLACEMENT OF THE LEVITICAL PRIESTHOOD. vii. 11-19

(11) If then perfection were attainable through the levitical priesthood, in close connection with which the Law was given, what further need would there have been for a different kind of priest to arise, 'in the rank of Melchisedek', and for him not to be described as 'in the rank of Aaron'? (12) Now when the priesthood is changed, there must also be a change of the Law. (13) The one here spoken of belonged to a different tribe, from which no one has served at the altar. (14) For it is obvious that our Lord has

sprung from Judah, and in connection with this tribe Moses said nothing about priests. (15) The argument is much clearer still if another kind of priest arises, resembling Melchisedek, (16) a priest not in virtue of a law consisting of a commandment concerning the flesh but in virtue of the power of a life that nothing can destroy. (17) For it is affirmed: 'Thou art a priest for ever in the rank of Melchisedek'. (18) The foregoing commandment has been annulled because it was weak and unprofitable (19) (for the law perfected nothing), and a better hope has been introduced, through which we draw near to God.

The next stages of the argument (*vv.* 11-25) show the replacement of the levitical priesthood by Jesus' Melchisedekian priesthood. Our author takes in turn the key words of Psalm cx. 4: 'The Lord has sworn and will not go back on his word, Thou art a priest for ever in the rank of Melchisedek'.

He first deals with Melchisedek, making the same kind of point as Paul did in connection with the promise given to Abraham (Ro. iv.; Gal. iii. 1-22). Paul wished to show that the Law had been abrogated, and in order to do this he had to go behind the Law to the period before it was given, to prove that, although it was given by God, it had only transitory authority and limited efficacy. Our author makes use of Melchisedek, again going behind the Law to the period before it was given in order to prove his point. But his application is necessarily different from that of Paul. Paul could show that the promise to Abraham's offspring had not been fulfilled, and that, since God could not break his promise, its fulfilment was to be found outside the Law. Our author, however, has to meet the difficulty that the Melchisedekian priesthood, which was in existence before the Law, might have been superseded by the Law when it established the levitical priesthood. He counters this objection by Psalm cx, which was commonly believed to have been written by David (cf. iv. 7) and which was therefore later in date than the Mosaic Law. Verse 4 of this Psalm establishes Melchisedek's rank of priesthood (cf. *v.* 28); and so this rank of priesthood could not have been abolished by the Law, since it

was established later than Law. It would not have been estab-
11 lished unless it had been needed. **If then perfection were
attainable through the levitical priesthood, in close connection with which the Law was given, what further need
would there have been for a different kind of priest to
arise 'in the rank of Melchisedek', and for him not to be
described as 'in the rank of Aaron'?** The Law was regarded
by Jews as the perfect expression of God's will for his people.
Our author bravely contests this. **The perfection** which the
Law cannot give is the power to cleanse, sanctify and bring men
to God. The sacrificial system established by the Law was
powerless to expiate sins (x. 1), or to cleanse the conscience (ix. 9).

The Law had not, of course, been given simply in order to
establish the levitical priesthood; but the two were closely
12 connected together, so that **when the priesthood is changed,
there must also be a change of the Law.** So the fact that
a new rank of priesthood has been established by God shows
that the Law too is changed; indeed it will shortly disappear
(viii. 13). That which is imperfect is to be superseded by that
which is perfect (1 Cor. xiii. 10).

The priestly office had not, of course, disappeared. That
could not happen, for it represents a permanent need of man in
his relations with God. What had happened was a change in
the priesthood from one priestly order to another, indeed
13 from one tribe to another. **For the one here spoken of
belonged to a different tribe, from which no one has
served at the altar.** It was well known that no Jew could hold
the high priestly office unless he was descended from Aaron
14 (Josephus, *Antiq.* 20. 10. 1). Yet **it is obvious that our Lord
has sprung from Judah, and in connection with this tribe
Moses said nothing about priests.** The human lineage of
Jesus must have been well known early in the Apostolic Age
(cf. Ro. i. 3). This was not the first time that our author's
interest in the details of the historical Jesus has been noted
(cf. ii. 3; v. 7). There is perhaps just a hint of Jesus' messianic
status in his use of the phrase **has sprung,** for the Messiah is
called a Sprig in Zech. vi. 12 (cf. Philo, *de Conf. Ling.* 62).
Genealogies were important to the Jews, and thus were necessary
for Messianic claims; but the statement that **our Lord has**

sprung from Judah does not necessarily imply that Jesus had a human father, for our author also regarded Jesus as belonging to a class of priest who has no father and no mother. He may have been referring here to Jesus' adopted lineage of the tribe of Judah.

The expectation of a priest from the tribe of Judah is unknown in the Old Testament. In T. Levi viii. 14 there is this prophecy: 'A king will rise from Judah and will establish a new priest-hood', but this does not furnish a real parallel. In its context it is a prophecy about a priest exercising royal prerogatives, not about a king assuming priesthood. Jesus, however, was at once both Priest and King, thereby superseding the levitical priest-hood.

Our author, still basing his arguments on Psalm cx. 4, examines next the phrase 'for ever', which is found to yield a further proof of the superiority of the Melchisedekian priest-hood. **The argument is much clearer still if another kind 15 of priest arises, resembling Melchisedek, a priest not in 16 virtue of a law consisting of a commandment concerning the flesh, but in virtue of the power of a life that nothing can destroy. For it is affirmed: 'Thou art a priest for ever 17 in the rank of Melchisedek'.** The levitical priests were appointed to their office on the hereditary principle which finds expression in a **commandment** of the Law (Ex. xxviii. 1 ff.). The only prerequisites for a levitical priest (apart from legiti-macy and the absence of physical defects) were that his mother should have been an Israelite and his father a priest before him. This commandment was external, outward, **concerning the flesh.** This use of flesh is free from the Pauline overtones of sin, but it does convey something of the transitoriness and earth-bound nature of the commandment.

Melchisedek himself is not contrasted with this levitical priesthood, for he is regarded as a scriptural figure, a type of an actual person still to come. The argument concerns the case **if another kind of priest arises, resembling Melchisedek.** Such a priest would not be appointed because he conformed to certain legal requirements. 'He was made priest because of his inherent nature' (Westcott). He was not in priestly succession: he simply **arises,** as it were, out of the blue. His divine nature, united to his humanity, conferred upon the latter **the power of a life that nothing can destroy.** (Philo uses a very similar phrase in describing God's creation of Adam, *Leg. All.* 1. 32.) This union of natures took place when the Son came into the world, and it was then that he was given his priestly office (x. 5). The levitical priesthood had been appointed an 'everlasting priesthood' (Ex. xl. 15), but it was everlasting only in virtue of priestly succession. Jesus' priesthood, however, is eternal because of the indestructible life of a single priest, and for this reason it supersedes the levitical priesthood.

18   **The foregoing commandment has been annulled be-**
19 **cause it was weak and unprofitable (for the Law perfected nothing), and a better hope has been introduced.** Since the argument concerns law, a legal term is introduced to declare that the commandment **has been annulled.** The reasons for annulment were both negative and positive. Negatively the Law was **weak** because it was powerless to give life (Gal. iii. 21) and because it dealt with earth-bound matters of outward observance (Ro. viii. 3). It was **profitless** precisely because it was law and not love; and without love nothing is profitable (1 Cor. xiii. 3). The Law expressed God's will but hindered its execution (Ro. vii. 7). Thus **the Law perfected nothing.** It was not bad in itself. Later the writer will show how the Law performed the useful function of being the 'type' of what superseded it. But the Law could not achieve its proper end. It could not help men to draw near to God. Its inherent imperfection meant that through it God's purposes could only be imperfectly realised. There was also a positive reason why the Law was annulled: because **a better hope has been introduced.** The legal terminology is continued here, for the word ἐπεισαγωγή, translated **introduced,** is found in the papyri in a legal sense.

The Christian hope was not in itself better than the Jewish hope. For Christians and for Jews, hope signified the same, the realisation of God's final destiny for his people. But the Christian hope was better than the Jewish law, and that in two ways. Firstly, the Jewish law was fixed and static, expressing how men should obey God; while the Christian hope is eschatological, looking beyond the present to man's ultimate goal. Secondly, according to the Jewish law only priests could draw

near to God (Ex. xix. 22); but under the Christian dispensation
all Christians share in priesthood (1 Peter ii. 5). Thus in hope
a Christian can do what could never be fully achieved under
the Jewish law: he can **draw near to God.**

21. THE SUPERIORITY OF JESUS' PRIESTHOOD.
vii. 20-28

**(20) And how important that this was not done without
the taking of an oath! For they became priests without
the taking of an oath, (21) but he with the taking of an
oath, through the One who says to him: 'The Lord has
sworn and will not go back on his word: "Thou art a priest
for ever"'. (22) So much better, then, is the covenant of
which the guarantor is Jesus! (23) They indeed became
priests in large numbers because they were prevented
by death from remaining in office; (24) but he has a
priesthood which cannot pass to another, because he
remains for ever. (25) And so he is able to save for all
time those who approach God through him, because he
lives for ever to plead on their behalf. (26) Such a high
priest was suited to our condition, devout, innocent,
undefiled, separated from sinners, and exalted above the
heavens. (27) He does not need, as high priests do, to offer
up sacrifices daily, first for his own sins, and then for
those of the people: this he did once for all when he
offered up himself. (28) The Law appoints as high priests
men who are frail, but the words of the oath which came
after the Law appoint for ever the perfected Son.**

Having shown how Jesus' priesthood replaced the levitical
priesthood, our author next shows its superiority. The third
part of Psalm cx. 4 still remains to be examined, that is, the
first part of the verse which introduces the declaration of priesthood: 'The Lord has sworn and will not go back on his word'.
And how important that this was not done without the 20
taking of an oath! According to Ex. xxix. 9 (LXX) the sons of

Aaron had been given a priesthood that would last 'for ever'.
Similarly, according to Psalm cx, the Melchisedekian priesthood had been appointed 'for ever'. If God had superseded the
Aaronic priesthood, even though it had been given 'for ever',
what certainty could there be that God would not also supersede
the Melchisedekian priesthood? If he had changed his mind
once, might he not change it again? Fortunately scripture pro-
21 vided a proof that this could never happen since **he** (Jesus)
became priest **with the taking of an oath, through the One
who says to him: 'The Lord has sworn and will not go
back on his word: "Thou art a priest for ever"'**. A lot
of ceremonial was required at the consecration of Aaron and his
sons (Ex. xxviii-xxix; Lev. viii-ix), but there was no oath. **They
became priests without the taking of an oath,** and so their
22 priesthood could be annulled. **So much better, then, is the
covenant of which the guarantor is Jesus!** The word **Jesus,**
standing emphatically here at the end of the sentence, stresses
the human nature which was prerequisite for his high priesthood (ii. 17).

Characteristically our author mentions in passing the **covenant,** preparatory to an extended exposition of the subject in
the next chapter. In calling the covenant **better** he is using one
of the key words of this Epistle (twelve times in all). He is not
attempting to deny the usefulness of the old covenant, but
showing a covenant which is even better. It is **better** because
Jesus' priesthood is permanent and immutable, and Jesus him-
23 self its guarantor (another legal term). **They indeed became
priests in large numbers because they were prevented by
24 death from remaining in office, but he has a priesthood
which cannot pass to another because he remains for
ever.** The author here is not thinking of a large number of
priests officiating at once, but a long 'historic succession' of
priests contrasted with Jesus' one inalienable priesthood. The
ascription to Jesus of an eternal nature (cf. John viii. 35) is
tantamount to ascription of divinity (cf. John viii. 58), since
eternal life is an attribute of God himself (Psalm xciii. 2).

The eternal nature of his priesthood results in continual and
25 continued activity. **And so he is able to save for all time
those who approach God through him, because he lives**

for ever to plead on their behalf. In our author's view the whole mission of the Son of God, comprising his advent, ministry, death and ascension, was not primarily undertaken to express God's nature but to achieve a specific object; to bring men to God. His eternal session in heaven, since his ascension, results in the ceaseless maintenance of this priestly ministry.

Previously men had used the levitical priesthood in their attempt to draw near to God through the sacrificial cultus; but now Jesus, by fulfilling all that both priests and sacrifices stood for, **is able to save for all time those who approach God through him.** He saves by pleading on men's behalf. Whether he intercedes for help or for forgiveness is left open here (cf. Ro. viii. 26 ff.; 1 John ii. 1); and indeed the two, if not identical, at least overlap. It is in virtue of his glorified and perfected humanity that Jesus intercedes, as will be shown in the following verse. His intercession is not the humble prayer of a suppliant, but the confident plea of an advocate. Aaron bore the names of the children of Israel on the breastplate of judgement when he went into the Holy Place, for a memorial before the Lord continually (Ex. xxviii. 29); but Jesus, the high priest of the heavenly sanctuary, lives for ever to intercede for all time with God himself.

Our author, having shown Melchisedek's superiority over Abraham and Levi (*vv.* 4-10), and Jesus' superiority over the levitical priesthood (*vv.* 11-25), now describes the perfection of Jesus' high priesthood and of his self-offering (*vv.* 26-28), thereby preparing the way for an explanation of the heavenly sanctuary (chapter viii), and of Jesus' self-sacrifice (chapters ix and x).

In describing the perfection of Jesus, our author even dares to comment on the appropriateness of the Incarnation (cf. ii. 10, 17). **Such a high priest was suited to our condition,** 26 **devout, innocent, undefiled, separated from sinners, and exalted above the heavens.** Jesus' character perfectly answered the needs of men. A mediator was required between God and men to bring men to God; and, if the Son was to fulfil this role properly, he must be humanly perfect as well as perfectly human. Our author contrasts the spiritual and moral perfection of Jesus with the outward characteristics of the levitical high priesthood. Jesus was **devout** in the sense that he participated in the divine holiness; while Aaron and his sons were holy in the sense that they were consecrated to perform certain visible functions. Jesus was **innocent** in that he was pure in heart and incapable of conceiving hurt against anyone; while the Aaronic high priest was innocent in that he had been ritually purged of sin. Jesus was **undefiled** because he was morally and spiritually flawless; while the levitical high priest was undefiled because he kept the regulations against defilement. Jesus was **separated from sinners** because he who never sinned had entered heaven and thus had left sin and sinners behind (cf. ix. 28); while the sons of Aaron were separated from sinners because they had to obey the strict rules of Lev. xxi. 10-15. (There is no need to see here a reference to the week's seclusion prescribed for the high priest by postbiblical tradition before he could officiate on the Day of Atonement (cf. Yoma 1. 1); for our author is interested not in rabbinic prescriptions but in biblical exegesis.) Finally Jesus was **exalted above the heavens** (cf. iv. 14; Eph. iv. 10) while the levitical high priest was merely 'great' compared with the other priests.

These contrasts, although only implicit, are significant; but they do not go to the heart of the matter. Jesus' paramount 27 superiority is shown by his sacrifice of himself. **He does not need, as high priests do, to offer up sacrifices daily, first for his own sins, and then for those of the people: this he did once for all when he offered up himself.** Once again our author mentions in passing for the first time a doctrine which will, in a later chapter, receive extended explanation. The self-sacrifice of Jesus is expounded in chapters ix and x.

The **daily** offering of sacrifice by the high priest, mentioned here by our author, has caused difficulty among commentators. For it was on the Day of Atonement alone that the high priest offered sacrifice for himself before offering for the people (Lev. xvi. 6). Our author could hardly have been ignorant of this fact; nor can the Greek text here be forced to mean that the high priest offered sacrifice not daily, but 'on the appointed day'; nor can the difficulty be evaded by pointing out that the high priest is not specifically stated to offer sacrifice daily. If our author did not precisely specify this, he certainly intended it.

The true explanation is to be found in Lev. vi. 13 (LXX), where the offering of the high priest on the occasion of his anointing is commanded to be offered 'continually'. Philo among others believed that the high priest offered daily sacrifice (*de Spec. Leg.* 3. 131; cf. Ecclus. 45. 14). Here again there is no need to adduce post-biblical ordinances, such as the requirement of the high priest that he should offer daily sacrifices for the week preceding the Day of Atonement (Yoma 1. 2), or that he should officiate on sabbaths, new moons, national festivals and days of solemn assembly (Josephus, *Bell. Jud.* 5. 5. 7). In the first place, our author was not interested in rabbinic laws, and, besides, neither of these requirements provides an explanation of the phrase **daily.**

Contrasted with the daily offerings of the high priest, Jesus **offered up himself.** (Worshippers offer gifts, but priests offer them up.) This is the first time that Jesus is described in terms of a sacrifice. **This he did** refers not to what he offered for himself (which would have been unnecessary because of his sinlessness), but to his self-offering for the people. He did this **once for all.** This word ἐφάπαξ, together with the simpler form ἅπαξ, is another of the key concepts of this Epistle. (Taken together, both words are used eleven times.)

Our author ends the chapter with a summary and a contrast. **The Law appoints as high priests men who are frail, but 28 the words of the oath which came after the Law appoint for ever the perfected Son.** 'This "weakness" includes both the actual limitations of humanity as it is, and the personal imperfections and sins of the particular priest' (Westcott). **The oath** of Psalm cx. 4 supersedes **the Law,** just as the frailty of the levitical high priesthood is superseded by the eternal priesthood of **the perfected Son.**

22. PRIESTHOOD AND CULTUS. viii. 1-6

(1) The main point of what is being said is this: we have indeed such a high priest. He has taken his seat at the right hand of the throne of Majesty in the heavens, (2) a

minister of the sanctuary, the real Tent which the Lord and not man set up. (3) Every high priest is appointed to offer gifts and sacrifices; hence it was necessary for him too to have had something to offer. (4) Now if he were on earth, he would not even be a priest, since there are priests who offer the gifts according to the Law. (5) These priests are serving that which is a model and shadow of the heavenly places, as Moses was instructed when he was about to make the Tent, in the words, 'See that you do everything in accordance with the pattern shown to you on the mountain'. (6) But in fact he has obtained a ministry which is as far superior as the covenant of which he is the mediator is better, for it is a covenant which has been legally secured on better promises.

The previous chapter contained a detailed argument concerning the superiority of the Melchisedekian priesthood, and the pre-eminence of Jesus as high priest. The reasoning was complex, and our author, instead of giving a summary of it all, underlines its salient point so that he can build upon it the next

1 stage of his argument. **The main point of what is being said is this: we have indeed such a high priest,** that is, the Son installed in the rank of the Melchisedekian priesthood (cf. vii. 26). **He has taken his seat at the right hand of the throne of Majesty in the heavens.** This phrase here is almost identical with i. 4 (*q.v.*), and possibly it was not uncommon in the primitive church. Earlier in the Epistle, Jesus has been described as 'having passed through the heavens' (iv. 14), or as being 'higher than the heavens' (vii. 26). The actual details of celestial geography have no intrinsic importance. All these phrases are used to symbolise that Jesus is now in the very presence of God himself. Our present passage has the same meaning; for even if Jesus is still **in the heavens,** he is in the presence of God because **he has taken his seat at the right hand of the throne of Majesty.** From this point onwards our author has to insist that Jesus is now in heaven itself, for heaven

2 is the celestial Tent (ix. 24) and Jesus is **a minister of the sanctuary, the real Tent which the Lord and not man set up.**

It is perhaps surprising that one who is described as officiating in a sanctuary should be seated. It is unlikely that there is a particular distinction meant between Jesus and Michael (believed in late rabbinic writings to be the heavenly high priest). It is Jesus' unique status which provides the explanation of his session. He is not merely high priest, but enthroned as King and Son of God (cf. Psalm cx. 1). It is appropriate to his divine and regal status that he should have taken his seat (cf. Rev. iii. 21). The occasion when this happened was, of course, his ascension into the heavens.

The word λειτουργός, translated **minister** here, has previously been used of the angels (cf. i. 6, citing Psalm cix. 4). It signified one who performs a public service, often with reference to a sacred function; and thus in the LXX the noun λειτουργία describes the service of priests officiating in the Temple (cf. Nu. vii. 5). The phrase τῶν ἁγίων λειτουργός, here translated **a minister of the sanctuary,** could also mean 'a minister among the saints' or 'a minister of holy things'. Philo uses the phrase in the latter sense when writing of Aaron (*Leg. All.* 3. 135; cf. *de Fuga et Inv.* 93). Here, however, the meaning is defined by the words which follow, **the real Tent which the Lord and not man set up.** (The Lord here refers to God, contrary to our author's customary usage, according to which 'the Lord' should refer to Jesus and 'Lord' to God.)

The thought of Jesus' priestly function leads naturally to his priestly offering, and our author recapitulates what he has already written at v. 1: **Every high priest is appointed to offer 3 gifts and sacrifices.** This generalisation must include Jesus. **Hence it was necessary for him too to have had something to offer.** The Greek here could equally well be rendered 'hence it is necessary for him too to have something to offer'; and the distinction of tense is of some importance. The latter rendering, however, does not reflect the thought of our author. Westcott's words must still stand: 'The modern concept of Christ pleading in heaven His Passion, "offering his blood" on behalf of men has no foundation in the Epistle. His glorified humanity is the eternal pledge of the absolute efficacy of his accomplished work. He pleads as older writers truly expressed the thought, by His Presence on the Father's throne.'

Our author expresses his argument rigorously and logically. On Calvary Jesus offered himself (and the next chapter explains how this happened). With animals immolation can be distinguished from oblation; but in the case of a personal self-offering involving the sacrifice of life, this distinction is impossible. A man cannot offer himself after he is dead. He can only offer himself up to the point of death. The sacrifice of himself having once and for all been offered on Calvary, Jesus lives for ever as high priest at God's right hand. He could not continually offer his blood in heaven; for heaven is the sphere not of flesh and blood but of ultimate reality.

In the Hellenistic Jewish thought of our author's day, the offering in the heavenly temple was specifically stated not to be of blood, but 'a reasonable and bloodless offering' (T. Levi iii. 6, longer text).[1] This spiritual offering consisted of the prayers of the saints (Rev. viii. 3 ff.; cf. Tobit xii. 15), and, according to later Jewish thought, the souls of the righteous (Beth Hamidrash 3. 137). According to some Talmudic authorities, the Archangel Michael ministered as high priest in the fourth heaven of Zebul (Chag. 12b, Zeb. 62a, Men. 110a), while others said he ministered in the upper heaven of Arabot (Beth Hamidrash 3. 137). The idea of an actual sacrifice in heaven is only found much later in Cabbalistic Judaism (Hach. Harazim, 113. 2), when speculation ran riot.

In the Epistle to the Hebrews the work of the heavenly high priest is explicitly described as intercession on behalf of men (vii. 25; cf. ix. 24), so that they can receive mercy and find grace to help in time of need (iv. 16). (When the purpose of Jesus' high priesthood was described in ii. 17 as 'to expiate the sins of the people', this was intended as an explanation of his priestly function and it was not meant to imply continual and continuing acts of expiation.) Jesus' present ministry in heaven is intercession, not offering; and so it was in the past that he had to have had something to offer. This **something** was not simply his blood. In ix. 14 it is said that the blood of Jesus will be able

[1] According to R. H. Charles (*The Greek Versions of the Testaments of the XII Patriarchs*, 1908, p. xlv.) these Testaments were current in the Greek version by A.D. 50; and Paul twice cites them (Ro. i. 32 = T. Ash. vi. 2, 1 Thess. ii. 16 = T. Lev. vi. 11). M. de Jonge, however, believes that these documents are quoting from Paul (*Testaments of the XII Patriarchs*, 1953).

to cleanse the conscience; but cleansing is not the same as offering. What Jesus offered on Calvary was himself, his soul and body, in his entirety.

The thought of Jesus' self-oblation leads our author to consider the difference between the offering of Jesus and that of the levitical priesthood. For him to have offered what the levitical priests offer would have been to usurp their functions. **Now if 4 he were on earth, he would not even be a priest, since there are priests who offer the gifts according to the Law.** Jesus is a priest in heaven, not on earth; and the perpetual exercise of his heavenly priesthood involves him in a ceaseless activity which is not identical with, but which issues from, the act of self-oblation which inaugurated it. Our author shows here, once again, that he does not regard the levitical priesthood as valueless. It had been established by God's Law, and it performed a useful function, and no one had any right to infringe its divinely appointed prerogatives. 'It is assumed that there cannot be two divinely appointed orders of earthly priests' (Westcott). It follows that Jesus' priesthood must be exercised in heaven, since the levitical priesthood has been established to officiate on earth.

These priests are serving that which is a model and 5 shadow of the heavenly places. The idea of a heavenly temple, with an earthly temple as its counterpart, is very ancient indeed. It can be traced right back to Babylonia, where, according to Hammurabi (Code 2.31), the temple at Sippar was 'like the heavenly dwelling' (cf. R. Buchanan Gray, *Sacrifice in the Old Testament* (1925), p. 151). Centuries later, in New Testament times, Josephus expressed the same idea with reference to the contents of the Jewish temple: 'Each of these things is meant to imitate and represent the universe' (*Antiq.* 3. 7. 7). A refinement of this idea was that an earthly temple was built according to a divine building plan or model. Thus about 3000 B.C., King Gudea in Babylonia built a temple according to a building plan divinely revealed in a dream; while, in biblical times, Ezekiel was visited by an angel who revealed to him the dimensions of the temple to be built (Ez. xl. 4 ff.). Solomon had been instructed by David to build the first Temple 'by the writing from the hand of the Lord concerning it, all the work to be done according to the plan' (1 Chron. xxviii. 19; cf. Wisd. Sol. ix. 8). Long before this the Tent of Meeting in the wilderness was said to have been constructed according to a heavenly model, **as Moses was instructed when he was about to make the Tent, in the words, 'See that you do everything in accordance with the pattern shown to you on the mountain'.** This quotation is taken from Ex. xxv. 40 (LXX), with one word added: See that you do **everything**. . . .; an addition which Philo also made to the text when he cited it (*Leg. All.* 3. 102) and which may have stood in the LXX version used at that time at Alexandria. In this biblical text nothing is said about a heavenly antitype to which the Tent of Meeting was an earthly counterpart. It is merely stated that the tent was made according to a pattern shown by God to Moses (cf. Acts vii. 44). The use of the word τύπον for pattern in the LXX suggested, however, an earthly type and heavenly antitype. By New Testament times this had become a common Jewish belief, and the earliest reference to a heavenly temple is probably that in T. Levi v. 1. In later rabbinic speculation the belief was held that the heavenly temple had the same contents as the earthly temple, and that the earthly temple was a reproduction of all that was found in the heavenly (cf. Men. 29a).

In Alexandrian Judaism, however, the interpretation of Ex. xxv. 40 took a rather different turn. Philo also speculated on the significance of the model which Moses was shown on the mountain. His way of thinking was coloured by Platonism. For him the idea of the Tent which Moses saw belonged to the pure world of incorporeal and invisible ideas and to the sphere of intelligible reality (*de Vita Moys.* 2. 76); while the actual Tent made in the desert was only an imperfect copy and 'shadow of the reality' (*de Somn.* 1. 206). Indeed, Philo even used Hebrew eponymy to interpret Bezalel's name so as to mean 'in the shadow of God' (*Leg. All. ibid.*). While Moses saw the vision of true reality, Bezalel constructed an actual tent (Ex. xxxvi. 1 ff.) that was only in the shadow of God. Similarly our writer states that the levitical priests minister in what is only **a model and shadow of the heavenly places.**

In fact the correspondence between our author and Philo is closer than this. Our writer, like Philo but unlike the rabbis, did not commit himself to the view that the earthly Tent exactly reproduces the heavenly Tent. Indeed his later equation of the heavenly Tent with heaven itself (ix. 24) suggests that he did not share this view. He has, however, already spoken of the real Tent, which the Lord and not man set up (v. 2). There is a passing reference here to Nu. xxiv. 6 (LXX).

The use of ἀληθινός for **real** in v. 2, to signify the real world of ultimate reality, is found frequently in the Johannine writings. Philo too contrasts the world of reality with what 'is made with hands'. According to him the temple made with hands is the earthly Jewish temple, while the highest and real temple is the whole universe (de Spec. Leg. i. 66). This might seem far removed from the thought of our writer, but in fact there is a close similarity. For Philo, in the passage already cited, goes on to state that, while the whole universe forms the true temple of God, heaven is its sanctuary. This is almost what our writer will shortly show. For him heaven is not the antitype of the two tents which Moses was instructed to build, but the antitype of the second tent only, which formed the sanctuary; while the first tent is 'a symbol, pointing to the present time' (ix. 9).

The thought of our author must be distinguished here from that of the Fourth Evangelist and from that of Paul. For Paul the congregation of Christians formed the Temple of God (1 Cor. iii. 16; 2 Cor. vi. 16; Eph. ii. 21). According to the Fourth Evangelist, Jesus when he prophesied that in three days he would raise up the temple, was speaking 'of the temple of his body' (John ii. 21). But for our author, heaven is to be identified with the heavenly sanctuary, and Jesus entered it at his ascension.

Our author does not even mention the Temple: he is concerned about the mobile desert sanctuary constructed in the wilderness wanderings, just as Stephen is reported to have spoken about the Tent which Moses was appointed to make (Acts vii. 44). Much has been made of this correspondence between the Epistle to the Hebrews and the speech of Stephen. It is perhaps not so significant as has been often thought. In the first place Stephen is reported to have disapproved of the building of the Temple as an example of Jewish rebelliousness, whereas in our Epistle the Temple is not even so much as mentioned. Probably the coincidence of thought, such as it is,

can be explained by the fact that both Stephen and our author
were converted Hellenistic Jews. They had lived in the Diaspora,
and had known the irrelevance of temple worship: they had
found that it was possible to be a good Jew without any intercourse with the Jewish Temple. Yet all good Jews believed in
the inspiration of their bible, with its account of the institution
of the Temple. The resolution of this conflict lay in a preference
for the earlier Tent over the later Temple, a view not without
biblical foundation. The preference for the Tent over the
Temple in our Epistle has been thought by some scholars to
show a connection with the Essenes. But the Essenes did not
object to the Temple as such: they only objected to the wicked
priests who ministered there. Our author, on the other hand,
shows indifference to the Temple but great respect for the
levitical priesthood, although he regards their ministry as superfluous now that Jesus has entered upon his ministry. The ideas
of our author and the Essenes are quite different.

Consideration of the new sanctuary led the writer on to
discuss the new covenant which inaugurated its use. The
superiority of Jesus' ministry over the levitical priesthood has
already been demonstrated (vii. 11-26). It is now affirmed to be
6 as far superior as the new covenant is better than the old. **In
fact he has obtained a ministry which is as far superior
as the covenant of which he is the mediator is better, for
it is a covenant which has been legally secured on better
promises.** A covenant differs from an agreement in that the
latter results from discussions between the parties, while
the former is a binding compact which requires the consent
of both parties but which has not necessarily been preceded
by mutual discussion. The entire relationship of the Israelites
towards God was founded on the conviction of a sacred covenant
between them, according to which God would care for them
and they would be obedient to him. There is a sense in which
the whole of the Old Testament is a record of this covenant
relationship which was often broken by the Jews but which had
never been finally abrogated. A covenant requires someone to
bring together the contracting parties, and because Jesus brings
together God and his people, he is here called **the mediator**
of the new covenant, as Moses was the mediator of the old (cf.

Gal. iii. 19; cf. Philo, *Vita Moys*. 2. 166). This new covenant
has been legally secured (cf. vii. 11, where the same Greek legal
term is used), and Jesus has already been cited as its guarantor
(vii. 22). The use of legal terms in connection with the new
covenant is, in a sense, paradoxical; for the new covenant, in
contrast to the old, is not legalistic. **The better promises** on
which it rests (and which are guaranteed by Jesus) are about to
be described in the prophetic words of Jeremiah; they consist
in (*a*) the promise of a new spiritual and moral relationship with
God (*v.* 10); (*b*) the promise of universal scope (*v.* 11); and (*c*),
the promise of absolute relief from all past sins (*v.* 12).

23. THE INADEQUACY OF THE OLD COVENANT.
viii. 7-13

**(7) For if the first covenant had been faultless, there would
have been no desire for a second to take its place. (8) But
God finds fault with them, and says, 'Behold, the days
are coming, says the Lord, when I will conclude a new
covenant with the house of Israel and with the house of
Judah, (9) not like the covenant which I made with their
fathers when I took them by the hand and led them out
of the land of Egypt; for they did not abide by my covenant,
and I ceased to care for them, says the Lord. (10) This is
the covenant which I will make with the house of Israel
after those days, says the Lord: I will put my laws in their
minds and I will write them upon their hearts, and I will
be their God and they shall be my people. (11) And each
man shall not teach his neighbour or his brother, saying,
"Know the Lord", because from small to great they shall
all know me. (12) For I will be merciful to their wrong
doings, and their sins I will remember no more.' (13) By
saying new he has made the first covenant old; and that
which is antiquated and ageing has nearly disappeared.**

The fact that a new covenant was promised at all shows that
there must have been something imperfect about the first one.

(The Essenes, who accepted the old covenant, spoke, in connection with their initiation, not about a new covenant but simply about 'entering the covenant'.) Imperfection did not so much lie in the terms of the old covenant as in its impotence and

7 inefficacy (cf. Ro. vii. 11 f.). **For if the first covenant had been faultless, there would have been no desire for a second to take its place.** Our author does not specify whether this desire for a new covenant was felt by God or by Jeremiah the prophet or by the Israelites generally: probably he meant by God speaking through Jeremiah, for he goes on immediately to cite Jer. xxxi. 31-34, preceding the quotation with the words,

8 **but God finds fault with them and says.**

Our writer was not troubled by matters of source criticism concerning the prophecy which he quoted. It was sufficient for him that the words were found in the bible, and therefore were inspired. Nevertheless there is a certain significance about the context in which the words of this prophecy were uttered. In the dark days of the Babylonian captivity, after the fulfilment of his sombre prophecies of national disaster, Jeremiah might well have despaired. Instead he looked forward to a future full of hope, and he saw present difficulties as a springboard for God's new initiative towards his people. God would give them what the old covenant had been powerless to effect. Our author too wrote in dark days, when his readers were threatened with the calamity of lapsing from their Christian faith; and Jeremiah's message of hope was relevant to them in their own situation.

Behold, the days are coming, says the Lord, when I will conclude a new covenant with the house of Israel and with the house of Judah. The opening words comprise an eschatological formula common in the writings of Jeremiah. The **new** covenant of which he spoke was not so much a novelty as different in kind from the old covenant. Despite the fact that Israel had gone into Assyrian captivity over a century before Judah's conquest by Babylon, this new covenant would

9 bind together both Israel and Judah. It would **not** be **like the covenant which I made with their fathers when I took them by the hand and led them out of the land of Egypt.** That covenant was intrinsically good, but disastrous in its

effects. It was legal in outlook, and by commanding obedience it provoked disobedience (cf. Ro. vii. 7). As a result, the covenant was revoked and God's wrath was visited upon the Jews. As God says in Jeremiah's prophecy, **they did not abide by my covenant, and I ceased to care for them, says the Lord.** Here the LXX differs from the Hebrew text, which reads 'although I was their husband'. Possibly the Massoretic text used by the Septuagintal translators had been softened in meaning by a slight alteration to the Hebrew verb in question.

The new covenant is next described. **This is the covenant 10 which I will make with the house of Israel after those days, says the Lord.** In this new covenant the distinction between Israel and Judah will have disappeared. **I will put my laws in their minds and I will write them upon their hearts and I will be their God and they shall be my people.** There is nothing new about this relationship between God and his people. In Ex. iv. 22 Israel is described as Jahwe's first-born son, and in 2 Sam. vii. 14 the relationship of father and son, hitherto applied to the nation as a whole, is renewed individually for David. The object of the old covenant was precisely to establish Israel as God's people and Jahwe as their God (Lev. xxvi. 12). The new covenant succeeds in this because, in the first place, it establishes not a legal status, but an inward relationship of a moral and spiritual kind. God's laws will not merely be written on tablets of stone: they will be impressed upon the workings of the **mind,** and they will be engraved in the **heart,** the centre of the human personality (cf. 2 Cor. iii. 3). Secondly, this new relationship will be universal in scope; not universal, so far as Jeremiah conceived it, because it would include both Gentile and Jew, but universal in as much as it would include all sorts and conditions of men not only in Judah but also in Israel. **And each man shall not teach his 11 neighbour or his brother, saying, "Know the Lord", because from small to great they shall all know me.** This knowledge can be revealed even to babes (cf. Matt. xi. 25), because it is not mediated or theoretical but direct and experiential (cf. John vii. 17). In the third place the new covenant will bring an absolute forgiveness (involving even God's blotting all

past sins out of his remembrance. This was something impossible under the old covenant, which could only deal with sins which were not committed with 'a high hand'. There is no distinction
12 here between venial and mortal sins. **I will be merciful to their wrong doings and their sins I will remember no more.**

Our author was not the only person in the New Testament who saw in the work of Christ the fulfilment of Jer. xxxi. 31-34. Paul's account to the Corinthians of Jesus' words of institution at the Last Supper (1 Cor. xi. 25), together with the longer version of the Lucan account (Luke xxii. 20), suggest that Jesus himself viewed his own death as the inaugurating sacrifice which fulfilled Jeremiah's prophecy. Paul also spoke of himself as a 'minister of the new covenant' which belongs to the sphere of spiritual reality and not of written ordinances (2 Cor. iii. 6). In this passage Paul compared the glory of the new covenant with the glory of the old, which he described as 'passing away' (2 Cor. iii. 7). Our writer compares the two covenants in rather
13 similar terms. **By saying new he has made the first covenant old,** for if a thing is called new, it may be presumed that its predecessor is regarded as old; **and that which is antiquated and ageing has nearly disappeared.** There is no reference here to the fall of Jerusalem or to the consequent cessation of the temple sacrifices. Our author never referred to contemporary events in Israel's history, and, in any case, his argument concerned not the Temple but the Tent. He believed that the end of the age was near, and thus he held that the old covenant had **nearly disappeared.** The Day was drawing near (x. 25), and the time of reformation was approaching (ix. 10), when Christ would shortly appear (x. 37; cf. ix. 28), and would make his enemies a footstool for his feet (x. 13). And already the new age had begun, and Christians had tasted the powers of the age to come (vi. 5) and had drawn near to the city which marked the end of their journey (xii. 22). Christians were living at the overlap between the two ages (1 Cor. x. 11). The new age had begun, and the old age was ending. The old covenant was still in existence, but it had already been superseded. It was not merely old; it was **antiquated** and decrepit. Because it was *passé*, it would soon pass out of existence.

(1) The first covenant had indeed regulations for worship and a sanctuary, an earthly one. (2) For a Tent was made —the first Tent, in which was the lampstand and the table with the bread of the Presence; and this Tent is called Holy. (3) Beyond the second veil was a Tent which is called Holy of Holies. (4) It had a golden altar of incense and the ark of the covenant, covered all over in gold. In the ark was a golden jar containing the manna, Aaron's staff which sprouted, and the stone tablets of the covenant. (5) Above it were the Cherubim of the Glory overshadowing the Place of Expiation. It is not possible now to speak of these in detail.

At the end of the last chapter there was quoted Jeremiah's prophecy of the new covenant. This chapter is concerned with the contrast between the cultus of the two covenants, the old and the new. Verses 1-10 summarise the cultus of the old covenant, and the remainder of the chapter explains the difference between this and Jesus' high priestly work in the heavenly sanctuary.

The first covenant had indeed regulations for worship. 1 The use of the past tense does not imply that this covenant is no longer in existence. It merely affirms that these regulations are ancient in origin. The **regulations for worship** mentioned here are those which are found in the Pentateuch. A cultus needs a place where it is performed, and the old covenant had **a sanctuary, an earthly one.** The word κοσμικόν, translated earthly, could also mean costly; or it could refer to the world-wide efficacy of the Jewish cultus; or it might contain an allusion to the belief, held by Josephus and Philo, that the earthly tent was symbolic of the universe. In fact, it merely stresses the earthly nature of the worship under the first covenant, and implies a contrast between this and the heavenly worship under the new covenant.

There follows a description of the wilderness tabernacle,

2 based on Ex. xxv-xxvi. First **a Tent was made** (cf. Philo, *de Vita Moys.* 2. 89, where the same phrase is used). There is in Ex. xxv f. a single tent, with a covering at its entrance and a veil inside which divides it into two. Our author, however, instead of speaking about an outer and an inner part of the Tent, prefers to speak of a first and a second Tent. **The first Tent** contained **the lampstand,** which is described in Ex. xxv. 31-37 (cf. Ex. xxxvii. 17-24). Its distinctive feature was its seven branches. When the Tent was superseded by the Temple, there were ten candlesticks (1 Kings vii. 49); but our author is concerned not with the Temple but with the Tent. Also in the outer Tent was **the table,** called in the bible 'the pure table' (Lev. xxiv. 6) or 'the table of the Presence' (Nu. iv. 7). On this table was placed **the bread of the Presence,** better known as the Shewbread, twelve loaves in all, one for each tribe, in two piles of six. These were renewed every sabbath and consumed by the priests (Lev. xxiv. 5-9). According to our author **this Tent is called Holy.** The Greek word ἁγία translated here **Holy** could be construed either as a feminine singular (in which case it is used adjectively and descriptive of the Tent), or as a neuter plural (used as a noun and meaning a sanctuary). The latter usage, however, would be unparalleled in the anarthrous form in which it appears here; and, in any case, our author consistently uses the neuter plural with the article to mean the sanctuary, that is, the inner and not (as here) the outer Tent (cf. ix. 25; xiii. 11, etc.). If the word is construed as a feminine singular (as in the translation *supra*), the passage makes sense and our author is seen to maintain his consistency, which is such a marked feature of his style (cf. F. C. Synge, *Hebrews and the Scriptures* (1959), p. 26 f.).

The outer or first Tent was divided from the inner or second
3 Tent by a veil (Ex. xxvi. 31-35), called here **the second veil** to distinguish it from the curtain at the entrance (cf. Ex. xxvi. 36). **Beyond the second veil was an** inner **Tent,** called in Greek **the Holy of Holies** (a literal translation of the Hebrew phrase, which means Holiest). Our author henceforth refers to this
4 inner Tent as the sanctuary. He says that it **had a golden altar of incense.** The Greek word θυμιατήριον, translated here **alter of incense,** was more often used to designate a censer, and some

have supposed that our author is referring to the golden censer used in the ritual of the Day of Atonement (Lev. xvi. 12). Such a minor object of the cultus would not, however, have been mentioned here; and the word could also be used (e.g. by Philo, *de Vita Moys.* 2. 94) to signify the altar of incense. This altar, however, was not situated in the sanctuary but in the outer Tent (Ex. xxx. 6; cf. Philo, *Quis Rer. Div.* 226). Possibly our author has made a slight slip and placed the altar in the wrong part of the Tent, relying on the vague language of the LXX at this point. He may have been misled by the fact that this altar is not mentioned in Exodus along with the rest of the furniture of the outer Tent, but is described in a passage which refers to the use of its incense in the inner sanctuary on the Day of Atonement (Ex. xxx. 1-10). This would have been an easy mistake for someone, like our author, who had no personal knowledge of the Herodian Temple and who was describing the desert Tent simply from its description in the Septuagint. In any case our author does not actually commit himself to the view that the altar of incense is situated in the sanctuary: he merely says that it belonged to the sanctuary.

The sanctuary also had **the ark of the covenant, covered all over in gold.** This ark was a chest, made of acacia wood, measuring about four feet long and two and a half feet wide and two and a half feet high. There was also **a jar** (Ex. xvi. 33), described in the Septuagint (but not in the Hebrew) text as being **golden.** According to the biblical description, this jar contained a measure of **manna** from the wilderness wanderings (Ex. xvi. 32-34). Also there was **Aaron's rod which sprouted,** the divine proof of Aaron's exclusive right to the priesthood, vouchsafed when Moses issued a challenge after a rebellion in the desert against Aaron and himself (Nu. xvii. 1-11). Also there were **the stone tablets of the covenant,** on which were written the Ten Commandments and which were ordered to be kept in the Ark (Deut. x. 5). According to the biblical description, these stone tablets were the only objects to be placed inside the Ark (1 Kings viii. 9). The other objects were kept near by in the sanctuary, but not in the Ark itself.

Above it were the Cherubim of the Glory, overshadow- 5 ing the Place of Expiation. According to Ex. xxv. 18-20, these

two Cherubs were made of gold and were all of one piece with
the Place of Expiation. They faced each other, and their wings
were spread out to overshadow it, as though to protect it. These
Cherubim kept watch over the very dwelling place of God himself. They are called Cherubim of the Glory, because Glory here
is a synonym for God; an apt periphrasis, since the mystery of
this inner sanctuary, together with its gold furnishings, suggests
the divine glory. The Place of Expiation itself was literally a
covering of pure gold on top of the Ark. The Hebrew verb
'cover', however, can mean either to cover or to expiate sins,
and from the latter meaning is derived the Greek word
ἱλαστήριον, used in the LXX and translated here as **the Place
of Expiation** (cf. Ro. iii. 25, where this word is applied direct
to Christ).

Our author wants to get back to the main course of his argument, and he is unwilling to particularise more about these
sacred objects. **It is not possible now to speak of these in
detail.** Philo too had used an almost identical phrase when he
wished to break off a description of the Temple (*Quis Rer.
Div.* 221). But our author was not interested in allegorical interpretations of the sanctuary such as those which Josephus and
Philo gave. These two, for example, regarded the four-fold
fabric of which the veil was made as symbolic of the four
elements (Philo, *de Vita Moys.* 2. 88; Josephus, *Antiq.* 3. 7. 7;
Bell. Jud. 5. 5. 4). They both regarded the seven branches of the
candlestick as symbolic of the seven planets with the sun at the
centre (Philo, *Quis Rer. Div.* 221; Josephus, *ibid.*). For Philo
the altar of incense was four-sided because it was used for
thanksgiving for the four elements (*Quis Rer. Div.* 226); and
the manna in the golden jar represented perception, word and
mind (*De Congr.* 100); and the proportions of the Ark symbolised
the power, purpose and understanding of God revealed in
his mercy at the Place of Expiation (*de Vita Moys.* 2. 96). As for
the Cherubim, some said that they represented the two hemi-
spheres, but Philo asserted in one passage that they represented
the creative and royal powers of God (*de Vita Moys.* 2. 99),
and he also put forward his own idea that they represented the
goodness and the governance of God (*de Cher.* 28).

Our author abjures here this allegorical method of interpretation. He borrowed much from Philo; but his Christian faith provided him with a better method of understanding the scriptures than allegorical interpretation.

25. THE INSUFFICIENCY OF THE OLD CULTUS.
ix. 6-10

(6) Under these arrangements the priests continually enter the first Tent as they carry out the duties of their service, (7) but the second Tent is entered only once a year by the high priest alone, and that only with the blood which he offers for himself and for the people's sins of ignorance. (8) By this the Holy Spirit shows that the way into the sanctuary was not open while the first Tent was in existence. (9) This is a symbol, pointing to the present time. It entails the offering of gifts and sacrifices which could not give the worshipper a perfectly clear conscience, (10) since they were concerned only with food and drink and washing rites of different kinds—regulations concerning the body in force until the time of reformation.

After a brief description of the objects of the cultus under the old covenant, there is now a short consideration of this cultus itself (*vv.* 6-10). Firstly, an important distinction is made between the duties of the priests and those of the high priest. The priests may not, on pain of death, penetrate into the sanctuary itself: their work is done in the outer Tent (Nu. xviii. 3-7). They have exclusive charge of the outer Tent, and the proper discharge of their duties results in a continual ministry of worship there. They have to offer incense morning and evening on the altar of incense; they have to see that the seven-branched candlestick is continually alight; they have to change each sabbath the bread of the Presence. **Under these arrangements 6 the priests continually enter the first Tent as they carry out the duties of their service.**

The worship in this outer tent has no counterpart in the heavenly cultus, since Jesus is not regarded as a priest, but as

high priest, and it is in the second or inner sanctuary that the
7 high priest ministers. **The second Tent is entered only once
a year by the high priest alone.** The occasion was the ritual
of the Day of Atonement (Lev. xvi). **Once** refers to the one day
of the year on which the high priest entered, not to one single
occasion, for the bible prescribed at least three entrances on
that day; first, to bring in the censer of incense (Lev. xvi. 13);
secondly, to make expiation for himself and for the priests (*v.*
14 f.); and thirdly to make expiation for the people (*v.* 16); and,
although a fourth visit is not prescribed in scripture, the censer
of incense had later to be removed (Yoma 5. 1-4; 7. 4; but cf.
Philo, *Leg. ad Gai.* 307).

It was not without danger even for the high priest to enter
so numinous and sacred a place (cf. Lev. xvi. 2). He needed, as
it were, protection as he approached. He entered alone, **and that
only with the blood which he offers for himself and for
the people's sins of ignorance.** Our author follows here a
habit which has been noticed earlier in his Epistle. He introduces casually a theme which he will treat at greater length later
on. The importance of **the blood** in the sacrificial cultus will
receive great emphasis in the course of the exposition of Jesus'
self-sacrifice (it is mentioned twelve times more in this and
the following chapter). **The blood** which the high priest takes
into the inner sanctuary is, firstly, the blood of a bullock for his
own purification and for that of the priests (Lev. xvi. 14), and,
secondly, the blood of a goat for the purification of the people
(Lev. xvi. 15 f.). The method of purification is explained in
Lev. xvi. 14 f. The further elaborations of the ritual according
to Jewish tradition are not the concern of our author who, here
as elsewhere, argues from the biblical account.

This blood can make expiation only for **sins of ignorance,**
in accordance with the biblical precept that sins committed with
a high hand are unforgivable (Nu. xv. 30). Probably a contrast is intended between the different kind of sins expiated
by the old, as opposed to the new, covenant. These sins of
ignorance may be very grave both in their nature and in their
consequences; but they can be forgiven because they have not
been committed with the settled and deliberate intention of
disobedience.

The old covenant, with its inner and outer Tent, is symbolic of the conditions under which human existence must be lived. (Here our author seems to approach the belief of Philo and Josephus that the Temple is a symbol of the universe, cf. comment on *v.* 5.) It was part of God's providence that the Tent should represent something more than itself. **The Holy 8 Spirit,** who is the guarantor and agent of biblical inspiration, **shows that the way into the sanctuary was not open while the first Tent was in existence.** The very fact that there was an outer and an inner Tent shows that the two parts of the Tent could be distinguished and that there was a curtain which divided them from each other. There was no free passage from one to the other; and it was only on one day of the year that one person was permitted to go from the inner to the outer Tent, and that only after considerable preparation.

This state of affairs points beyond itself: it **is a symbol, 9 pointing to the present time.** (The Greek here could be construed to mean that this had been symbolic of the old covenant up till the present time, i.e. before the coming of Jesus: but this exegesis is forced and unnecessary.) It will not be until the full establishment of the world to come that the way to God will be absolutely open. Of course it has been opened already through the sacrifice that Jesus has offered. But his sacrifice belongs properly not to this present time but to the 'world to come': and the accomplishment of Jesus' sacrifice is in itself a proof that the 'world to come' has already broken into this present time (cf. Gal. i. 4).

The cultus of the earthly sanctuary is therefore a symbol of human existence under the old covenant which has 'nearly disappeared' (viii. 13), but which still exists at **the present time** when this Epistle was written, even if it was antiquated and out of date. It is symbolic (or as we might say, 'typical') because **it entails the offering of gifts and sacrifices which could not give the worshipper a perfectly clear conscience.** Unless the conscience has been cauterised (1 Tim. iv. 2), sin brings consciousness of guilt. The main purpose of the cultus under the old covenant was to remove guilt and thereby clear the conscience. This purpose could, however, be achieved only in an extremely limited sphere. By these sacrifices the

10 conscience could only be cleansed from the kind of guilt which had been incurred through ritual offences, **since they were concerned only with food and drink and washing rites of different kinds.** The Pentateuch contains a mass of regulations about what foods should be regarded as unclean (Lev. xi; Deut. xiv. 3-21); and there is also a number of laws concerning washing rites of various kinds (Lev. vi. 27; xiv. 8; Nu. viii. 7; xix. 17 f.), those which concern the person and those which concern objects. The regulations became more complex as tradition developed, but there is no reason to suppose that there is an allusion here to any but Pentateuchal regulations. There are, however, no general laws in the Pentateuch concerning the drinking of intoxicating liquors, only regulations for priests (Lev. x. 9) and for Nazirites (Nu. vi. 3). Possibly our author was referring to the drink-offerings, mentioned occasionally in the Pentateuch (e.g. Nu. vi. 15).

These laws are all **regulations concerning the body.** They can therefore only remove a guilty conscience caused by offences which are merely ritual. The validity of these ritual laws is not questioned by our author. Paul, too, never ordered Jewish Christians to give up the Jewish food laws, and he forbad liberal-minded Christians to despise those who did keep them (Ro. xiv. 10). Our author would seem to be more explicit than Paul; for he affirms that these regulations are still **in force,** although they had already become antiquated and out of date in as much as they belong to the old covenant. They will vanish altogether at **the time of reformation,** when this world order will be completely superseded. This is what the author of St Matthew's Gospel described as 'the new world' (Matt. xix. 28), and what is called in Acts 'the time of universal restoration' (Acts iii. 21).

26. THE CULTUS OF CHRIST. ix. 11-14

(11) But Christ has appeared, high priest of good things to come. By means of the greater and more perfect Tent, not made with human hands, that is, not of this created

world, (12) and not by the blood of goats and calves, but by his own blood he entered the sanctuary once for all, and secured a deliverance that is everlasting. (13) For if the blood of goats and bulls and the sprinkled ashes of a heifer can hallow those who have been defiled and restore their external purity, (14) how much more shall the blood of Christ, who in his eternal nature gave himself to God as a spotless self-oblation, purify our conscience from dead works to serve the living God?

In the last section a brief description was given of the sacred objects and cultus of the old covenant. There now follows a series of contrasts between the old and the new: in verses 11-14, between the old and the new cultus; in verses 15-22 between the old and the new covenants; in verses 23-26 between the many sacrifices of the old covenant and the one sacrifice of the new; and in verses 27-28 there is a rather different kind of contrast between men and Christ concerning the hereafter.

The first contrast is between the mode and *locus* of sacrifice in the two covenants. **But Christ has appeared, high priest of good things to come.** The text adopted here is $\tau\hat{\omega}\nu\ \mu\epsilon\lambda\lambda\acute{o}\nu\tau\omega\nu\ \mathring{a}\gamma\alpha\theta\hat{\omega}\nu$. B D* *1611 1739 2005 pc* it syᵖ ʰ ᵖᵃˡ Or Chr Cyr read $\tau\hat{\omega}\nu\ \gamma\epsilon\nu o\mu\acute{\epsilon}\nu\omega\nu\ \mathring{a}\gamma\alpha\theta\hat{\omega}\nu$ (*p*⁴⁶ $\gamma\epsilon\nu\alpha\mu\acute{\epsilon}\nu\omega\nu$). This reading would mean that Christ is the high priest of good things that have already come. According to our author, however, Christians have tasted the powers of the age to come (vi. 5), yet their salvation still lies in the future (i. 14). The variant $\gamma\epsilon\nu o\mu\acute{\epsilon}\nu\omega\nu$, although well attested, is intrinsically improbable, and it was probably caused by a primitive corruption of the text by dittography from the preceding $\pi\alpha\rho\alpha\gamma\epsilon\nu\acute{o}\mu\epsilon\nu os$.

The contrast here between the person of Christ and the officiants of the earthly Tent is very marked, so that **Christ** could almost be rendered 'the Christ'. He is not in the succession of these levitical priests. Like Melchisedek of old, mysteriously he **has appeared** on the scene of history. All that the levitical priests could achieve has been achieved; but Christ is **high priest of good things** still **to come** in the near future, when this world-order will be ended.

Christ's ministry is not on earth. **By means of the greater**

and more perfect Tent, not made with human hands,
12 that is, not of this created world, and not by the blood of
goats and calves, but by his own blood he entered the
sanctuary once for all. Four possible translations of this
difficult passage may here be considered.

(a) The first phrase of the sentence may be rendered 'through
the greater and more perfect Tent . . . he entered'. The verbs
of motion in this and in the preceding sentence are in favour of
this rendering. Two objections are, however, decisive: (i) While
διά with the genitive can signify 'passage through', it would be
bad style and unparalleled N.T. usage to use the same preposition twice in the same sentence with the same case but with
different meanings ('through the Tent . . . not by the blood, but
by his own blood'). (ii) It is the priests on earth who minister in
the outer court, and so an outer court would be irrelevant in
heaven, since Christ is high priest, not a priest. In fact our
author is not interested in distinguishing the different parts of
the heavenly Tent, as this translation would suggest. In any
case the sanctuary is heaven itself (v. 24), and Christ could
hardly have passed through the greater and more perfect Tent
of heaven in order to arrive in heaven!

(b) Assuming that the preposition διά is used instrumentally
and not with the meaning of 'passage through', it would be
possible to take the first phrase of this sentence with the last
phrase of the last sentence, thus: 'high priest of good things to
come by means of the greater and more perfect Tent'. The
difficulty of this rendering is that the good things to come are
achieved not through the instrumentality of the heavenly Tent,
but solely through the self-sacrifice of its high priest.

(c) It would be possible to identify 'the greater and more
perfect Tent' with Jesus' humanity, and even by extension to
equate it with his exalted Body in which is included the church
militant and triumphant. Such an ecclesiastical reference, however, would be uncharacteristic of our author, who thinks of the
church not as the Body of Christ but as a family or city or
assembly. So far as Christ's humanity is concerned, although it
was united with the divine nature of the Son (vii. 16), it is
stressed so strongly (ii. 17; iv. 18) that to designate it 'made
without human hands' or 'not of this created world' would be

to run counter to one of our author's deepest convictions.

(d) In viii. 2 the heavenly Tent is identified with the sanctuary. It follows that, since there is no contrary indication, the same identity is intended here. Our author consistently holds that the heavenly things are 'better' than their earthly counterparts. The heavenly Tent is **greater and more perfect** because the earthly one is its model and copy. It might at first sight seem slightly clumsy to say, in effect, that by means of the heavenly Tent Jesus entered into the heavenly Tent. But the emphasis of the sentence is not on his entry into the Tent, but on the eternal salvation that was procured there, and the sanctuary is mentioned instrumentally as well as locally so as to form a contrast with the means whereby the mode and the place of the earthly cultus was maintained.

The Greek word χειροποίητος, translated **made with human hands,** was probably used by Jewish writers in the Hellenistic world to describe idols (cf. Acts xvii. 24), and in the New Testament it is applied by Jesus and by his followers to the Jewish Temple (Mark xiv. 58; Acts vii. 48). The negative form of the word, on the other hand, can describe Jesus' resurrection body (Mark xiv. 58), the church triumphant (2 Cor. v. 1), or Christian baptism (Col. ii. 11) contrasted with Jewish circumcision (cf. Eph. ii. 11).

Unlike the levitical high priest, who on the Day of Atonement entered the earthly sanctuary **by the blood of goats** for the sins of the people **and** by the blood **of calves** for his own sins and for those of the priests, Christ **entered by his own blood.**[1] For both, it was blood that enabled entrance to be gained, but in Jesus' case it was his own blood. Although our author puts very great weight on the efficacy of the blood of Jesus, in fact Jesus died an almost bloodless death, apart from what was shed when he was nailed to the cross. But for our author any self-sacrifice which culminates in death presupposes blood-shedding (cf. ix. 22). Jesus did not enter the sanctuary in order to offer his blood, but **by his own blood** he gained

[1] This comparison between Jesus' sacrificial death and the Day of Atonement sacrifice would suggest itself more easily to anyone accustomed to the old Jewish calendar, according to which Jesus' death and the Day of Atonement fell on the same day of the week (A. Jaubert, *La Date de la Cène* (1957), p. 35 n. 2).

access to the heavenly sanctuary. The fact that Jesus **secured a deliverance that is everlasting** means that he entered heaven **once for all.** It was not merely that he obtained a deliverance in the eternal sphere, but that his deliverance has eternal force and therefore can never be repeated. The word λύτρωσις, translated **deliverance,** means literally redemption. In Paul it is usually connected with the idea of sacral manumission (cf. A. Deissmann, *Light from the Ancient East* (1910), pp. 331 ff.), but here the word is used, as in the LXX, more generally of a costly liberation (cf. Luke i. 68, ii. 38).

The eternal validity of Christ's sacrifice has been thus asserted, but it requires further explanation. Why is this redemption everlasting? Our author uses the sacrifices of the old covenant as the starting-point of his answer to this question. He does not deny the limited efficacy of these sacrifices: indeed, it is on the basis of this partial efficacy that he argues *a fortiori*

13 to the sacrifice of Christ. **The blood of goats and bulls and the sprinkled ashes of a heifer can hallow those who have been defiled and restore their external purity.** The blood of goats and bulls was used in the sacrifices of the Day of Atonement (Lev. xvi. 14 f.). **The sprinkled ashes of a heifer** were used in the making of 'water of impurity' for the cleansing of persons and vessels and clothes ritually polluted by contact with a dead body (cf. Nu. xix). After seven days **those who have been defiled** are reckoned, after treatment, to be clean again (Nu. xix. 19), and so they regain their **external purity.** If the ritual sacrifices of the old covenant result in ritual

14 cleansing, **how much more shall the blood of Christ, who in his eternal nature gave himself to God as a spotless self-oblation, purify our conscience from dead works to serve the living God?** Westcott here differentiates four ways in which the sacrifice of Christ is superior to those of animals; it was voluntary, rational, spontaneous and moral. But, true though this is, the eternal efficacy of Christ's sacrifice still remains to be explained; and the only true explanation of it is that self-sacrifice was offered by Christ in his **eternal nature.**

The phrase πνεῦμα αἰώνιον means literally 'eternal spirit' and is translated here **eternal nature,** because πνεῦμα is understood in the common New Testament sense of a man's ego or very

self. It does not mean here 'the Holy Spirit', or Christ's dis-
position, or his soul. It refers to 'the power of a life that nothing
can destroy' (vii. 16). The complete humanity of Jesus is
always assumed by our author, and this is not here in question.
The point is this: that he, who in self-sacrifice offered to God
his full and perfect humanity, was himself eternal by nature;
and because of this, the salvation that he procured is everlasting. This salvation has not been gained merely by suffering,
but by blood, that is, by life offered in death. Now if ritual
sacrifices can cleanse the body from ritual sins, the personal
self-sacrifice of one who is by nature eternal will cleanse for
ever the soul from personal sins. The guilt incurred by these
personal sins leaves its mark upon the conscience; but the blood
of Christ will cleanse the stain of those sins which are committed in **works** which are **dead** because they are done apart
from God (cf. vi. 1). Released from a life which is no life, the
sinner is freed to serve God, who is the source of all life. It is
characteristic of our author that he sees this service of God
not as a fellowship but as a quasi-liturgical activity, 'a sacred
ministry of complete surrender' (Westcott).

27. THE COVENANT SACRIFICE. ix. 15-22

**(15) Therefore he is the mediator of the new covenant or
testament, in order that, as a death has taken place to
secure deliverance from transgressions committed under
the first covenant, those who have been called may
receive the promise of the eternal inheritance. (16) For
where there is a testament, it is essential for the testator's
death to be established; (17) for a testament is valid only
after death, since it never has force while the testator is
alive. (18) That is why even the first covenant or testament was not inaugurated without blood. (19) For when
every commandment of the Law had been declared by
Moses to all the people, he took the blood of the calves
and the goats, with water, scarlet wool and marjoram,
and sprinkled both the scroll itself and all the people,**

saying, (20) 'This is the blood of the covenant which God commanded you'. (21) In the same way he sprinkled with the blood both the Tent and all the vessels of divine service. (22) Indeed almost everything is cleansed with blood according to the Law, and without outpouring of blood there is no remission of sins.

Having shown the efficacy of Christ's blood, our author next considers why it was necessary for blood to have been shed. The answer was not hard to find. A covenant requires a blood
15 sacrifice; and such was Jesus' death. **Therefore he is the mediator of the new covenant** (cf. viii. 6). He is its guarantor (vii. 22) because the efficacy of his sacrifice guarantees the establishment of the new covenant. The word διαθήκη means either **covenant** or **testament.** In the next verse the necessity of Christ's death will be derived from the idea of a valid testament. Here, however, the reference is still to the new covenant prophesied by Jeremiah and inaugurated by Christ. His death is described (literally) as a ransom. The word ἀπολύτρωσις is employed because of its associations of cost and sacrifice and liberation. The use of this word does not imply that a debt was actually paid to God or to the devil or to anyone or anything else. This **deliverance** that Christ effects removes men from the guilt of **transgressions committed under the first covenant** (cf. Acts xiii. 39).

The covenant with Noah (Gen. vi. 18) and with Abraham (Gen. xv. 7 ff.) preceded the Mosaic covenant; but Noah's was universal in scope and Abraham's was universal in promise, so that the Mosaic covenant can be called God's **first covenant** with the Jewish people. This covenant, although it forbad sin, was itself the occasion of sin (Ro. vii. 8-12), and from such sin Christ's death effected deliverance. Its benefits were not only for Christians, but for all **those who have been called,** including those who had lived under the old covenant. They too **may receive the promise** which consists in their inheritance which belongs to the world to come.

The word **inheritance** suggests a will; and it is this meaning of διαθήκη which is intended here. A will is not valid until it is
16 'proved'. **Where there is a testament, it is essential for**

the testator's death to be established; for a testament is **17**
valid only after death, since it never has force while the
testator is alive. (Actually, under rabbinic law, a man could
give away his inheritance while he was alive (cf. Luke xv. 12),
but our author is not interested in rabbinic law.) While the
testator is living, he will still want to own his possessions and
property, and he may wish to alter his testamentary dispositions.
Death is necessary for a will to be effective; and **that is why 18
even the first covenant or testament was not inaugurated
without blood.** The author's argument here seems weaker in
English than in his Greek original, for in English there is no word,
as there is in Greek, which can mean both covenant and will.

Having shown the necessity of a sacrifice at the inauguration
of a covenant, our author proceeds to describe this sacrifice,
not of the Abrahamic (Gen. xv. 9 f.), but of the Mosaic covenant. **For when every commandment of the law had 19
been declared by Moses to all the people, he took the
blood of the calves and the goats.** Our author uncharacter-
istically alters and embroiders the biblical record at this point
(Ex. xxiv. 3-8), but he does this in a way unknown in rabbinic
haggadah. According to Exodus, after Moses had read the
words and ordinances of the Lord, young men (representing
the twelve tribes) sacrificed young oxen. The Bible does not
mention goats in this connection. Perhaps they are added here
because of associations with the Day of Atonement, or because
'calves and goats' formed a common expression (cf. ix. 13), or
because our author was using some oral tradition since lost.
Furthermore, according to Exodus, there is no mention here of
water, scarlet wool and marjoram. These were prescribed
for the cleansing of a leper (Lev. xiv. 4-7) and in connection
with the 'water for impurity' (Nu. xix. 6, 17). According to
Exodus, Moses only sprinkled the people and the altar (Ex.
xxiv. 8, 6); but our author substitutes for the altar of the
biblical account **the scroll itself.**

According to our author, Moses says to the people, **'This is 20
the blood of the covenant which God commanded you'.**
There is a subtle change here from the text of Ex. xxiv. 8, which
reads: 'Behold the blood of the covenant . . .'. There is possibly
an unconscious assimilation of the LXX text to the dominical

words of institution at the Last Supper (cf. Mark xiv. 24); but the fact that our author makes absolutely no use of these words of institution with reference to the new covenant shows, as has been noted earlier (cf. comment on vii. 3), that he is not concerned in this Epistle with the Christian Eucharist.

21 According to our author, Moses **in the same way** also **sprinkled with the blood both the Tent and all the vessels of divine service.** In fact, when the Mosaic covenant was made, the Tent was not yet in existence; and when it was made it was consecrated with oil, not blood, and so were its sacred vessels (Ex. xl. 9 f.). Josephus, however, knows of a tradition that it was consecrated both with oil, with water and with blood (*Antiq.* 3. 8. 6).

After this description of the Mosaic covenant's inaugurating sacrifice, two generalisations of the utmost importance are

22 added. The first one is that **almost everything is cleansed with blood according to the Law.** This is a fair statement: **almost everything;** for there are a few ablutions by means of water (e.g. Lev. xv. 10) and fire (e.g. Nu. xxxi. 22 f.) which are also found in the Law. The second generalisation is stated without any qualification. **Without outpouring of blood there is no remission of sins.** Our author here coins a word for **outpouring of blood,** and he actually wrote simply **remission,** but the context makes it plain that he intended to refer to remission **of sins.**

No explanation is given of this principle that forgiveness necessitates the blood of sacrifice. It is not even true, for there are other means of receiving forgiveness actually prescribed in the Old Testament, such as prayer (Dan. ix. 19), fasting (Joel ii. 12), almsgiving (Ecclus. iii. 30), penitence (Psalm li. 17). The prophets demand penitence and promise forgiveness, but they do not regard blood sacrifice as the only or even as a desirable means of receiving divine absolution. Our writer, however, is here primarily concerned with the Pentateuch, and his interests are liturgical and sacerdotal, and so he is led to make this unqualified generalisation that **without outpouring of blood there is no remission of sins.** For him this is a self-evident datum (cf. Yoma 5a; Men. 93b). It forms the ground of his whole doctrinal argument. It may be presumed that the ideas underlying it are that the blood is the life (cf. Gen. ix. 4) and therefore it is sacred; and that by the release of life through death and by the sprinkling of blood the victim (and the sinners who identify themselves with the victim) are brought into the presence of God. Such is the theory; but it is a theory constructed by scholars, not a doctrine found in the O.T. scriptures.

There is no explanation of sacrifice in the Old Testament. Its efficacy is assumed. Our author does not question it for a moment: he simply takes it for granted, and to query the validity of the sacrificial system is to ask a question which would never have occurred to him.

28. THE SACRIFICE OF CHRIST. ix. 23-28

(23) It was necessary then that the copies of the heavenly things should be purified by these means, but the heavenly things themselves by better sacrifices than these. (24) For Christ did not enter into a sanctuary made by human hands, a mere copy of the real one, but into heaven itself, now to appear in God's presence on our behalf; (25) nor is he there to offer himself time after time, like the high priest who enters the sanctuary every year with blood that is not his own; (26) otherwise he would have had to suffer time after time from the creation of the world. But now at the consummation of the ages he has appeared once and for all to annul sin through the sacrifice of himself. (27) And as it is the lot of men to die once, and after that the Judgement, (28) so too the Christ who was offered once to bear the sins of many will appear a second time, not to deal with sin, but to bring salvation to those who await him.

Having contrasted the inaugurating sacrifices of both covenants, our author now bends the argument towards a comparison between the cultus of each covenant. **It was necessary 23 then that the copies of the heavenly things should be purified by these means.** This is a reference to the purifications described in the last section and believed by our author to have taken place at the inauguration of the first covenant. A rather unhappy comparison is now adduced between the heavenly things—that is, the whole heavenly cultus—and their earthly copies. For, he argues, the earthly copies had to be purified thus, **but the heavenly things themselves by better sacrifices than these.** As the sentence is phrased in the Greek, there is a clear implication that the heavenly things themselves had to be purified. Attempts have been made to explain this by citing the shaking of heaven (xii. 26) (but this is quite a different matter from purification), or by the assumption that the Fall had infected heaven, which was now the abode of evil powers, so that this too needed purification by the heavenly high priest. 'There is no place, however near to God, where His will is not working against opposition' (Nairne). This may or may not be true; but it certainly does not form part of the author's argument here. In any case, the heavenly work of Christ is effective for men, according to our author, and not for angels or evil powers. What our author meant was this: the purification of men's consciences, made by means of the heavenly cultus, needed a better sacrifice to make it effective than those which sufficed for the earthly cultus, which was a mere copy of the heavenly. Our author, however, has not expressed himself with his usual felicity, and hence the contortions of commentators at this point.

Our author has baldly asserted the necessity of a 'better sacrifice'. But why, it may be asked, *must* the heavenly cultus have this better sacrifice? The answer is given in terms of a contrast between the cultus of both covenants. A better sanc-
24 tuary demands a better sacrifice. **For Christ did not enter into a sanctuary made by human hands, a mere copy of the real one, but into heaven itself, now to appear in God's presence on our behalf.** The contrast between sanctuaries which have been made or not **made by human hands** has already been noted (cf. comment on ix. 11). The Greek word, ἀντίτυπον, translated here **copy,** is used in the opposite sense from that of 1 Peter iii. 21, where it means a prototype. The contrast between the **real** Tent and its copy has been noted earlier (cf. comment on viii. 2). For the first time the heavenly sanctuary is identified with heaven itself, a key point for understanding our author's argument.

The object of Christ's heavenly ministry is **to appear in God's presence on our behalf.** It is unlikely that a contrast is intended here between the clouds of incense obscuring the earthly sanctuary and the pellucid brightness of the heavenly courts. More probably Christ is said to appear not so that he may be visible to God (for God can see everyone everywhere) but in order that he may **appear** as counsel on **our behalf** (cf. vii. 25; Ro. viii. 34; 1 John ii. 1). The nature of his plea is not stated, and it is unprofitable to speculate on what our author may have thought its content to be. To plead on our behalf is Christ's present work as heavenly high priest. He does it **now,** for in the eternal world there is no passage of time, and every moment is an eternal **now.**

Two further contrasts of the cultus are added: firstly between Jesus' own blood and the high priest's use of animal blood, and secondly between Jesus' single entry into heaven, and the high priest's entry, annually repeated, into the earthly sanctuary. These points recapitulate the earlier argument of chapter ix, and especially ix. 11 f. **Nor is he there to offer himself time 25 after time, like the high priest who enters the sanctuary every year with blood that is not his own.** Our author does not mean by this (and indeed he does not state) that Christ offered his own blood in heaven, like the levitical high priest who offered the blood of animals in the sanctuary. Christ's self-oblation is identified in x. 14 with his death (cf. also the comment on viii. 3).

The argument at this point is particularly subtle. Earlier on, the question whether Jesus could have a successor as high priest was answered in terms of his eternal nature (vii. 24). The question now is slightly different. How, it might be asked, can there be any certainty that Jesus will only enter the heavenly sanctuary once? He can have no successor; but might he not, like the levitical high priest, repeat his sacrifice? The answer suggested to this question is that the time is now too late for this to happen. The ordinances of this world have already nearly passed away (viii. 13). If Jesus had intended to offer himself more than once, he would have had to do this before the present time. Indeed, **he would have had to suffer time 26 after time from the creation of the world** itself. The

opportunity, such as it was, has now passed. **Now at the consummation of the ages he has appeared once and for all.**
The wording here implies the personal manifestation of a preexistent being (cf. 1 Tim. iii. 16). The purpose of Christ's first advent is put here in legal terms; **to annul sin through the sacrifice of himself.**

The writer next passes from a contrast of opposites to a com-
27 parison of similarities. **It is the lot of men to die once, and after that the Judgement.** There is but one life. Death is irrevocable; and it leads to final judgement. On this matter our author has more to say later (x. 27 ff.). At first sight it might seem that the Christ should be contrasted with men, rather than compared with them; for, unlike men, the Christ is triumphant over death, and, unlike men, he does not come under final judgement. Yet there is a similarity between the Christ and mankind. For both of them, death opens the portals to a fresh kind of existence, and, since it is a new mode of life, our author confirms the point that Christ cannot return to earth to offer himself in sacrifice all over again, but can only return for a
28 fresh purpose. **So too the Christ who was offered once to bear the sins of many will appear a second time, not to deal with sin, but to bring salvation to those who await him.**

There is in the Greek a play here on the two words, προσεν-
εχθείς translated **offered,** and ἀνενεγκεῖν rendered **to bear.** The passive form of the verb **was offered** seems strange, for Christ offered himself. It suggests not so much the pressure of Christ's enemies forcing him to his death as the fulfilment of divine destiny in his freely willed self-oblation. The phrase translated **to bear the sins of many** is a passing allusion to Is. liii. 12 (cf. 1 Peter ii. 24), but it could also be translated 'to offer the sins of many'. **Many** is used here, as elsewhere in the New Testament, to indicate people in general (cf. Mark x. 45; xiv. 24). The idea of vicarious sin-bearing is prominent in this passage, but there is no hint of vicarious punishment.

The future appearance of Christ, mentioned in this passage, is not merely the advent of one 'who is separated from sinners' (vii. 26). The second advent of Christ will have no reference to sin at all, since he dealt with that at his first advent. The return

of Christ will be **to bring salvation,** the fulfilment of the
eschatological promise, **to those who await him** in patience
and in hope. Nothing is said here about the fate of unbelievers,
for they are not, at this point, in the author's mind. It is possible
to see here a parallel between the second advent of Christ and
the return of the high priest to the people when he has completed
his ritual duties in the sanctuary on the Day of Atonement
(Lev. xvi. 24). **So too the Christ** will return to his people (the
use of Christ here is more than a mere name) **a second time**
to bring them salvation, the fruit of his self-sacrifice in the
heavenly cultus.

29. SHADOW OF GOOD THINGS. x. 1-4

**(1) The Law contains but a shadow of the good things to
come instead of the true form of these realities. It can
never, by the same sacrifices which they offer year after
year, bring the worshippers to perfection for all time. (2)
Otherwise would they not have ceased to be offered,
since the worshippers, being purified once and for all,
would no longer have had consciousness of sins? (3) But
in fact in these sacrifices there is a reminder of sins year
after year; (4) for it is an impossibility for the blood of
bulls and goats to remove sins.**

The exposition of the work of Christ has now been nearly
completed. In the first half of this chapter the previous arguments are summed up, with special emphasis on the one,
perfect and sufficient self-oblation of Christ compared with the
multiplicity of levitical sacrifices. If the keynote of the last
chapter was the efficacy of blood offered in sacrifice, the main
theme of this chapter is the once-for-all character of Christ's
saving death. Only one fresh point in the argument emerges in
this section: that God was pleased not with the involuntary
sacrifices of animals but with the personal freely given act of
obedience to God's will which constituted the essence of Christ's
self-oblation.

The starting-point of recapitulation is the Law, since it was the Law that established the levitical sacrificial system (cf. vii.
1 11). **The Law contains but a shadow of the good things to come instead of the true form of these realities.** Earthly institutions have previously (in viii. 5) been distinguished from their heavenly archetypes by the use of the word **shadow** (which Philo also uses in this sense in e.g. *de Migr. Abr.* 12; cf. Col. ii. 17, where 'shadow' is contrasted with 'body'). **The good things to come** are not to be identified with the Christian dispensation which has superseded the abrogated Law. There is no comparison here between the 'types' of the old covenant and the 'sacraments' of the new covenant. The good things will come at the consummation of the age, i.e. they are the 'promises' (cf. ix. 11). **The true form of these realities** is contrasted with the shadow as a complete and accurate representation might be contrasted with a dark outline figure. The author means that the Law cannot give an accurate embodiment of these heavenly realities. It can only provide an insubstantial and distorted expression of the future promises. The reading of p^{46}, according to which the Law contains 'a shadow and likeness' of the good things to come, is an attempt to evade the exegetical difficulty of the passage.

The impotence of the Law finds expression in the multiplicity of its sacrifices. Probably the author is still at this stage thinking of the Day of Atonement, following up his train of thought from the last chapter. The Law **can never, by the same sacrifices which they offer year after year, bring the worshippers to perfection for all time.** 'The identical repetition was a sign of the powerlessness of the whole system' (Westcott). It is tempting to take **for all time** with the subordinate clause ('which they are for ever offering'), but the order of Greek words and the use of the same phrase later in the chapter (*vv.* 12, 14) forbid this.

In fact the levitical sacrifices can only cleanse ritual sins (ix. 13), and they can never, even for a moment, effect a perfectly clear conscience (ix. 9): still less can they **bring worshippers to**
2 **perfection for all time. Otherwise would they not have ceased to be offered?** It is noteworthy that, in this passage, sacrifices are regarded as being offered under the pressure of

human needs rather than in obedience to the will of God. It is assumed that if these needs had been allayed, sacrifices would have ended. But this point must not be pressed. The question is rhetorical and implies a *reductio ad absurdum*. In such circumstances God would have ordered sacrifices to cease, **since the worshippers, being purified once and for all, would no longer have had consciousness of sins.** Chrysostom suggested here the analogy of a sickness which is cured by a single dose of perfect medicine. Even then, God would still have had his **worshippers,** for nothing can end the worship of God. Yet men would have had no further need of sacrifice; for when men have perfectly clear consciences, further purification is not required.

All this, however, bears no relation to the actual situation. **In 3 fact in these sacrifices there is a reminder of sins year after year.** This is not a particular reference to the 'law of jealousy', whereby a jealous husband can bring to remembrance the iniquity he suspects in his wife (Nu. v. 15), nor is it a reminder reserved solely for the wicked (cf. Philo, *de Vita Moys.* 2. 107). It is a generalisation which applies to all who offer sacrifices under the old covenant. These sacrifices actually recall the sins which they are intended to cleanse but which they are powerless to remove. This may be better than cauterising the conscience (1 Tim. iv. 2), but it leads to a pitiable frustration. For this reminder of sins is not merely a mental recollection. The cultic rites actually bring past sins into the present (cf. Lev. xvi. 21; contrast, Philo *de Spec. Leg.* 1. 215), not unlike the way in which Jesus' saving death at the Christian Eucharist is brought to remembrance (Luke xxii. 19).

It was inevitable that these sacrifices should have had such a result. **For it is an impossibility for the blood of bulls and 4 goats to remove sins.** This sentence is, in the original Greek, remarkable for its terse finality. It is more uncompromising in tone than Essene sentiments (1QS 3. 4-6). It expresses a typical prophetic sentiment (cf. Mic. vi. 7), diametrically opposed to later Jewish thought (cf. Jub. v. 17 f.). The reference to **bulls and goats** is possibly a general phrase, but it probably indicates that the author is still thinking in terms of the sacrifices of the Day of Atonement.

(5) Consequently, when he comes into the world, he says, 'Sacrifice and offering thou didst not desire, but a body thou hast prepared for me; (6) whole burnt offerings and sin-offerings thou didst take no pleasure in. (7) Then I said, "See, I have come" as in the roll of the book it is written about me, "to do thy will, O God".' (8) First he says, 'Sacrifices and offerings and whole burnt offerings and sin-offerings thou didst not desire nor take pleasure in'—and these are offered according to Law. (9) Then he said, 'See I have come to do thy will.' (10) He abolishes the former in order to establish the latter, and by that will we have been consecrated through the offering of the body of Jesus Christ once for all.

Since levitical sacrifices were doomed to failure, some other means had to be found, and a more personal way of reconciliation was required, if persons, alienated by sin, were to be brought back to God. This need found fulfilment in the personal self-offering of Christ; and our author finds confirmation of this in the words of Psalm xl. 6-8 which are put into the mouth of

5 Christ. **Consequently, when he comes into the world, he says.** . . . It is very improbable that our author here intended a reference to the Messiah as 'he who comes' (cf. Mark xi. 9). The phrase was intended, rather, to give a context for the quotation. It has been suggested that the words of the Psalm which are quoted were intended to apply generally to Jesus' response of loving obedience to God throughout his life, or to certain particular crises of his ministry. This is not, however, the meaning of the text, which gives the words of the Son **when he comes into the world,** i.e. at his human conception or at his human birth. They are spoken by the pre-incarnate Son to the Father. They give the reason for the Incarnation. They underline the Son's obedience in carrying out the human role which the Father had destined for him (cf. John vi. 38).

Psalm xl may have originally been concerned with the situation of the Jewish people at the time of the Return from Babylon, but more probably with David in his troubles. The sentiments of the verses about to be cited are reminiscent of Samuel's words of Saul (1 Sam. xv. 22) and can be paralleled in the prophetic literature (Is. i. 11; Amos v. 2 ff.; Hos. vi. 6). This quotation seems to be another instance of our author's original use of the Old Testament, for this Psalm is not cited elsewhere in the New Testament.

In the verses quoted, three points are made: (i) God's dis-approval of sacrifices, (ii) his preparation of a body for the speaker in the Psalm, and (iii) the promise of obedience to God's will on the part of the speaker. Our author identifies the speaker with the Son. **Sacrifice and offering thou didst not desire, but a body thou hast prepared for me; whole burnt 6 offerings and sin-offerings thou didst take no pleasure in.** Two main classes of sacrifices are mentioned here; the euchar-istic offering of animals (**sacrifices**) and of meal (**offering**), and the expiatory sacrifices of **whole burnt offerings and sin-offerings.** The LXX phrase which is rendered here **a body thou hast prepared for me** translates the Hebrew 'thou hast dug mine ears'. The meaning of this is obscure, but it probably refers to God's gift of hearing to enable men to obey him. Commentators have suggested that there was here a primitive corruption of the LXX text, and they have pointed out simi-larities in the appearance of the Greek words for 'ears' and 'body'. Another suggestion has been that the LXX text has been intentionally altered in the interests of Jewish Messianism. This hypothesis is strengthened by a small point of detail in the second half of the quotation: **Then I said, 'See, I have come', 7 as in the roll of the book it is written about me, 'to do thy will, O God'.** The Hebrew text reads 'it was written for me', and the subtle LXX alteration **about me** suggests the divine predestination of the Messiah. The Greek words ἐν κεφαλίδι βιβλίου, translated here **in the roll of the book,** might con-ceivably mean 'in the beginning of the book'; and a reference has been seen here to Gen. i. 1, Psalm i. 1, Lev. i. 3, etc. In the LXX the phrase in question can be used to describe a manu-script rolled up on a shaft (Ez. ii. 9), and this is determinative for the meaning here. If any particular passage of scripture is thought to be in the author's mind when he wrote about this avowal of interior obedience to God, Deut. vi. 5 or Jer. xv. 16 is likely to be as good a guess as any.

This passage is cited by our author to show that it was God's will, attested by the words of scripture, that instead of the present sacrifices the coming Messiah should offer to God the 8 body which was to be given him. **First he says, 'Sacrifices and offerings and whole burnt offerings and sin-offerings thou didst not desire nor take pleasure in'—and these are offered according to Law.** Our author is not thinking here of particular ordinances: he is referring rather to divine 9 disapproval of the Law itself. **Then he said, 'See, I have come to do thy will'.** It is the personal offering that is accept- 10 able to God. **He abolishes the former in order to establish the latter.** Animal sacrifices have been superseded by the personal self-sacrifice of Jesus. God himself took this initiative to help man. Because of God's will for our salvation (cf. 1 Tim. ii. 4) and Christ's obedience to that will (cf. John v. 30), men have been cleansed. **By that will we have been consecrated through the offering of the body of Jesus Christ once for all.** God's will was the efficient cause and Christ's self-oblation the instrumental cause of our consecration. This consecration was perfected in the past through the sacrifice of Christ. The perfect tense is used here, and whenever that tense is used in this Epistle, it is significant. Here it refers to the completed work of Christ. This self-oblation of Christ is more than the offering of his flesh and blood. The word σῶμα, translated here **body,** signifies the whole incarnate personality of the Son. Animals were sacrificed involuntarily, but Jesus, by his act of freely willed obedience, offered himself entire to God in a final and unrepeatable sacrifice.

31. CHRIST'S UNIQUE OBLATION. x. 11-14

(11) Further, every priest stands ministering day after day and offering time after time the same sacrifices which can never take away sins; (12) but Christ, having

**offered for all time one sacrifice for sins, took his seat at
the right hand of God, (13) where he waits henceforth
until his enemies are made a footstool for his feet. (14)
For by a single offering he has made perfect for all time
those whom he consecrates.**

A fresh argument is now elaborated in order to show the
completeness of Christ's finished work. Psalm cx. 1 has already
been cited (i. 13; cf. i. 3, viii. 1), but no special emphasis was
then laid on Christ's posture as seated. This point is here
elaborated. **Every priest stands ministering day after day** 11
**and offering time after time the same sacrifices which
can never take away sins.** The whole range of Jewish priesthood is now included in the argument. The proper posture of a
priest during his ministrations was 'to stand before the Lord
to minister unto him' (Nu. xvi. 9). Even angels stood in worship
before the divine throne (Is. vi. 2; Rev. vii. 11). David, however,
sat before the Lord (2 Sam. vii. 18) and **Christ,** the Messiah of 12
the house of Judah (vii. 14), **having offered for all time one
sacrifice for sins, took his seat at the right hand of God.**
This heavenly session implies (i) God's approval for the earthly
work of Jesus and (ii) Jesus' divine status at God's right hand
and (iii) Jesus' rest from work which has now been completed.
The priests on earth busy themselves with endless comings
and goings; but the heavenly high priest has taken his seat in
heaven after having finally completed his work of ministry.
He is still high priest, because this is his role for ever (cf. vii.
16 f.); but his work of offering was completed by his death,
and his eternal function in heaven is that of pleading (vii. 25;
ix. 24).

In view of Christ's divine status, this work of advocacy is
quite compatible with his heavenly session. Christ sits in
heaven **where he waits henceforth until his enemies are** 13
made a footstool for his feet. The **enemies** are not specified.
According to ii. 14 the devil has been destroyed. The suggestion
that the enemies of Christ should be identified with the ministering angels of i. 14 seems little short of fantastic. The fact is that,
although there is much in the rest of the New Testament about
the evil powers opposed to Christ, they are not specifically

mentioned in this Epistle, although their existence is not denied. The citation of this part of Psalm cx. 1 here and elsewhere in this Epistle (i. 13) suggests that our author took over without comment a common belief of the early church in Christ's final victory and a common use of this *testimonium* (cf. Acts ii. 35; 1 Cor. xv. 25). The opposition of heavenly powers to the heavenly high priest has no place in this argument.

14   The main conclusion of our author's doctrinal exposition is now stated in a positive form. **By a single offering he has made perfect for all time those whom he consecrates.** Each particular phrase in this sentence has been the subject of full exposition earlier in the Epistle.

32. THE FINAL SACRIFICE. x. 15-18

(15) The Holy Spirit also bears witness for us, for after having said: (16) 'This is the covenant which I will make with them after those days, says the Lord: I will put my laws in their hearts and write them upon their minds', (17) he then continues: 'And I will remember their sins and their evil deeds no more'. (18) Where there is remission of these, there is no longer any offering for sin.

The fact of divine forgiveness, obtained by Christ's offering, is proved once again by a further reference to Jeremiah's prophecy of the new covenant, already cited at length in the previous chapter. Here it is quoted from memory, so that it does not conform quite so exactly to the LXX text as the previous citation (viii. 10 ff.); but the meaning is the same.

   The text is adduced as having the authority of the Holy Spirit (cf. iii. 7), and it was written for our benefit (cf. 1 Cor. x.

15 11). **The Holy Spirit bears witness for us.** The use of witness in this connection was not uncommon (cf. Philo, *Leg. All.* 3. 4).

16   The passage from Jer. xxxi. 33 is then quoted. **'This is the covenant which I will make with them after those days, says the Lord: I will put my laws in their hearts and write**

them upon their minds'. This quotation is introduced with the phrase **after having said,** which strictly speaking requires a main verb; unless it be assumed that our author has (uncharacter-istically) broken off with an anacoluthon. In fact the last part of the quotation from Jeremiah does supply the missing main verb. In English (not in the Greek) it is necessary to add the words **he then continues** before the last section of Jeremiah's 17 prophecy, which runs: **'And I will remember their sins and their evil deeds no more'.** This gives excellent sense, for the next sentence is about forgiveness, and the main point of this sentence is also forgiveness.

After the promise of a new inward relationship with God, there is a further promise of a total obliteration from God's memory of all past transgressions, something that the sacrifices of the Law could never achieve (cf. *v.* 3). This leads naturally to the same generalising conclusion as that in verse 12, expressed here negatively. **Where there is remission of these** sins, 18 **there is no longer any offering for sin.** The completed self-oblation of Christ has rendered any other sin-offering superfluous.

33. FAITH, HOPE AND LOVE. x. 19-25

(19) Since therefore, brothers, we have confidence to enter the sanctuary by the blood of Jesus, (20) through a new and living way which he inaugurated for us through the curtain, that is, through the sacrifice of his flesh, (21) and since we have a great priest over the house of God, (22) let us make our approach with a sincere heart in full assurance of faith, with our hearts sprinkled clean from a bad conscience and our bodies washed with pure water. (23) Let us hold fast, without swerving, to the confession of our hope, for he who promised is trustworthy; (24) and let us take thought for one another so as to stimulate love and good deeds, (25) not deserting our meetings when we assemble together,

as some habitually do, but encouraging one another, especially as you see the Day drawing near.

Our writer has finished his dogmatic exposition. He now turns to a prolonged exhortation to his readers to persevere in their faith (x. 19-xii. 13). This summons to perseverance is the main moral theme of the Epistle, and it has appeared earlier in hortatory sections (iii. 12 ff.; iv. 11 ff.; vi. 11 ff.).

As Paul in his Epistles draws moral imperatives from doctrinal assertions about the finished work of Christ, so our author bases his demand for perseverance on his doctrine of the work and person of Jesus. His readers are to persevere because of what Christ did and does for them. Two grounds for this perseverance are adduced, of which the first is confidence

19 in direct and unimpeded access to God in heaven. **Therefore, brothers, we have confidence to enter the sanctuary by**

20 **the blood of Jesus, through a new and living way which he inaugurated for us through the curtain, that is, through the sacrifice of his flesh** (literally, 'that is, his flesh'). Our author associates himself with his readers whom he calls brothers, as in iii. 1; xiii. 22, and with whom he shares this privilege. He has already urged them to show boldness and confidence (iii. 6; iv. 16; cf. x. 35), and expounded how **the blood of Jesus** gives access to the heavenly sanctuary (ix. 7-12).

This entry (literally, 'way in') is now described as **a new and living way,** an idea which closely approaches the conception of Jesus as 'the way, the truth and the life' (John xiv. 6). The way to heaven is **new** because Jesus only opened it up at the consummation of the age (ix. 26) and it is **living** because it is the way opened up through death of him who lives for ever (ix. 14). The word ἐνεκαίνισεν, translated **inaugurated,** is a sacrificial term. The new and living way was inaugurated in the same kind of manner as a sanctuary is consecrated by a sacrifice. Jesus opened this way by passing through the curtain which marks off the heavenly sanctuary (vi. 19 f.). Through this curtain Jesus passed at death (cf. Mark xv. 38), and in the power of his sacrificial blood he entered the heavenly sanctuary (ix. 12). This way which he inaugurated was a way through death: it was a new and living way which consisted in the sacrifice of his flesh-and-blood humanity, a self-oblation symbolised in the offering of his blood.

In the light of this, the exegesis of this particular passage becomes less difficult. The words 'that is, his flesh' have been understood in two ways: (i) in apposition to **through the curtain,** or (ii) explanatory of the **way,** i.e. **a new and living way** of his flesh **which he inaugurated through the curtain.**

(i) The Greek words of the text might be rendered: 'through the curtain, that is, by means of (the offering of) his flesh', understanding both nouns to be governed by the same preposition, but giving **the curtain** a local sense of 'passage through' and **his flesh** an instrumental sense of 'by means of'. This is stylistically extremely awkward, and quite uncharacteristic of our author (cf. comments on ix. 11).

A different interpretation is possible, by still taking **his flesh** in apposition to **the curtain,** but understanding the preposition to signify 'passage through' in both cases: **through the curtain, that is, through his flesh.** On this interpretation **the curtain** is identified with **his flesh.** There are three insuperable objections to this: (*a*) elsewhere in this Epistle the function of the curtain is to hide the sanctuary from view, not to reveal what is within (ix. 3). In later gnostic speculations the Curtain became regarded as a Divine Emanation (cf. Gospel of Philip, 132. 25; cf. Work without Title from Nag-Hammadi, ed. Boehlig and Labib, 1963), but such is not the view of our author. (*b*) Elsewhere in this Epistle the Incarnate Son does not hide the glory of God, but God speaks through him (i. 3). (*c*) Elsewhere in this Epistle, Jesus is assumed to have ascended into heaven *in* his glorified humanity (iii. 1; iv. 14; vi. 20); and so it is difficult to understand how he could have passed 'through' his flesh.

(ii) **His flesh** should be understood as dependent on and explanatory of the **new and living way.** Most commentators adopt this interpretation. They understand our author to mean that the new and living way that Jesus inaugurated consisted of his human nature. But our author is here recalling his doctrine of Christ's sacrifice; and according to his exposition Christ's human nature as such, although prerequisite for his self-sacrifice, was not what he sacrificed. It was not the human life as such but that human life offered in death that constituted Jesus' sacrifice. Jesus shared our flesh and blood (ii. 14); and in offering his blood he sacrificed his flesh (cf. Mark xiv. 22-24). It is best therefore to take **his flesh** here as the correlate of the blood of Jesus (mentioned in the previous verse) and to understand by it the flesh of Jesus offered in sacrifice.

21 The second ground for perseverance concerns the present not the past work of Jesus. **We have a great priest over the house of God.** There is no need to see here a reminiscence of Zech. vi. 11 ff., where Jozedek is said to be a great priest who helps in building the house of God. Our author is merely recapitulating what he has written earlier. He has already shown that Jesus is **a great** high **priest** (iv. 14), and that he is set over the house of God (iii. 6); and here the two ideas are brought together.

22 On these two grounds the readers are encouraged first to faith, then to hope, and then to love. First, faith. **Let us make our approach with a sincere heart in full assurance of faith.** As yet neither the author nor his readers can enter heaven itself. So long as this world order remains, they will have to pass through the curtain of death, following in the steps of their forerunner. As yet they can only **make** their **approach** to God through worship. The author encourages them in words reminiscent of their baptism (cf. x. 32 f.). He asks for the right interior attitudes; for sincerity of heart and **full assurance of faith** (cf. vi. 11), both prerequisite for baptisands. Sincerity without faith is not Christianity; while full assurance of faith without sincerity of heart is merely emotional self-indulgence.

These two qualities are subjective. Our author next reminds his readers of the objective work of God, actualised in them through baptism. In the old covenant priests at consecration were outwardly sprinkled with blood (Ex. xxix. 21), and when the first covenant was made the people were also sprinkled with blood (Ex. xxiv. 8): but Christians at their baptism have had their **hearts sprinkled clean** with the blood of Christ, and so have been inwardly cleansed **from a bad conscience.** The reference here is not eucharistic but baptismal. It is perhaps strange that the author should also remind his readers that their **bodies** had been **washed with pure water.** Ablutions under

the old covenant took place at the consecration of priests (Ex.
xxix. 4), as well as for the high priest on the Day of Atonement
(Lev. xvi. 4); but Christian baptism, alluded to here, is a very
different kind of ablution. It is indeed described in the New
Testament in terms of washing (1 Cor. vi. 11; Eph. v. 26; Titus
iii. 5), but as a spiritual washing to be contrasted with the outward washing of the body (1 Peter iii. 21). Yet our author seems
to mean here an outward rite.

If, however, this Epistle was written by Apollos, who had,
until only a short time beforehand, known only the baptism of
John (cf. comment on vi. 2), then an explanation of his language
may be given as follows. According to Josephus, John baptised
'as a means of purifying the body, supposing the soul to have
been thoroughly cleansed beforehand by righteousness' (*Antiq.*
18. 5. 2). Possibly Apollos slipped back here to old ideas of
Johannite baptism. The perfect participle λελουσμένοι, translated **washed,** refers to an action completed in the past, and
so the repeated ablutions of the Essenes are irrelevant here,
despite apparent similarities of language (cf. 1QS 3. 4 f., 9;
4. 21).

The second exhortation concerns hope, and baptismal allusions are continued. Baptism was the occasion of solemn pro-
fession of faith in Christ (cf. iii. 1; iv. 14) concerning his past
work, his present lordship and his future promise. Our author
stressed the future aspect (cf. iii. 6; vi. 11, 18). **Let us hold fast,** 23
without swerving, to the confession of our hope. It is
characteristic of him that he should use **unswerving,** a word
which could well describe his own unbending logic and pastoral
rigorism. Such constancy of purpose is based not merely on
subjective feelings of assurance but on the faithfulness of God:
for he who promised is trustworthy (cf. 1 Cor. x. 13).

The third exhortation is to show love. The trio, faith, hope
and love, is found elsewhere in the New Testament (1 Cor.
xiii. 13; 1 Thess. i. 3), and these three theological virtues may
have been commonly connected in the circles in which Paul and
our author moved. **Let us take thought for one another so as** 24
to stimulate love and good deeds. It is not universal charity
but mutual love within the Christian community that is meant
here (cf. xiii. 1). Good deeds are the natural expression of this

love. Such deeds are not merely good in themselves but attractive to others. Love evokes love; and genuine benevolence begets in turn further good deeds. The word παροξυσμὸν, translated **stimulate,** usually denotes an activity which provokes unpleasant reactions, but not so here.

Our author has heard that certain people have been absenting themselves from church meetings. According to Acts, gatherings of the Christian congregation took place daily (Acts ii. 46) or weekly (Acts xx. 7). It may be presumed that at these meetings bread was broken and probably wine was consecrated (cf. 1 Cor. xi. 17 ff.). The purpose of regular attendance was not only to offer worship to the glory of God, but also for the mutual encouragement of the church members. Worship that is sparsely attended, or offered by a laggard congregation, can chill the heart of a devout believer. By contrast a 'full house' confirms and strengthens the individuals who attend.

The duty of attendance at public worship was emphasised by Jewish writers (cf. Philo, *de Migr. Abr.* 91). It is not stated here whether some of the recipients of this letter had withdrawn from public worship for fear of Jews or pagans, or because of syncretistic, schismatic or shallow Christian convictions. It has been suggested that a small group regarded themselves as too superior to worship with the rest, and even that they formed a small congregation of their own. Since, however, the whole tenor of this Epistle is against lapsing into Judaism, it seems probable that these absentees were Jewish Christians who were in danger of so lapsing.

Mutual encouragement, recommended here by our author, had been the subject of an earlier exhortation (iii. 13; cf. 1 Thess. v. 11), although not in connection with public worship. On both occasions the urgency of the need is occasioned by the pressure of the times. Here the eschatological motif is openly expressed, 25 **especially as you see the Day drawing near.** Such eschatological expectations should not alter present activities, but give them special urgency and importance. The **Day** is used elsewhere in the New Testament for 'the Day of the Lord' (cf. 1 Cor. iii. 13; 1 Thess. v. 4). The word **drawing near** had become common Christian usage in this connection (cf. Ro. xiii. 12 and the Synoptic Gospels, *passim*).

(26) For if we go on sinning deliberately after we have received knowledge of the truth, no further sin-offering remains, (27) but only a terrifying expectation of the Judgement, and a fury of fire which will surely consume God's adversaries. (28) Anyone who has set aside the law of Moses is put to death on the evidence of two or three witnesses. (29) Think how much more severe a punishment a man will deserve who has trampled on the Son of God, profaned the blood of the covenant by which he was consecrated, and insulted the gracious Spirit of God. (30) For we know who it was who said: 'Vengeance belongs to me: I will repay'; and again, 'The Lord will judge his people'. (31) It is terrible to fall into the hands of the living God.

The significance of withdrawal from public meetings of worship is now explained. **For if we go on sinning deliber-** 26 **ately after we have received knowledge of the truth, no further sin-offering remains.** It is unlikely that our author has explicitly in mind at this stage of his argument the impossibility of rebaptism or the consequences of open apostasy (cf. vi. 4 ff.); for the conjunction at the beginning of this sentence connects it with the last, which was concerned specifically with the problem of persistent absenteeism from Christian meetings. This may have been almost tantamount to apostasy, but it is not to be equated with it. Such conduct could not be called 'unwitting sin' (Lev. iv. 1; v. 15), but sin committed 'with a high hand' (Deut. xvii. 12) for which no forgiveness was possible. According to our author, if such people had never become Christians, their sins could have been blotted out; but there is **no further sin-offering** for them **after** they **have received knowledge of the truth.** This last phrase is found also in 1 Tim. ii. 4. Its use here suggests the personal acceptance of an objective revelation. Christianity is often called 'the truth' in the New Testament.

People in such a plight have **only a terrifying expectation** 27

of the Judgement. No doubt it was some such expectation that made many of the Corinthians weak and caused some to die as a result of falling under judgement at the Christian Eucharist (1 Cor. xi. 29 f.); but, whereas our writer keeps undeviatingly to a stern rigorism, Paul held that disgraceful behaviour at the Eucharist would not merit final condemnation (1 Cor. xi. 32).

Our author reinforces his point by a free adaptation of Is. xxvi. 11 and Zeph. i. 18, threatening that the fate of such people is **a fury of fire which will surely consume God's adversaries.** The idea that the Day of Judgement entails fire has already been mentioned (vi. 8), and this is found elsewhere in early Christian literature (2 Thess. i. 8), taken over from Jewish apocalyptic. The Greek phrase $\pi\upsilon\rho\grave{o}s$ $\zeta\tilde{\eta}\lambda os$, translated **fury of fire,** has a semitic flavour, but it is a secondary semitism of the type often found in the LXX. It suggests the passionate jealousy of wounded love.

The argument *a fortiori* from the old covenant to the new, so often used in this Epistle, is employed here to show the 28 propriety of such savage divine retribution. **Anyone who has set aside the law of Moses is put to death on the evidence of two or three witnesses.** The offence alluded to here is not merely the breach of the law, but a denial of its authority and validity. The old covenant prescribed capital punishment for several offences, to be inflicted without mercy; and for these evidence was required from more than one witness (Nu. xxxv. 30; Deut. xvii. 6; cf. Matt. xviii. 16, CD 10. 14). Our author would seem to be referring here to the sin of apostasy involving the abrogation of the entire Law (Deut. xiii. 6 ff.; xvii. 2-7). That argument here, *mutatis mutandis*, can be paralleled in 29 the writings of Philo (*de Fuga et Inv.* 84). **Think how much more severe a punishment a man will deserve who has trampled on the Son of God, profaned the blood of the covenant by which he was consecrated, and insulted the gracious Spirit of God.** The punishment is worse in proportion as Jesus is greater than Moses (cf. iii. 1 ff.), and the new covenant better than the old.

Abrogation of the new covenant, not the Christian Eucharist, is in the author's mind by now. Yet it was precisely the prolonged absence of some of his readers from Christian meetings (which included the Eucharist) which has led him to describe the punishment appropriate for a sin which is unforgivable. His language, therefore, while it refers to the new covenant, is tinged with eucharistic overtones. For one who has deliberately absented himself from the Eucharist has trampled on the Son of God, in a similar way as anyone who eats or drinks unworthily at the Christian Eucharist is guilty of desecrating the body and blood of the Lord (1 Cor. xi. 27). Whereas the apostate has **profaned the blood of the covenant by which he was consecrated,** the desecrator of the Christian Eucharist regards as common the consecrated wine of which Jesus said: This cup is the new covenant in my blood (1 Cor. xi. 25). **The gracious Spirit of God** whom he has **insulted** translates the Greek τὸ πνεῦμα τῆς χάριτος. The phrase signifies the Holy Spirit through whom God communicates his grace and favour. The concept is a personal one. It is not possible to insult a thing, only a person; and this particular outrage is unforgivable (cf. Mark iii. 29). A contrast is meant here between the gracious action of God and the contemptuous insult of the apostate.

Our author, according to his custom, proves his point from scripture. **For we know who it was who said: 'Vengeance belongs to me: I will repay'.** The citation is from Deut. xxxii. 35. Exactly the same quotation and text is employed by Paul in Ro. xii. 19; but Paul uses it to prove that Christians must not take vengeance into their own hands, while our author proves by it that divine retribution is inevitable. This is the only occasion when our author cites a text closer to the Hebrew than to the LXX version of the scriptures. In fact, this is not an exact translation of either the Massoretic or the Samaritan text ('To me belong vengeance and recompense') or of the Targumic version ('Vengeance is before me, and I will repay'). Our author, unless he borrowed from the Epistle to the Romans (for which there is no other evidence), or unless he had in front of him a Hebrew or Aramaic text (of which, again, there is no other evidence), was probably using a Greek text of the bible now unknown to us. It is not necessary to assume that our author always used the same text of the LXX as we have now. Philo usually, but not always, kept

to our LXX text. The divergences which appear in certain
treatises have been explained as due to the use of an indepen-
dent version of the Old Testament, or a late revision of the
LXX influenced by the version of Aquila. For the latter view
cf. P. Katz, *Philo's Bible* (1950).

The next verse of Deuteronomy (Deut. xxxii. 36) is also cited
as this point, and the two consecutive verses of Deuteronomy
are joined together by the phrase **and again** (cf. ii. 13). In the
original context the author of Deuteronomy is expressing his
conviction that God will champion his people: **The Lord will
judge his people** and repent himself for his servants. Here,
however, this quotation is used out of its context to prove that
God will show not mercy but justice to his people if they
abrogate his covenant. *Corruptio optimi pessima.* The fact that
they have been chosen to be God's people increases, not lessens,
the punishment which they will receive.

Our author is not averse to the use of fear in order to inculcate
obedience and evoke perseverance. He prefers warning to
encouragement, and he emphasises the stimulus of fear rather
than the attraction of love. According to 2 Sam. xxiv. 14 David,
after carrying out the census, spoke these words: 'Let us now
fall into the hands of God, for his mercies are great: and let me
not fall into the hands of man' (cf. Ecclus. ii. 18). This was an
expression of confidence on the part of a believer. Our author
makes use of the phrase to deal with the situation not of a
31 believer but an apostate. For him **it is terrible to fall into
the hands of the living God.** It is fearful in prospect (cf.
verse 27) and terrifying in fact (cf. xii. 29). The phrase **living
God** suggests the power of God to exact retribution. Our author
never questions the propriety of ascribing to God a jealous wrath
and a vengeful desire for retributive justice. Jesus is described as
merciful and compassionate. But God is conceived primarily as
holy and just.

35. A REMINDER OF THEIR PAST. x. 32-35

**(32) Remember the earlier days, when, after you were
enlightened, you remained steadfast in a hard and pain-**

ful struggle. (33) Not only were you made a public spectacle with taunts and afflictions, but also you associated yourselves with those who were being treated in this way; (34) for you suffered with those who were in prison, and also accepted joyfully the seizure of your possessions, realising that you possessed something better and more lasting. (35) So do not throw away your confidence: it brings great reward.

After a passage of extreme rigorism our author turns to encouragement and hope, as in an earlier passage (vi. 9 ff.). Chrysostom adduces here the analogy of a surgeon who comforts the patient after making a painful incision. Earlier in the chapter there were baptismal allusions (*v.* 22 f.). Here, however, reference is not to baptism but to the days of fervent faith and exemplary conduct which followed hard on the baptism of our author's readers. They attained, then, as others have done at such a time, a very high level of enthusiasm. Our author hopes to encourage them now by reminding them of this. **Remember** 32 **the earlier days, when, after you were enlightened, you remained steadfast in a hard and painful struggle.** (Baptism has already been alluded to as an enlightenment (vi. 4).) The hardness of their struggle was due to the intensity and frequency of the assaults which they withstood. The troubles were caused partly by the treatment which the readers received from their enemies and partly by their own behaviour, which provoked further ill-treatment. Like contestants in a stadium, they were **made a public spectacle** (cf. 1 Cor. iv. 9). There is 33 no reference here to such persecutions as Nero's burning of Christians in the public gardens at Rome (Tacitus, *Annals*, 15. 44) or to a personal appearance in an arena (cf. 1 Cor. xv. 32). It is purely a metaphor of a public contest in the stadium which is introduced here. It is continued in the next verse and employed again at xii. 1.

The suffering was partly the result of their enemies' insulting and contemptuous attitude (**taunts**) and partly due to actual bodily assaults (**afflictions**). In this state of affairs the readers of this Epistle had not merely played a passive role: they had actively **associated** themselves **with those who were being**

treated in this way. They had made clear, by their witness and practical help, their kinship with those who bore the brunt of these misfortunes.

Our author enlarges on their exemplary behaviour under
34 persecution. **For you suffered with those who were in prison, and also accepted joyfully the seizure of your possessions, realising that you possessed something better and more lasting.** The situation described here is obscure (for a reconstruction, see Introduction, pp. 19f.). It seems that some of the members of the congregation, probably when the church was originally founded, had been cast into prison. Possibly their possessions had been confiscated along with those of the recipients of this letter; but, more probably, there had been looting by the mob in the homes of those imprisoned and of other Christians as well (for a description of the Alexandrine (anti-semitic) riot, cf. Philo, *in Flacc.* 7 ff.). In this way those still at liberty **suffered with** those in prison. Such disaster was not met passively, with stoic indifference: it was accepted **joyfully** (cf. Matt. v. 11). Through the loss of personal possessions the recipients of this letter had come to realise that they **possessed something better and more lasting.** Their treasure was in heaven (Matt. vi. 20), a city that lasts (xiii. 14), the heavenly Jerusalem (xii. 22).

The reading adopted here is ἑαυτοὺς, 'realising that *you* possessed something better and more lasting'. This is found in $p^{13, 46}$ ℵ A H *1912 pc* lat bo Cl Or. It gives excellent sense, but the reflexive pronoun is unusual. So attempts have been made to emend the text, thereby weakening the sense. The dative ἑαυτοῖς is found in D K L *pm*, preceded by ἐν in I *al*; while the reflexive pronoun is omitted altogether by P co. Many texts add ἐν οὐρανοῖς, a gloss from Matt. xix. 21 (cf. Luke xii. 33).

The reminder of the past was intended to evoke perseverance
35 in the future. **So do not throw away your confidence: it brings great reward.** The word ἀποβάλητε, translated **throw away,** can be used in connection with an inheritance. Chrysostom, commenting on this passage, adduced the analogy of one who has won a contest at the games, but who is so provoked by the interval of time before he is actually given the prize that he is tempted to leave the arena. Our author's readers have been

given the promise of eternal life: they need to show perseverance for a short time longer before the promise is actually realised. And so they must **not throw away** their **confidence: it brings great reward** (contrast ii. 2). This confidence cannot in itself merit a reward (cf. comment on vi. 10), but its maintenance by our author's readers will make possible the realisation of what has already been promised (cf. xi. 26).

36. PRESENT NEED FOR FAITH. x. 36-39

(36) Steadfastness is what you need, that you may do God's will and obtain his promise. (37) For 'in a very little time now the Coming One will have come, he will not be long. (38) My righteous one shall live through faith; if he draws back, I take no pleasure in him'. (39) But we are not among those who draw back and are lost; we are among those who have faith and obtain life.

Our author hopes that a reminder of his readers' past may steady them now. **Steadfastness is what you need, that you** 36 **may do God's will and obtain his promise.** In the New Testament **God's will** is a phrase which can be used to express a divine summons which runs counter to natural human inclination (cf. Matt. xxvi. 42). **Steadfastness** is recommended as a virtue elsewhere in the New Testament (cf. Ro. v. 3; 1 Tim. vi. 11; James i. 3, etc.).

The point is driven home by means of scriptural proof. The reference to **steadfastness** brings to our author's mind some verses from Habakkuk, to which a phrase from Is. xxvi. 20 has been added so that together they seem like one quotation from a single source. Previously in this Epistle (ii. 13) two adjacent citations have been joined by the phrase 'and again'. Either these two passages had been joined together in Christian tradition before this Epistle was written, or possibly by sheer inadvertence our author has forgotten to insert 'and again'. The explanation may well be, however, that he was quoting inaccurately from memory.

The first quotation, taken from Is. xxvi. 20 (LXX), consists of a very short phrase which is, however, so distinctive that it could not have been taken from anywhere else. The prophet Isaiah had warned his people to go indoors and hide themselves for a very little while until the wrath of the Lord had passed by.

37 Of this our author cites only the words **in a very little time now,** which he uses as a preface to a quotation from Habakkuk ii. 3 f. The Lord had granted to Habakkuk a vision which he was ordered to write down so that others might read it (cf. Mark xiii. 14). The Hebrew text may be rendered as follows: 'For still the vision awaits its time: it hastens to its end—it will not lie. If it seem slow, wait for it; it will surely come, it will not delay. Behold, he whose soul is not upright in him shall fail, but the righteous shall live by his faith.'

The text used by our author is much closer to the LXX's free rendering of the Hebrew. It reads as follows: **The Coming One**
38 **will have come, he will not be long. My righteous one shall live through faith; if he draws back, I take no pleasure in him.** Our author's text agrees with the LXX in as much as the prophecy is made to refer not to the fulfilment of Habakkuk's vision, but to the advent of God or his Messiah. Our author uses the first part of this quotation to prove the imminence of Jesus' return. The remaining part of the quotation differs from that of the LXX in three important ways: (i) the LXX has 'coming he will have come'; but in our text, by the addition of the definite article, this becomes a messianic prophecy of **the Coming One.** (ii) In our text the first and second halves of Hab. ii. 4 have been transposed so as to emphasise the difference it makes whether a man is faithful or shrinks back. (iii) The Hebrew text has 'the righteous shall live through his faith': the LXX has 'the righteous shall live through faith'; and our author has 'my righteous shall live through faith'. (The MSS A C of the LXX have the same reading here as our author, and it is uncertain whether he used a similar manuscript tradition or whether A C have been influenced by this citation. Some MSS of this Epistle attempt to assimilate this text to that cited by Paul in Ro. i. 17 and Gal. iii. 11, but this is a corruption of the text of this Epistle.)

The Hebrew text means that the righteous man will by his

faithfulness keep his life. According to the Qumran exegesis of this Hebrew text the righteous man will live through faithfulness to the Teacher of Righteousness. Presumably this means that he will be faithful to his teaching (cf. 1Qp Hab col. viii, lines 1-3). Paul, however, omits all personal references, and cites the verse thus: 'The righteous shall live through faith'. He used the verse to prove that the quality of life evoked by a faith-relationship with God is superior to life lived out under law.

Our author, although he is nearer to the LXX than to the Hebrew, interprets the text in a sense approximating to that of the Hebrew. He means that the righteous man will be preserved in life by his loyalty and faithfulness to God. If he wavers and shrinks back he incurs the divine disapproval. To **take no pleasure in** someone is tantamount to condemnation (cf. x. 6).

The passage ends with an expression of hope and confidence, preparatory for the next great section about the perseverance and faith of the heroes of old. **But we are not among those 39 who draw back and are lost: we are among those who have faith and obtain life.** The Greek word ψυχῆς, translated **life,** can also mean 'soul'; but here the author is expressing the hope not that his readers will keep their souls, but that they will not lose their promise of eternal life (cf. Luke xxi. 19).

37. FAITH: DEFINITION AND PRESUPPOSITION.
xi. 1-3

(1) What is faith? It is certainty concerning what is hoped for, the proving of what is not seen. (2) Because of it men of old gained their testimony. (3) By faith we perceive that the universe was fashioned by God's word, so that what is visible has come into being from what is not visible.

There is no real break between the end of the last and the beginning of this chapter. Chapter x is mostly taken up with an exhortation to steadfastness and a warning against apostasy. It concludes with a contrast between fearfulness and faith which forms an introduction for the theme of chapter xi. Before an account is given of the heroes of old who have been notable for their faith, a short definition of the word is attempted. This is intended to be neither philosophical in language nor exhaustive in scope. Rather it provides a rough summary of the main aspects of faith which are manifested in the inspiring examples to follow.

1 **What is faith? It is certainty concerning what is hoped for, the proving of what is not seen.** The order of words in the Greek suggests a formal definition, and the mention of **faith** without an article shows that a generalisation is intended. It is, however, a description not of any kind of faith whatever, but of specially religious faith.

The word ὑπόστασις, translated here as **certainty,** has already been used twice in this Epistle; in i. 3 where it refers to the being or essence of God, and in iii. 14 where it means confidence. The latter meaning is to be preferred here. The Greek fathers, however, with their philosophical leanings, understood the clause to mean: 'faith gives substance to things hoped for'. This rendering is intrinsically improbable, since **what is hoped for** exists independently of and prior to faith. Other commentators, supposing that the phrase is parallel in meaning as well as in structure to what follows it, understand the word in a sense found in the papyri: 'faith is the objective guarantee (or the title deeds) of what is hoped for'. These renderings although possible are not as probable as one which retains the more usual meaning of **certainty.**

This Epistle is as much concerned with invisible realities as with future hopes, and faith is further defined here in terms which are spatial rather than temporal. Faith is the **proving of what is not seen.** This addition gives further extension rather than greater precision to the concept of faith. It might make a special appeal to those whose background has been Greek philosophy rather than Hebrew prophetism. Faith is not in itself the proof, still less the evidence, of what is unseen. Rather it is the mode by which invisible realities become real for men. Thus faith is not inferior to knowledge: on the contrary, it is the proper mode of knowledge in relation to unseen realities.

This twofold description of faith is not unlike Paul's conception of hope (Ro. viii. 24). Faith, however, is a very rich and varied conception in the New Testament. It is itself closely connected with hope (Ro. iv. 18) as well as with love (Gal. v. 6). In Pauline thought the idea of faith is so rich that there is what Bultmann has called a 'structure of faith', although the distinctive Pauline usage describes faith-union with Christ. In the New Testament the same word can designate faithfulness (1 Peter i. 7), trust (Ro. iv. 3) and loyalty (Rev. xiii. 10). Faith can represent the mode of belief (Ro. iii. 23) or its content (Ro. x. 8). 'To believe' can range in meaning from the act of bare intellectual assent (James ii. 19) to personal commitment (John i. 12). Faith can be used generally to signify 'Christianity' (Gal. vi. 10), or it can stand for the body of Christian doctrine which forms the deposit of faith (Jude 3). Not all these meanings can be found in the examples of faith which constitute the rest of this chapter. Nevertheless the faith which is there depicted cannot be confined within the working definition with which this chapter opens.

Before the heroes of the past are cited, a summary is given of their relationship to faith. **Because of it the men of old 2 gained their testimony.** The supreme example of faith is that of Jesus himself (xii. 2); but here it is the heroes of the past who fall under review. **The men of old** are the same as 'the fathers' mentioned in i. 1, the great men of the *Heilsgeschichte*, among whom Abraham was, of course, pre-eminent. It is, however, noteworthy that in the scriptures faith itself is not mentioned in connection with any of the incidents which follow. Yet the **testimony** which these heroes **gained** through their faith is pre-eminently the testimony of scripture.

The first example of faith to be given is, in fact, prerequisite to all the rest. Just as in Genesis the account of creation precedes the record of revelation (cf. John i. 1-14), so here faith in the Creator is placed before the examples of faith shown by the biblical heroes. 'The belief in creation—the belief in a divine will manifested in the existence of the world—is the necessary foundation for the life of faith in all its manifestations' (Westcott). There can be no proper theology of revelation without the foundation of natural theology.

Belief in creation is not a matter of proof by scientific logic

3 but of spiritual preception through faith. **By faith we perceive that the universe was fashioned by God's word.** Faith illumines the mind to recognise the design of its Creator (cf. Wisd. Sol. xiii. 4; Ro. i. 20). According to this Epistle it is not acceptance of the Creator which leads to recognition of his design in creation. The process works the other way round. Faith moves the mind to recognise the supernatural ordering of nature. As yet the universe is only perceived as **fashioned** (the Greek word κατηρτίσθαι does not mean created) by the divine command. **God's word** is not to be equated here with the pre-existent Word. It refers to the single creative utterance of God omnipotent which fashioned the universe (cf. i. 3). Ugliness and suffering and the predatory character of the natural world cast no shadow over our author's argument. Consideration of God's design in nature leads him to the conclusion that **what is visible has come into being from what is not visible.** God is not merely the Divine Architect (cf. Gen. i. 2; Wisd. Sol. xi. 17; Philo, *passim*), but the Divine Creator (cf. Wisd. Sol. ix. 1; Philo, *de Aet. Mundi* 1).

The Greek words of this verse could be rendered merely to mean that 'the visible has not been created out of material things'. This would leave open the doctrine of creation *ex nihilo*, but it is a less probable meaning of the Greek words. It is best to take the clause to mean that God creates **from what is not visible.** It would be hazardous to assume that our author means by this phrase the invisible world of the heavenlies (cf. ix. 23) or the intelligible world which, in Philonic thought, is the archetype of the physical universe (cf. Philo, *de Vita Moys.* 2. 74). These invisible realities are not particularised.

38. THE FAITH OF ABEL, ENOCH AND NOAH.
xi. 4-7

(4) By faith Abel offered to God a sacrifice greater than that of Cain, through which he has received testimony as a righteous man, for God approved of him in virtue of his gifts. This is why, although he is dead, he still speaks. (5)

By faith Enoch was taken away, so that he did not see death, and he was not found because God had taken him away. For it is testified that, before he was taken away, he had been pleasing to God, (6) and without faith it is impossible to please him; for anyone who comes to God must have faith that he exists and that he rewards those who seek him. (7) By faith Noah, divinely warned about what he did not yet see, took good heed and built an ark to save his household. By this he condemned the world and became the possessor of the righteousness that comes through faith.

The 'roll-call of heroes' now begins. It is a much longer list than those found in 4 Macc. xvi. 18 ff. and xviii. 11 ff., but not so wide in scope as that of Ecclus. xliv–l. Adam and Eve do not head it, presumably because both sinned; and in any case their relationship to God in Paradise was one of sight not faith. Cain and Abel were sons of Adam and Eve; and, although Cain was the older, Abel's sacrifice was preferred. **By faith Abel offered 4 to God a sacrifice greater than that of Cain** (although it was of course vastly inferior to that of Jesus, as is pointed out in xii. 24). There has been speculation whether Abel's sacrifice was better than Cain's in quantity or quality. The biblical record gives no reason for God's acceptance of Abel's and his rejection of Cain's. Some have seen significance in Abel's earlier offerings of firstlings of the flock contrasted with Cain's later gift of cereal offerings (cf. Gen. iv. 3 f.); while others have supposed that God preferred the offering of cattle to gifts of produce. Our writer, however, states that Abel's was preferred because he offered it **by faith;** although the mode by which God indicated his preference is left open, just as it is left open too in the scriptures.

It was the spirit in which the sacrifice was made which determined its acceptance or rejection by God. Because of Abel's faith, manifested in his sacrificial offering, **he has received testimony as a righteous man, for God approved of him in virtue of his gifts** (cf. Gen. iv. 4). In fact Noah, not Abel, is the first person in the bible to be called righteous (Gen. vii. 1); but Abel is regarded both in Jewish tradition (Josephus,

Antiq. i. 2. 1) as well as in New Testament literature (Matt. xxiii. 35; 1 John iii. 12); as having obtained a reputation for righteousness, while Cain was celebrated as an awful example of wickedness (1 John iii. 12; Jude 11).

According to Gen. iv. 11 God said to Cain, 'The voice of your brother's blood is crying to me from the ground'. In Genesis this is probably a cry to God for vengeance; but in this Epistle the blood of martyred Abel neither cries to God for revenge nor intercedes with God for men: the meaning is rather that Abel's faith still speaks to men by way of illustrious example. His faith manifested in sacrificial offerings remains even now as a witness and encouragement to men; and **this is why, although he is dead, he still speaks.**

After Abel, Enoch. Enoch enjoyed great popularity in both Jewish and Christian literature, especially in apocalyptic works. Enoch was regarded as the revealer of divine secrets, the exemplar of wisdom and knowledge, and even an intercessor in the presence of God. Our author however keeps, according to his

5 custom, within the biblical tradition. **By faith Enoch was taken away, so that he did not see death, and he was not found, because God had taken him away.** It is not explicitly stated in our text of the bible that Enoch did not die, but this was generally assumed to be the meaning of Gen. v. 24, and it probably stood in the text used by Clement of Rome, Origen and Tertullian. Enoch's earthly life was much shorter than those of the other antediluvian heroes, a mere 365 years compared with his father's 962 or his son Methuselah's 969. In the Hebrew text it is said that 'he walked with God', and this signal honour of translation to God's immediate presence was given to no one else in the Old Testament except Elijah (2 Kings ii. 11) and possibly Moses, whose body was not found on earth (Deut. xxxiv. 6; cf. Jude 9).

A second point about Enoch is adduced from Gen. v. 24 (LXX). **For it is testified that, before he was taken away, he had been pleasing to God.** In fact it was because Enoch had pleased God that he was removed to God's immediate presence. According to Wisd. Sol. iv. 10 f. Enoch was taken when still (comparatively) young lest he should be contaminated by sin; according to Ecclus. xliv. 16 he was translated because he was 'an example of repentance to all generations' (cf. Philo, *de Abr.* 18 f.); but according to our author his faith was the reason behind his removal. As the biblical record contains no record of Enoch's faith, our author has to prove the point. Since it is axiomatic that **without faith it is impossible to please** 6 God, and since it has been testified that Enoch did please God before he was removed to heaven, therefore Enoch must have had faith. Indeed faith is a prerequisite not merely for satisfying God, but for approaching him at all. **Anyone who comes to God must have faith that he exists and that he rewards those who seek him.** Bare assent to his existence is insufficient. It must be joined to a lively faith in God as a person and in his moral nature, especially in God's active benevolence towards all who turn to him. Before man can enter into a true relationship with God, he must realise that God can give to man far more than man can give to him (cf. x. 35; xi. 26). Such faith cannot of course be confined within the Judaeo-Christian revelation. It could, for instance, be found in the ancient world among stoic writers (Epictetus, 2. 14. 11); but the fate of those outside the Judaeo-Christian revelation does not come within the purview of this Epistle.

The example of **Noah** follows that of Enoch as in Ecclus. 7 xliv. 17 and Philo, *de Abr.* 27. It provides an excellent instance of faith as the proving of what is not seen (cf. xi. 1). It would have been unreasonable for Noah to expect a universal flood. And so when he was **divinely warned about** its coming by God, his acceptance of the warning and his obedience in building an ark **to save his household** gave a signal example of a man's faith about **what he did not yet see.** As the sacrifice of Abel showed Abel's faith in action, so Noah's construction and fitting of the ark was a practical manifestation of Noah's faith. This differentiated Noah from the world. Noah was obedient to God, while **the world** consisted of human society organised apart from God. **By this he condemned the world** (cf. Josephus, *Antiq.* 1. 3. 2), not by judicial act or word but by showing up the wickedness of the world in contrast to himself (cf. John xvi. 8) in as much as he **became the possessor of righteousness that comes through faith.** This righteousness is not the achievement of man but the gift of God. It can only

be given to a man who has faith in God (cf. Ro. iv. 13). Such
faith is not self-reliance but reliance on the promises of the
invisible God.

39. THE FAITH OF ABRAHAM. xi. 8-12

**(8) By faith Abraham obeyed the call to go out to the place
which he was to receive as his possession and he went
out without knowing where he was going to. (9) By faith he
settled in the land of promise as a stranger in a strange
country, living in tents, with Isaac and Jacob who shared
the same promise; (10) for he was looking forward to the
City with foundations, whose maker and designer is God.
(11) By faith even Sarah herself received power to conceive, and that although past the time of life, because she
regarded him who promised as trustworthy. (12) So from
one man, and him dead in this respect, came descendants as numerous as the stars in the sky or as the countless grains of sand on the sea-shore.**

Abraham is next instanced. He is the greatest Old Testament
exemplar of faith (Ro. iv. 3; Gal. iii. 6; James ii. 23; cf. Acts vii.
5). Several instances of Abraham's faith are given, as might be
expected of one who was the father of the Jewish people and
to whom was given the promise which was fulfilled in Christ.
8 First comes the faith of obedience. **By faith Abraham obeyed
the call to go out to the place which he was to receive
as his possession.** It was in Mesopotamia, in Ur of the
Chaldees, that the call first came to sally forth (Gen. xi. 31).
The tenses used here have been nicely calculated to show
Abraham's immediate obedience, so that 'the word of God was
still resounding in his ears as Abraham set out on his journey'
(Spicq). **He went out without knowing where he was
going to.** It was not until Abraham had settled in Haran that
Canaan was designated as the goal of his wanderings (Gen. xii.
5; cf. Philo, *de Migr. Abr.* 43). Abraham's faith was more dis-
interested than that of Noah, for Abraham went forth, not

knowing the things that would befall him (cf. Acts xx. 22). His courage did not consist so much in putting home and civilisation behind him as in venturing forth in faith to the unknown.

If the first instance of Abraham's faith shows obedience, the second shows endurance. **By faith he settled in the land of** 9 **promise as a stranger in a strange country.** The land of promise is, of course, Canaan, although Canaan is never so designated in the Old Testament. Abraham had been promised possession of the land, but he continued to live as 'a stranger and a sojourner' (Gen. xxiii. 4). His faith was shown in that he did not question the promise of God, but he knew that this was not his true home. The fact that he was **living in tents** shows his temporary and unsettled mode of life in this world. Associated with him are **Isaac and Jacob.** They are mentioned because they **shared the same promise** of possession (Gen. xxvi. 3; xxviii. 13).

In one sense the promise of God was fulfilled during Abraham's lifetime, in as much as he saw his descendants multiply (cf. vi. 15). But in another sense the promise could never be fulfilled on earth. Our author suggests that he was content to dwell in tents not because he preferred the nomadic life but because he did not expect too much of this world. **For he was** 10 **looking forward to the City with foundations.** 'The object of his desire was social and not personal only' (Westcott). It was the celestial City to which he looked forward (cf. *v.* 16; xii, 22). Compared with the tabernacle of human existence, it has permanence and security (cf. 2 Cor. v. 1 ff.). Its **maker and designer is God.** These words (which are not used of God in the Old Testament) point to the Alexandrine milieu from which the author came (cf. Wisd. Sol. xiii. 1; Philo, *Quis Rer. Div.* 133). They also show that **the City with foundations** cannot be Canaan, for God is no more the **maker and designer** of Canaan than of any other part of the earth, while he is in a special sense the author of the heavenly Jerusalem (cf. Gal. iv. 26).

The third instance of Abraham's faith concerns his barren and aged wife. **By faith even Sarah herself received power** 11 **to conceive, and that although past the time of life, because she regarded him who promised as trustworthy.**

This passage contains several difficulties. (*a*) p⁴⁶ D*ψ *pc* lat sy add that Sarah was barren; but this seems a gloss which is not so unnecessary as not to have been added but which is sufficiently unnecessary to be otiose. (*b*) KLP *pl* sy add that Sarah bore a child. This is also a gloss, inserted because of a rather rare construction in the Greek text. (*c*) The Greek words translated **power to conceive** in fact attribute to Sarah the sexual act of a man, not of a woman. To obviate this difficulty, alternative textual emendations have been proposed; either the deletion of the reference to Sarah, thereby making Abraham the subject of the sentence as he is of the preceding one, or a slight textual addition according to which Sarah is read in the dative case αὐτῇ Σάρρα. In the latter case the rendering would be: 'along with Sarah Abraham received power to beget'. It is, however, extremely hazardous, when sense can be made, as here, of an existing text, to undertake textual emendation which is unevidenced by any manuscript reading. If a slight ellipse is understood, the translation **power to conceive** can stand. Elsewhere in the New Testament it is Sarah's rather than Abraham's old age that is emphasised in this connection (Ro. iv. 19; cf. Gen. xviii. 11). (*d*) According to this Epistle, it is precisely Sarah's faith that enabled an heir to be begotten and conceived. Sarah is said to have been given power to conceive **because she regarded him who promised as trustworthy.** But, according to Gen. xviii. 12, Sarah laughed at the promise of a child, just as Abraham had earlier laughed at the same prospect (Gen. xvii. 17). Possibly our author understood Sarah's mood to have changed from incredulity to faith; but more probably he had forgotten these two biblical incidents when he wrote this verse.

Abraham was so intimately associated with Sarah in the matter of an heir (cf. Gen. xvii. 19-21) that Sarah's promised fertility 12 was the ground of his own parenthood. **So from one man, and him dead in this respect,** came descendants. As Sarah had lost the power to conceive, so Abraham had lost the power to beget (Ro. iv. 19). Nevertheless God made their union fruitful, and so the divine promise of Gen. xxii. 17 was fulfilled, for his descendants are **as numerous as the stars in the sky or as the countless grains of sand on the sea-shore.**

(13) It was in faith that these all died. They had not got what had been promised, but they saw and welcomed it from afar, and they confessed that they were strangers and aliens on the earth. (14) For those who say such things make it clear that they are looking for a homeland. (15) If they had had in mind that from which they came out, they would have found opportunity to turn back; (16) but, as it is, they are eager for a better homeland, a heavenly one. And so God is not ashamed of them to be called their God; for he has made ready a City for them.

The security of heaven's everlasting commonwealth compared with the transitory nature of earthly existence is so deep a conviction of our author and so dear to his heart that a pause is made at this point of the roll-call of faith to emphasise its importance. This theme first appeared in chapter iii, when the wilderness wanderings of the people of God were contrasted with the heavenly rest which awaits them; and the same theme reappears again later in the Epistle (xiii. 14; cf. xi. 10).

The patriarchs had all lived lives of faith, and **it was in** **13** **faith that these all died.** Death, as the end of human life, marks the point beyond which human faith can no longer operate. Death is faith's final test; and a life of faith is crowned and completed by faith's acceptance of death, especially when, as in the case of the patriarchs, the fulfilment of God's promises has not yet taken place. They had not yet witnessed the universal blessing that God was to accomplish through them.

As yet they had not established themselves in Canaan as they had been promised, nor had they yet seen their descendants multiply in accordance with God's promise. **They had not got** **what had been promised, but they saw and welcomed it** **from afar.** It is improbable that a reference is intended here to the rabbinic interpretation of Gen. xxiv. 1 (M.T.) which under-lies the Johannine statement that Abraham saw the day of the

Messiah and rejoiced (John viii. 56). More probably the patriarchs' foresight and joy are inferred from their faithful lives and from the biblical accounts of the death of Abraham (Gen. xxv. 8), and Isaac (Gen. xxxv. 29), and of the blessing of Jacob (Gen. xlix. 18).

The patriarchs were content to die because they could see by the eye of faith the distant fulfilment of their promises, like mariners who are content to heave to, when they can see, with relief, their final destination on the distant horizon. The patriarchs, it is suggested, had known that their journey was not ended by death, for **they confessed that they were strangers and aliens on the earth.** So Abraham had said to the sons of Heth (Gen. xxiii. 4) and Jacob to Pharaoh (Gen. xlvii. 9), although it is improbable that they themselves meant more by this phrase than oriental self-depreciation. **Strangers** are foreigners temporarily resident from abroad, while **aliens** are foreigners who are domiciled, without rights of citizenship, in a country not their own. The symbolic use of these two words is found in stoic writings (cf. Marcus Aurelius 2. 17). According to Philo, men are aliens because their souls long to return to their pre-existent state in their homeland (*de Conf. Ling.* 77). By contrast, in Eph. ii. 12 ff. Christians are said no longer to be strangers and aliens because by their membership of the church they already share with the saints in the privileges of the household of God; yet 1 Peter (where the eschatology is futurist rather than realised) Christians are greeted as strangers and aliens in a way that suggests that the metaphorical usage of the phrase was well established (1 Peter i. 1; ii. 11).

Here, in the Epistle to the Hebrews, the words are given a scriptural foundation in the sayings of the patriarchs (cf. Psalm
14 xxxix. 12). **For those who say such things make it clear that they are looking for a homeland.** A homeland is a person's country of origin. Thus homeland for Jesus was Nazareth (cf. Mark vi. 1; contrast John iv. 44). By confessing that they were aliens, the patriarchs made it clear that they were not in their country of origin. It might be said that they considered themselves foreigners in as much as they lived in Canaan, for this was their country of adoption, not of origin. But this explanation can be dismissed because it is not supported

by the pattern of their lives. **If they had had in mind that** 15 **from which they came out, they would have found opportunity to turn back.** If they had attempted to return to Mesopotamia a different explanation of their words could be given; **but, as it is, they are eager for a better homeland, a** 16 **heavenly one.** What is heavenly is by its nature **better** (cf. ix. 11, etc.). Philo explains **homeland** in the same sense of **heavenly** when commenting on Gen. xlvii. 4 (*de Agric.* 65). Philo, however, believed in the pre-existence of souls. Our author does not commit himself to the doctrine of pre-existence by his explanation of **homeland** as heaven. Heaven is the **homeland** of God's people not because they have once lived there, but because it is the home of their heavenly Father who calls them to himself.

Since the patriarchs look forward with eagerness to God's final destiny for them, God in his turn acknowledges the patriarchs as his own. **And so God is not ashamed of them.** He is pleased **to be called their God,** that is, the God of Abraham, of Isaac and of Jacob (Ex. iii. 6, 15). According to Matt. xxii. 32, the very fact that God can be so called shows that the patriarchs are still alive; and, if alive, they may be assumed to have reached their homeland in heaven.

Far from being ashamed of them, God **has** actually **made ready a City for them.** This use of the word **City** is significant. It is an expression of the writer's concern, evidenced elsewhere in the Epistle, for the divine ordering of society (cf. ii. 5; xi. 10; xii. 22 ff., xiii. 14, etc.). Both in Pauline writings (Phil. iii. 20; Eph. ii. 19) and in the Apocalypse (xxi. 2 *et passim*) heaven is conceived of as a city. Westcott sees the three different conceptions of a city which belong to Jewish, Greek and Stoic thought combined in the Christian conception of a commonwealth. 'It is the seat of a Divine Presence which carries with it the fulfilment of a divine counsel in the fellowship of man with God. It is a community in which each citizen is endowed with the completest privileges and charged with the fullest responsibility for the general welfare. It is a world-wide organisation embracing in a communion of the largest hope "all thinking things, all objects of thought".'

(17) By faith Abraham, when he was being tested, offered up Isaac. He who was the recipient of the promises was offering up his only son, (18) although he had been told, 'Through Isaac your descendants will be named'. (19) He reckoned that God had power even to raise from the dead; and, as a result, he did in a figurative sense receive him back from the dead.

After this slight digression, a return is made to the faith of Abraham. According to Jewish tradition, his faith was tried ten times (Jub. xix. 8; Pirke Aboth v. 4). Two instances of testing have already been given, but the greatest test of all is now adduced. Abraham's sacrifice of his son Isaac was famed in Jewish literature (Wisd. Sol. x. 5; Ecclus. xliv. 20; 1 Macc. ii. 52); and Philo regarded it not merely as the greatest sacrifice that Abraham could make, but also as almost the greatest that
17 any religious person could offer (*de Abr.* 167). **By faith Abraham, when he was being tested, offered up Isaac.** The perfect tense of προσενήνοχεν shows that there was no reservation in Abraham's mind. His determination to offer up his son was complete, and (as the imperfect tense of προσέφερεν shows) he was actually in the process of doing this when he was stopped. **He who was the recipient of the promises was offering up his only son.**

His test was twofold. In the first place Abraham had to place obedience to divine command above the inclinations of natural affection (cf. Matt. x. 37). Isaac was not Abraham's only son (Gen. xvi. 15), but, so far as the promises were concerned, he was the only son through whom these could be effected (Gen. xvii. 19-21). The phrase **only son,** while it adequately renders the Hebrew of Gen. xxii. 2, is rendered in the LXX by 'beloved son'; but our author may have been following another text (like that underlying the version of Symmachus) which had the rendering **only son.** It seems improbable that the use of this word is intended to show Isaac's prefigurement of the sacrifice of the only Son of God (cf. John i. 18).

It was, secondly, with regard to the divine promises that Abraham's faith was most severely tested. **He who was the recipient of the promises** also had a certain responsibility for forwarding their fulfilment, as is implied by the use of the Greek verb ἀναδεξάμενος. He was told to sacrifice Isaac, **although he** 18 **had been** explicitly **told, 'Through Isaac** (and through nobody else) **your descendants shall be named'** (Gen. xxi. 12; cf. Ro. ix. 7). The Greek here could mean not 'to whom (Abraham) it had been told about this promise', but 'about whom (Isaac) this promise had been told'. The latter meaning, however, is not suggested by the structure of the Greek, nor does it bring out properly the poignancy of Abraham's choice.

Abraham's decision was so difficult because God seemed to be contradicting himself by giving an order which appeared to nullify a previous promise. In our author's view Abraham realised that God could not lie about a promise nor could God's command be disobeyed. As the aorist tense of the participle λογισάμενος shows, Abraham's decision was immediate. **He** 19 **reckoned that God had power even to raise from the dead.** For if God's command were to stand, this would be the only way by which his promise could be fulfilled.

In a manner of speaking Abraham was right; for, **as a result, he did in a figurative sense receive him back from the dead.** God's abrogation of his order for Isaac's sacrifice was the result of Abraham's palpable willingness to kill him. The consequent salvation of Isaac's life was, **in a figurative sense,** the resurrection of one who was as good as dead.

Not all commentators have understood this phrase in this sense. A general difficulty is whether ὅθεν should be understood locally to mean 'whence' or consecutively to mean **'as a result'.** Very different interpretations have been given to the clause. (a) On the ground that Isaac was originally dead, since he had been in the loins of the 'dead' Abraham (v. 12), the sentence has been understood to mean: 'Whence he had already got him, figuratively speaking'. This tortuous explanation sheds more light on its adherents than on the meaning of the text itself. (b) Some commentators understand ἐν παραβολῇ as a symbol which points forward (as in ix. 9), prefiguring here the general resurrection from the dead; but this seems weak. (c) Others have

supposed that Isaac's escape from death is meant to prefigure
the resurrection of Christ. But if an allusion to Christ is meant
here, it is hard to understand how such a brief and obscure
reference could suffice. In any case, it would be uncharacteristic of our author to regard the sacrifice and salvation of Isaac
as a type of Christ's death and resurrection, and the idea is
nowhere found in the New Testament. (*d*) It is best therefore to translate ἐν παραβολῇ **in a figurative sense,** qualifying
Isaac's escape as an instance of resurrection from the dead.

42. THE FAITH OF THE PATRIARCHS. xi. 20-22

**(20) By faith Isaac blessed Jacob and Esau, and that con-
cerning things to come. (21) By faith Jacob, when he was
dying, blessed each of Joseph's sons, and bowed in
worship, leaning on the top of his staff. (22) By faith
Joseph, as his life was ending, made mention of the
Exodus of the Israelites and gave directions concerning
his bones.**

From the period between Abraham and Moses three patriarchs are mentioned. None of these three incidents seems particularly apt to show faith in action; but, on further examination,
20 each can be seen to have its point. **By faith Isaac blessed
Jacob and Esau, and that concerning things to come.**
Isaac had faith not merely for the immediate future, but also
for **things to come.** He looked beyond himself to what God
would do through his sons. In fact he reversed the law of primo-
geniture by giving the older son Esau the blessing that belonged
to the younger son (Gen. xxvii. 1-41). In the ancient world the
final blessing of a dying father was prized as a quasi-physical
endowment. Through this final blessing God used Isaac's faith
as well as Jacob's deceit in order to work his strange providence.
21   **By faith** too **Jacob, when he was dying, blessed each of
Joseph's sons.** It is perhaps strange that, instead of Jacob's
more important blessing of the Twelve Patriarchs (Gen. xlix)
this earlier incident should have been selected (Gen. xlviii. 14-

16). Once again divine providence overruled the natural order
of things, for Jacob, to Joseph's annoyance, unwittingly laid his
right hand on Ephraim, his younger grandson, and his left hand
on the older Manasseh. In blessing his grandchildren Jacob was
looking two generations ahead, his faith fixed upon the future.

Our text continues: **and bowed in worship, leaning on
the top of his staff.** In fact this belongs to an earlier incident,
when Jacob gave directions about his burial (Gen. xlvii. 31). In
the Hebrew text of this passage it is said that Jacob bowed himself in worship on the bed's head. The Hebrew word for bed is
similar to that for **staff,** and the LXX, followed by our author,
has the latter in its text. It is necessary to supply the word
leaning as without it the Greek text would be translated: 'he
bowed in worship on the top of his staff'. It has been suggested
that the Greek text was intended to mean that Jacob, by bowing
his head towards Joseph's staff, recognised the authority which
it symbolised. The Greek, however, means not 'towards' but
on the top of his staff, and either the phrase indicates Jacob's
frailty or it is a symbol of his pilgrim status (cf. Gen. xxxii. 10).

As Isaac and Jacob had looked to the future in faith, so also
did Joseph. Although he had left Canaan at the age of 17 (Gen.
xxxvii. 2), and had lived in Egypt until his death at the age
of 110 (Gen. l. 26), yet he trusted that God would keep his
promise to Abraham that in the fourth generation his progeny
would return to the promised land (Gen. xv. 16). **By faith 22
Joseph, as his life was ending, made mention of the
Exodus of the Israelites and gave directions concerning
his bones.** This is a reference to Joseph's death-bed scene
recounted in Gen. l. 25 f. According to Ex. xiii. 19 Moses took
Joseph's bones with him in his wanderings, and according to
Josh. xxiv. 32 they were finally laid to rest in Shechem.

43. FIVE INSTANCES OF MOSES' FAITH. xi. 23-29

**(23) By faith Moses at his birth was hidden for three
months by his parents because they saw that the child
was beautiful, and they were not frightened of the king's**

order. (24) By faith Moses, when he grew up, refused to be
called the son of Pharaoh's daughter, (25) preferring
rather to suffer ill-treatment with God's people than to
enjoy the transient pleasures of sin. (26) He reckoned the
reproach incurred by God's Anointed greater wealth than
the treasures of Egypt: for he kept his eyes on his reward.
(27) By faith he left Egypt and did not fear the king's
wrath; he held to his purpose as one who sees him who
is invisible. (28) By faith he celebrated the Passover and
sprinkled the blood, in order that the Destroyer might not
touch their firstborn. (29) By faith they crossed the Red
Sea as if on dry land: when the Egyptians made the
attempt they were swallowed up.

Moses is next on the roll-call of witnesses. It is hardly surprising that no less than five instances of faith are taken from
his life, since Moses was the greatest figure of the old dispensation, and our author has already found it necessary to prove that
Jesus is superior to him (cf. iii. 2 ff.).

The first incident concerns the circumstances surrounding
Moses' birth. As with other great heroes of antiquity, legends
concerning his nativity grew up in Jewish haggadah (cf. *Moïse,
L'Homme de l'alliance* (Tournai, 1955), pp. 102-118). Our author,
however, follows his custom of keeping within the biblical
23 tradition. **By faith Moses at his birth was hidden for three
months by his parents.** This is an allusion, of course, to the
faith of the infant's parents, not of the babe itself. According
to Ex. ii. 2 f. only the mother is mentioned in this connection,
but she could have hardly hidden the infant without at least
the acquiescence of her husband. They did this **because they
saw that the child was beautiful.** Those who reproach the
parents for being moved merely by the outward appearance of
their infant might well ask themselves what other remarkable
characteristics could be found in a newborn baby. Pharaoh had
ordered that all male infants born to Jews should be drowned
in the waters of the Nile (Ex. i. 22), but Moses' parents **were
not frightened of the king's order.** Their faith consisted in
their conviction that God would preserve the baby and that he
would be used by divine providence.

The second instance of faith concerns Moses as a grown man. As an infant he had been rescued from his hiding-place and cared for by Pharaoh's daughter (Ex. ii. 5 ff.). **By faith Moses, 24 when he grew up, refused to be called the son of Pharaoh's daughter.** This was neither the awkwardness of a child nor the rebelliousness of an adolescent: it was the responsible choice of an adult.

As the result of an incident recorded in Ex. ii. 11-15 Moses chose to identify himself with his persecuted fellow-countrymen rather than with the royal family of his adoption, **preferring 25 rather to suffer ill-treatment with God's people than to enjoy the transient pleasures of sin.** Through the eye of faith he recognised in his enslaved fellow-countrymen a divine nation. He preferred to share spiritual security with them rather than to enjoy present material advantage from Pharaoh. He was more concerned with God's providence for his chosen people than with what, by comparison, were the less permanent privileges and pleasures that apostasy would have brought him. **Sin,** as in x. 26, means the sin of apostasy. **He reckoned the 26 reproach incurred by God's Anointed greater wealth than the treasures of Egypt.** Egypt's wealth was proverbial. **The reproach incurred by God's Anointed** is a reference to Psalm lxxxix. 51 f., where the chosen people are spoken of collectively as the Anointed. Doubtless our author saw their reproach as a prefiguring of the reproach which fell on Christ himself (cf. Ro. xv. 4). But our author, unlike Paul, has no doctrine of the mystical identity of Christ and the people of God. He does not mean that at the Exodus the Jews actually shared in the sufferings of Jesus Christ (cf. Col. i. 24), any more than Christians actually share his reproach (xiii. 13). He means rather that their reproach is a type of what Christ himself later suffered, and that God might be trusted to reward them, as he had later vindicated Christ. And so Moses, instead of looking for present profit, **kept his eyes on his** future **reward.** Moses did not act for the purpose of earning a reward but he remained faithful to God with the result that he was rewarded (cf. x. 35; xi. 6). The introduction of the word **reward** here is an allusion to Psalm lxxxix. 52 (LXX).

The third instance of Moses' faith shows him putting loyalty

to the invisible God before the wrath of a very visible Pharaoh.
27 **By faith he left Egypt and did not fear the king's wrath.**
Moses left Egypt on two occasions. The first was the outcome
of the incident to which reference was made in the previous
sentence. On this occasion the scriptural record specifically
states that he left because he was frightened of the king (Ex. ii.
15), and any attempt to harmonise this with the words of our
author that **he did not fear the king's wrath** is special
pleading. Because of this inconsistency, and because the incident has already been mentioned in the previous verse, the
passage must be understood as a reference to the second occasion
of Moses' departure from Egypt; that is, to the Exodus. On this
occasion Moses was absolutely unafraid whenever the king, in
his anger, hardened his heart. **He held to his purpose as one
who sees him who is invisible.** While Moses was actually to
see God (Ex. xxxiii. 23) and to speak with him face to face (Ex.
xxxiii. 11; cf. Num. xii. 8), this did not happen until afterwards.
It would therefore be incorrect to translate this phrase as an
oxymoron: 'in as much as he saw one who is invisible', for he
had not seen God when he left Egypt.

The fourth instance of Moses' faith concerns events immediately before the Exodus, so that this verse might have been
expected to have been placed before the previous sentence. But
the two events in question are so closely bound up with the
Exodus that the exact order of narration is of little importance.
The last of the ten plagues was to be the destruction of all male
first-born, of man and of beast (Ex. xii. 12). The Israelites were
ordered to take certain measures to prevent this fate befalling
28 their own first-born. And so **by faith** Moses **celebrated the
Passover and sprinkled the blood in order that the
Destroyer might not touch their firstborn.** Elsewhere in
the New Testament the Passover is the type of Christ's death
(1 Cor. v. 7), but it has no such meaning here. It is mentioned at
this point because it was the occasion when the paschal lamb was
slain, the blood of which, when splashed on the lintel and two side-
posts of the Israelites' houses, would be a sign for God to deny
access to the Destroying Angel (Ex. xii. 23). Moses' faith consisted
in his conviction of God's power to kill the first-born and in his
belief that God would pass over the Israelites' homes.

The final instance of Moses' faith, like its predecessor, concerns the Israelites as well as their leader. On this occasion Moses showed his pre-eminent faith by stretching his hand out over the Red Sea for the waters to go back so that the people could confidently cross over. **By faith they crossed the Red** 29 **Sea as if on dry land: when the Egyptians made the attempt they were swallowed up.** The faith that can move mountains (Matt. xvii. 20) succeeded in moving the ocean (Ex. xiv. 22). It was not the Egyptians' lack of faith that caused them to be **swallowed up** when they **made the attempt** to cross. It was rather Moses' faith that caused their destruction, for, according to Ex. xiv. 27, he raised his hand a second time so that the sea returned to its strength, and the Egyptians were engulfed.

44. FAITH IN THE DAYS OF JOSHUA. xi. 30-31

(30) Through faith the walls of Jericho collapsed after they had been encircled for seven days. (31) By faith Rahab the whore was not destroyed with the disobedient, since she had received the spies peaceably.

It might well be expected that Joshua would be mentioned by name after Moses, especially as his name in Greek is the same as that of Jesus. There are, however, references to two incidents both of which took place in the time of Joshua. The first concerns the fall of Jericho. **Through faith the walls of** 30 **Jericho collapsed after they had been encircled for seven days.** The extensive excavations of the ancient site of Jericho show no record of this event. Its identifiable remains pre-date this period, since the mud walls of Joshua's time easily disintegrated. According to Josh. vi the walls of the city fell in on the seventh day of the siege when, by divine command, the Israelites had processed round it seven times and the priests had blown on their trumpets and the people had uttered a great shout. Their faith consisted in their belief in the efficacy of these unprecedented proceedings.

Only one woman finds detailed mention on the roll of faith,
31 and she was a prostitute. **By faith Rahab the whore was not
destroyed with the disobedient, since she had received
the spies peaceably.** God's use of sexually immoral women
for the furtherance of his providence can be noted elsewhere in
the New Testament (e.g. Tamar in Matt. i. 3 and Rahab in
Matt. i. 5). The author of the Epistle of St. James regards this
particular incident as indicating Rahab's works rather than
showing her faith (James ii. 25; contrast Ro. iv. 3). Rahab's
faith, however, did not merely consist in her offer of hospitality
and of a hiding-place to the spies whom Joshua had sent to
Jericho. She also expressed an absolute conviction that the
Israelites' God was God of Heaven and earth, and that in his
providence he had given the land to his chosen people (Josh.
ii. 9 ff.). In return for her help she and her household were
spared when Jericho was taken, her house being identified by a
scarlet thread displayed in the window as an agreed sign (Josh.
ii. 18).

45. THE POWER OF FAITH. xi. 31-35a

**(32) What more am I to say? Time will fail me to tell of
Gideon, Barak, Samson, Jephthah, David, Samuel and the
prophets. (33) Through faith they overthrew kingdoms,
exercised justice, obtained the promises, muzzled the
mouths of lions, (34) quenched the force of flames,
escaped the edge of the sword, from being weak were
made powerful, became strong in war, turned back
armies of foreigners. (35a) Women received back their
dead by resurrection.**

Sixteen instances of faith have been given from the period
of biblical history between Adam and Joshua. Although even
by biblical chronology this is a long period of time, the bulk of
biblical history still lies ahead of it. And so the list is cut short
32 by the use of a classical formula: **What more am I to say?** In
the elevated style proper to a homiletic epistle it is not absolutely inappropriate to use this paraleipsis. **Time will fail**

me to tell of Gideon, Barak, Samson, Jephthah, David, Samuel and the prophets. The first four names are taken from Judges. They are not given in chronological order, but possibly in order of their popularity. **Gideon** with a hundred men put to flight the Midianites (Judges vii). **Barak,** at Deborah's command, routed the forces of Jabin, king of Canaan, which were under the command of Sisera (Judges iv f.). **Samson** both during his life and by his death troubled the Philistines (Judges xiii-xvi). **Jephthah** the Gileadite conquered the people of Ammon (Judges xi f.). These four judges witness to the gradual extension of Israelite power in Canaan. **David** and **Samuel** are 'here closely associated as the respective founders of theocracy and prophetism' (Spicq).

It is noteworthy that no king other than David features in this list. It seems that our author may have shared with Samuel doubts about the establishment of a Jewish monarchy (1 Sam. x. 17 ff.); for he prefers the royal type of Melchisedek, to which Jesus belongs (cf. vii. 1, 15), to the royal house of Judah. Similarly no priest figures in this roll of faith, perhaps also because true priesthood is to be found in the order of Melchisedek. But Melchisedek was not a prophet, so that our author feels quite free to mention **the prophets** among his list of heroes. Even if prophets are not mentioned by name (apart from Samuel) there are many allusions to them in what follows.

The first triplet of faith's examples stresses the social advantages that accrued. **Through faith they overthrew kingdoms,** 33 as when David conquered the Philistines, or when Gideon routed the Midianites or when Jephthah defeated the Ammonites. Faith lay here in the conviction that 'the Lord can save by many or by few' (1 Sam. xiv. 6). Through faith too **they exercised justice.** The Greek phrase ἠργάσαντο δικαιοσύνην refers neither to private piety nor to 'the righteousness that comes through faith' (v. 7). It signifies 'judging Israel', from which the Judges took their name. Samuel, for example, 'judged Israel all the days of his life' (1 Sam. vii. 15). In so doing, they were inspired by faith in God as the source of all righteousness and as the protector of Israel. By faith too they **obtained the promises.** These are not the same as 'the promise' of the heavenly city which it is expressly stated in *v.* 39 that they have not obtained. **The promises** refer more generally to promises of land and inheritance which they saw fulfilled in their lifetime (e.g. Josh. xxi. 43).

The next three instances of lives dominated by faith concern personal deliverance, not social advantage. David as a young man (1 Sam. xvii. 34 f.) and Daniel under duress (Dan. vi. 22) **muzzled the mouths of lions.** Shadrach, Meshach and
34 Abednego **quenched the force of flames** in the burning furnace (Dan. iii. 25). Even if these three, strictly speaking, cannot be included among the prophets, the record of this miracle is found in the book of the prophet Daniel. Others in the list, such as David, avoided a more conventional death and **escaped the edge of the sword** (Psalm cxliv. 10; cf. 1 Sam. xviii. 11).

The next three instances show how faith brought strength and vigour. **From being weak,** some **were made powerful.** The weakness is not further defined. It could be a woman's weakness which, like Judith's, was turned into the strength of a man (Judith xiii. 7), or the weakness of a blinded Samson miraculously strengthened for his final revenge (Judges xvi. 28). It could include the weakness of dying Hezekiah marvellously strengthened by divine decree (Is. xxxviii. 1-5). On the other hand others **became strong in war,** such as David when confronted by Goliath (1 Sam. xvii). Others too **turned back armies of foreigners.** This phrase might well apply to all those who were successful in routing the enemies of their nation; but the words used in the Greek are especially reminiscent of the language used about the Maccabean revolt (cf. 1 Macc. iii. 8, 15; iv. 10, etc.). The author is probably no longer confining his illustrations precisely to those whom he has enumerated in *v.* 32.

The next sentence stands on its own. 'The triplet of victorious faith is followed by a single, abrupt clause which presents
35a the highest conquest of faith' (Westcott). **Women received back their dead by resurrection.** The references here are to the widow's son from Sarepta whom Elijah returned to life (1 Kings xvii. 22), and the son of the Shunnamite woman whom Elisha restored by the 'kiss of life' (2 Kings iv. 34). The latter

story seems to have influenced the Lucan account of the widow's
son at Nain (Luke vii. 11 ff.).

46. FAITH UNDER DURESS. xi. 35b-38

**(35b) Other men were tortured, not accepting release,
that they might obtain a better resurrection. (36) Others
experienced mocking and flogging, and also chains and
imprisonment. (37) They were stoned, they were sawn
in two, they were put to death by the edge of the sword,
they went about in sheepskins, in goatskins, needy,
oppressed, suffering hardship, (38) (men of whom the
world was not worthy), wandering in uninhabited places,
mountains, caves and holes in the ground.**

The remaining examples of faith concern the hardships that
it can cause, in the first place through maltreatment by others.
Other men were tortured. The Greek word used here sug- 35b
gests stretching on a wheel. Our author is probably thinking of
Eleazar the scribe who refused to eat pork and who voluntarily
submitted to torture (2 Macc. vi. 19), or of the seven brothers
whose torture is described in 2 Macc. vii. 2 Maccabees formed
part of the Greek bible, so that our author is still taking his
examples from biblical records. Had these people complied with
the laws of the Seleucid ruler, they would have been released;
but they endured, not **accepting release.** They did this **that
they might obtain a better resurrection.** Three possible
interpretations of this phrase can be given. (1) They might have
hoped for a resurrection life better than the life they endured
on this earth. This sense is jejune. (2) They might have been
hoping for 'the resurrection to life' rather than run the risk,
through apostasy, of 'the resurrection to judgement' (cf. John
v. 29). It would seem improbable that so much could have been
intended by such a short phrase without a further explanation
in the text. (3) The most obvious and probable meaning of the
clause is to interpret **a better resurrection** by reference to the
resurrection mentioned in the previous sentence. The tortured

martyrs were encouraged to stand fast by their expectation
of a resurrection much better than the return to life which
was granted to the infants alluded to in the previous verse.
This explanation, moreover, accords with the words of one
of the seven brothers who suffered torture: 'It is good to
die at the hands of men and look for the hopes which are given
by God, that we shall be raised up again by him' (2 Macc. vii.
14).

36   Not all those who were persecuted were tortured. **Others
experienced mocking and flogging. Mocking** was not only
the fate of Maccabean heroes (1 Macc. vii. 34; ix. 26). Prophets
such as Micaiah ben Imlah (1 Kings xxii. 24) and Jeremiah
(Jer. xx. 2) suffered similar indignity. **Flogging,** although a
Roman punishment *par excellence*, is mentioned during the
Maccabean persecutions (2 Macc. vii. 1) and formed part of the
Suffering Servant prophecy (Is. l. 6). Acutely painful punishment, although agonising at the time, often does not last long.
The long-drawn-out tedium of prison is not necessarily a lighter
imposition. This was the fate of those who, like Jeremiah (Jer.
xxxviii. 13), endured **also chains and imprisonment.**

37   Others suffered different calamities. **They were stoned,** like
Zacharias the prophet (2 Chron. xxiv. 20 f.; cf. Matt. xxiii. 35).
(This is perhaps the most obvious way of causing death in a
country so full of stones as Israel.) They were **sawn in two,** like
the inhabitants of Rabbah of Ammon (2 Sam. xii. 31). No Jewish
martyr, however, suffered this fate according to the bible. This
must be one of the very few cases where our author draws on
non-biblical haggadah. According to Ascension of Isaiah v. 1-14,
as well as talmudic tradition (Sanh. 103b), Isaiah suffered this
terrible fate by the command of the king Manassah. The tradition is confirmed in the writings of Tertullian, Hippolytus and
Jerome. Others were killed in a more conventional manner.
They were put to death by the edge of the sword. Among
these should be numbered the prophet whom Jeremiah mentions
(Jer. xxvi. 20 ff.) and those whom Elijah laments (1 Kings xix.
10, cited in Ro. xi. 3).

In this verse there has been a certain amount of confusion in
the manuscripts. Dittography caused a primitive corruption.
ἐπειράσθησαν ἐπρίσθησαν is read by ℵ L 326 syʰ, and the two

words are transposed in p^{13} A *1739 pm* lat arm Or. In order to strengthen the sense this gave rise in *1923* bo to ἐπρήσθησαν ἐπειράσθησαν. The idea of temptation is alien to the context, and ἐπειράσθησαν should be omitted, as in p^{46} 2 *327 2423 pc* sy^p sa Hier Ps-Aug.

Instead of punishment and death at the hands of adversaries, some suffered hardship and privations in order to preserve their freedom and to escape torture. **They went about in sheepskins, in goatskins, needy, oppressed, suffering hardship.** This description, which could well fit the Maccabean rebels, also suits Elijah and Elisha; and Elijah's mantle, which was handed on to Elisha (2 Kings ii. 14), is described as a sheepskin (1 Kings xix. 13). All such people were **men of whom the** 38 **world was not worthy.** The meaning is not that there is nothing in the world to match the merit of these men. **The world** is used, as in *v.* 7, to signify human society organised without God. The sentence is ironical in intention. The world has rejected such people; and yet the world does not deserve to have them even if it were to accept them. (A similar phrase is found in Mech. 5a on Ex. xii. 6.) Outcasts, they were **wandering in uninhabited places, mountains, caves and holes in the ground.** This further description again suits the freedom fighters against the Seleucids (1 Macc. ii. 31; 2 Macc. v. 27; vi. 11; x. 6). Israel abounds in uninhabitable territory with excellent hiding-places for fugitives and outcasts, and these were later used in guerrilla warfare against Herod (cf. Josephus, *Bell. Jud.* 1. 16. 4) and against Rome (cf. P. Benoit and others, *Discoveries in the Judaean Desert*, II (Oxford, 1961), and Y. Yadin and others, *Judaean Desert Caves*, I and II (Jerusalem, 1961 and 1962)). The fact that Khirbet Qumran is situated in a desert spot is coincidental. Our author is concerned with those who suffered involuntary, not voluntary, hardship for their faith.

47. THE TESTIMONY OF FAITH. xi. 39-40

(39) All these have won testimony because of their faith, but they did not receive the promise, (40) God having

made a better plan including us, so that without us they should not be made perfect.

Our author has now made an imposing sweep of biblical history from its earliest beginnings to the latest events recorded in his Greek bible. He has painted an inspiring picture of faith and endurance and obedience. The whole point of the chapter is

39 now summed up. **All these have won testimony because of their faith.** The witness of their faith is in the scriptures. But they did not **receive the promise** (cf. *v.* 13). Particular promises had been fulfilled (cf. *v.* 33), but they had not yet

40 received the final reward of their faith, **God having made a better plan including us.** As elsewhere in the Epistle, **better** denotes what belongs to the new dispensation; and the **better plan** is none other than the better or new covenant (cf. viii. 6, 8).

This covenant specially concerns Christians. For their sake Christ was not manifested until the end of time (1 Peter i. 20), so that they too might be included among God's people. Christians seem to have the more favourable treatment. Living at the end of the age, they have already approached Mount Zion (cf. xii. 22 ff.); but the Jewish heroes have had to wait, and could only hail the promises from afar (cf. *v.* 13). This is all part of divine providence, **so that without us they should not be made perfect.** Commentators have explained this passage by reference to the human body, the perfection of which lies in the interdependence of all its members. This is certainly a Pauline concept (1 Cor. xii. 12 ff.; Eph. iv. 16; Col. ii. 19); but it is foreign to the thought of this Epistle. Our author prefers a social to an anatomical ecclesiology, thinking of the church not after the model of a human body but as a city or household. A family is not complete unless all its members are present. Our writer is not interested in matters concerning the waiting period for members of the household of faith who have died earlier. He is thinking of the inclusive nature of perfection and not of the passage of time that must elapse before it can be attained. By perfection he does not mean here either the perfect nature of the resurrection body or the perfection of Christ which will be bestowed on the church at the last day. His thought is at once simpler and deeper. God's plan is for all his elect, whether they belong to the old or the new dispensation. Salvation is social and not individualistic. So long as a single member of the family is not present, the household of faith can never be complete, and thus can never be **made perfect**.

48. SUMMONS TO ENDURANCE. xii. 1-3

(1) For this very reason then we too, with such a great cloud of witnesses around us, should lay aside every encumbrance and the sin which readily clings to us, and run with endurance the race that lies before us, (2) keeping our eyes on him who inspires our faith from the beginning to the end, Jesus, who in place of the joy which lay before him endured a cross, despising its shame, and has taken his seat at the right hand of the throne of God. (3) Consider him who has endured so great opposition from sinners against themselves, in order that you may not tire and lose heart.

The previous chapter on faith was hortatory in intention. The faith of past heroes is both an example and a stimulus to arouse faith and endurance. (The letter seems to have been written for first generation Christians, for there are as yet no followers of Christ on this roll-call of faith.) If these heroes could not obtain the promises although they had run their race, the present contestants have an added spur to their endeavours to complete their part of the course so that all may receive their reward. The imagery of the stadium is employed (cf. Phil. iii. 12; 1 Tim. vi. 12; 2 Tim. ii. 5). The present competitors are the last to take part in a kind of gigantic relay race. They are being watched by huge multitudes who have already handed on the baton of faith and who are waiting as invisible spectators to encourage those who run last. This **great cloud of witnesses** 1 are not merely onlookers of the present contest, but they have given their own witness of faith by their own past lives (cf. xi. 39), some even to the point of death. μάρτυς here is approaching its later sense of martyr.

213

No doubt for such a contest it is necessary to get into training (cf. 1 Cor. ix. 25) and to lose weight. This might be the meaning of ὄγκον ἀποθέμενοι, but here it signifies the removal of garments before a race so as to **lay aside every encumbrance** (cf. Philo, *Leg. All.* 3. 47). The nature of this encumbrance is explained by the additional phrase, **the sin which readily clings to us.** This is not the sin of apostasy (as in x. 26), for this would be a disqualification against running at all. Sin here is used, as in ix. 26, to describe that which acts as an impediment between man and God. The word εὐπερίστατον is unknown elsewhere in Greek literature. Its derivation has suggested many meanings, such as: readily besetting, easily discarded, popularly admired; but the sense here adopted, **which readily clings,** is more likely than most.

The imagery of putting off sin like a garment is found elsewhere in the New Testament (cf. Ro. xiii. 12; Eph. iv. 22, 25; Col. iii. 8; 1 Peter ii. 1; cf. James i. 21); and it formed an important part of early Christian catechesis. In such passages the metaphor is taken from the change of garments at baptism as an outward symbol of the change to the new life in Christ. Here, however, the metaphor is different, being derived from the stadium. It denotes stripping for action before a race. In this race the competitors are not being asked to put on a final spurt to the finishing-post, but doggedly to go on going on in the long-distance race of life. They are to **run with endurance the race that lies before** them.

The contestants are urged to take their attention off their own progress and to fix it instead on the person of Jesus. The use of his name emphasises the humanity of his person. We shall run 2 with faith only if we are **keeping our eyes on him who inspires faith from beginning to end, Jesus.** Since our author holds that Christ was presented to the heroes of old through the scriptures as well as manifested to Christians in the days of his flesh, he can speak of Jesus as the source, guide and perfector of faith for those who lived under either old or new dispensations. It is possible, however, that a reference is intended here not to their faith in God but to the faith of Jesus himself, in as much as he took the initiative of faith (cf. ii. 10) and by his sinless life and faultless death brought it to absolute perfection.

If this sense were to be adopted, Jesus might be described as 'the exemplar of faith from start to finish'. Since, however, the next clause is concerned only with the end of his life, this meaning is improbable.

The pattern of Jesus' death is the pattern of faith's response (cf. xi. 25 f.). **In place of the joy which lay before him he endured a cross, despising its shame.** It was not merely death that he had to bear (for all have to die) but a particularly dreadful and contemptible mode of death. Yet **despising its shame** he endured the last agonies reserved for criminals and slaves. Why did he do it? The preposition $\dot{a}\nu\tau\iota$ could be translated: 'in exchange for' (cf. xii. 16). In this case the meaning would be that Jesus endured a cross in exchange for the joy which would be his at his ascension and which he would then give to his disciples (cf. John xv. 11). Our author, however, has earlier so emphasised the human suffering of Jesus as to make it very improbable that he believed Jesus to have had anything in mind other than obedience when he died (cf. ii. 18). What then is the joy in place of which Jesus endured death? It could hardly be the joy of living, for Jesus did not exactly give up earthly happiness by submitting to death by crucifixion. The passage refers rather to the joy of eternal sonship in heaven which Jesus renounced in order to endure a cross, and thereby was given the highest honour of heaven. This whole passage describes the self-emptying of Jesus and his glorification in a movement of thought very similar to that of Phil. ii. 6-11 (cf. 2 Cor. viii. 9). For after the degradation of his death, Jesus **has taken his seat at the right hand of the throne of God.** The perfect tense here emphasises that while Jesus' death was a single past event, his heavenly session is a present reality. Jesus' enthronement in heaven is expressed in terms derived from Psalm cx. 1, and there is a certain progression in the use of this formula (i. 3; viii. 1; x. 12 and here). Coming here at the end of a sentence, the expression is very emphatic. It does not represent the repose of an athlete after running his race so much as Jesus' permanent glorification in heaven after his humiliating and truly human death on earth. This is the abiding theme and the theological presupposition of the whole Epistle.

The readers have been exhorted to keep their eyes on the

person of Jesus as they run in the race of life. This thought is
3 now further elaborated. They should **consider him who has
endured so great opposition from sinners against themselves.** The readers are not being instructed to seek out opposition so as to imitate Christ. On the contrary, opposition is
to be expected by those who are already imitating him. His
silent steadfastness under strain is not merely an example but
also an inspiration to those who suffer likewise. Furthermore,
readers can be encouraged by the thought that those who
caused opposition to Jesus brought judgement on themselves.
The word **opposition** has, in the Greek, a legal flavour about it,
and refers especially to the events preceding Jesus' death; his
trials at the hands of Caiaphas, the Sanhedrin, Herod and
Pilate. Meditation on these events brings courage and fortitude
to Christians at the hour of their trial. This suggests that the
readers of the Epistle are themselves undergoing testing of some
kind, but its nature is not here specified.

It is tempting to read here the singular pronoun εἰς ἑαυτόν
instead of the plural form εἰς ἑαυτούς, thus giving an easier
meaning: him who has endured so great opposition from sinners
against himself. The singular form ἑαυτόν is found in AP *326*
vg$^{s, cl}$ and αὐτόν in D^{c}KL *pl* sy^h ^{vld} sa. But the plural form is
better attested. ἑαυτούς is read here by ℵ* D* *pc* vg^w sy^p bo, and
αὐτούς by *p*$^{13, 46}$ ℵ^c *33*. Since the plural form has better
authority and gives the more difficult sense (and yet sense can
be made of it), it must be adopted. The idea of the self-contra-
diction of sinners is found in Greek thought (Xenophon, *Hell.*
1. 7. 19); and the hurt that sinners do to themselves is noted by
biblical writers (cf. Prov. viii. 36) and by Philo (*Quod Det. Pot.*
52). Moreover, according to Nu. xvii. 3 (LXX), the supporters
of Korah's rebellion are said to have been 'sinners in their own
souls', and in Jude 11 this revolt is described by the very same
word **opposition** (the only other instance of the word in the
New Testament). When our author wrote **opposition from
sinners against themselves,** he may well have been thinking
of the LXX passage about Korah and regarding it as a type of
what happened to Jesus. His thought is so steeped in the Old
Testament that this provides a likely explanation of what at
first sight appears a difficult phrase.

Our author has given advice to meditate on Jesus' attitude to his death **in order that you may not tire and lose heart.** The imagery of the stadium is continued. Both the Greek verbs used here are employed by Aristotle to describe the physical collapse of a runner after he has finished his race (*Rhet*. 3. 9. 2). The best way to avoid spiritual catastrophe in mid-career is to fix attention on the example of Jesus under test.

49. DISCIPLINE AND SONSHIP. xii. 4-8

(4) In your contest against sin, you have not yet contended to the point of bloodshed, (5) and you have forgotten the word of encouragement which is addressed to you as sons: 'My son, do not lightly regard the Lord's discipline nor lose heart when reproved by him. (6) For whom the Lord loves he disciplines; he lays the rod on every son whom he accepts.' (7) Endure it as discipline: God is dealing with you as sons. Is there a son whose father does not discipline him? (8) If you are without the discipline in which all sons share, then you are bastards and not sons.

So far in this chapter the imagery of the race-course has been employed. The metaphor of the stadium is still retained, but here the ring has been substituted for the track. Boxing formed part of Greek games as well as running; and in those days the pugilists' leather gloves were spiked with metal so that boxing was an even more dangerous and bloody sport then than it is now. Our author reminds his readers that they have not as yet met with serious opposition. **In your contest against sin, 4 you have not yet contended to the point of bloodshed.** Sin here must be the sin of apostasy, not the lighter forms of sin that can be laid aside by the contestant (cf. *v*. 1). Earlier, when the blood of Christ has been mentioned, a reference to his sacrificial death has been intended (ix. 14; x. 19). Here, where the reference is to boxing, there is no reason to think that death is meant. No doubt pugilists killed each other even more often than they do now; but death did not occur each time blood was shed. Our author means no more than that the recipients of this Epistle have not yet been seriously hurt in their struggle for faith against apostasy. There is, however, a suggestion that worse is still to come.

None the less there has been already considerable unpleasantness which the recipients of the Epistle have not accepted in the right spirit. The imagery of sport suggests to our author the concept of discipline; but he develops this not by reference to the stadium but in relation to a father's training of his son for
5 adult life. **You have forgotten the word of encouragement which is addressed to you as sons.** Stern words are to follow later, but first a warmer note of exhortation is struck. Two verses from Proverbs iii are quoted according to the LXX version. (The same verses are cited by Philo with the same intention (*de Congr.* 177).) The first verse runs: **My son, do not lightly regard the Lord's discipline nor lose heart when reproved by him** (Prov. iii. 11). **Son** is the normal title by which a Jewish teacher of wisdom would address his pupil. This verse contains a warning about two false attitudes towards suffering. In the first place, it is possible to make light of it, pretending either that it is non-existent, or that it has no part in God's providence. The second danger lies in the opposite extreme to indifference. The blows of God's discipline may be felt to be so crushing as to render further progress impossible. Reproof can lead to a godly or ungodly reaction (cf. 2 Cor. vii. 9). 'To endure rightly one must endure intelligently' (Moffatt). The next verse of Proverbs gives a positive explanation of
6 divine discipline: **Whom the Lord loves he disciplines; he lays the rod on every son whom he accepts** (Prov. iii. 12). The Hebrew version of *v.* 12b runs: 'as a father the son in whom he delights'; but the difference between the versions can be explained by an error on the part of the LXX translator.

In order to understand the teaching of this passage, it is necessary to appreciate the family ethos of the ancient world. The paterfamilias was not only the one on whom fell the prime responsibility for the welfare of his children: he was also the source of authority in the family. The education of children and of slaves was based on the stern realities of corporal punishment.

'Spare the rod and spoil the child' is a Jewish proverb (cf. Prov. xxiii. 13). The use of physical correction was unquestioned. The inculcation of fear was regarded as a necessary aspect of education.

The current 'father image' profoundly affected the theological understanding of divine fatherhood. If 'he that loves his son will continue to lay stripes upon him' (Ecclus. xxx. 1), it followed naturally that **whom the Lord loves he disciplines.** If 'foolishness is laid up in the heart of a child, but the rod of correction will drive it far from him' (Prov. xxii. 15), it followed also that our heavenly Father **lays the rod on every son that he accepts.** It must not be thought that such teaching about God was peculiar to Old Testament Judaism. It recurs in the New Testament (cf. Rev. iii. 19); and it was current in contemporary pagan teaching (Seneca, *de Prov.* 4. 7) as well as in Hellenistic Judaism (cf. Philo, *Quod Det. Pot.* 146). The ancient world did not feel the problem of evil with the same intensity as the modern world just because its 'father image' was different. Even the protest of the book of Job is not against the discipline of suffering as such, but against a surfeit of calamity inappropriate to Job's circumstances. It was not until ideas of liberal education began to have currency, and the value of corporal punishment and the inculcation of fear began to be questioned, that the full force of the theological problems concerning human suffering began to be felt.

Our author exhorts his readers to **endure it as discipline: 7 God is dealing with you as sons.** The unpleasantness of physical discipline can, if properly accepted, provide an opportunity for moral and spiritual growth. Such discipline is a sign that God is educating his children as a father educates his sons. Physical correction was universal in the ancient world. **Is there a son whose father does not discipline him?** The absence of such correction would not show the love of God, but rather his indifference; and since God could not be indifferent to his own children, it would mean that such people could not be God's rightful sons. **If you are without the discipline in 8 which all sons share, then you are bastards and not sons.** A natural son had no right to claim the name or inheritance of his father. The author has here taken for granted the moral and legal code of his day. He assumes that a father would not care about the education of his bastard and so would not bother to administer correction to him.

50. DIVINE DISCIPLINE. xii. 9-13

(9) Again, we had earthly fathers who disciplined us and we held them in respect; shall we not much more submit to the Father of spirits, and gain life? (10) They disciplined us for a short time as they chose, but he for our good, that we may share his holiness. (11) No discipline seems pleasant at the time but painful; yet afterwards it yields to those who have been trained by it the peaceful harvest of righteousness. (12) So 'stiffen your drooping hands' and 'straighten your failing knees' (13) and 'make straight paths for your feet', that the lame limb may not be dislocated, but may rather be cured.

Two further arguments about divine discipline based on the conception of human fatherhood are next propounded. The first is an argument *a fortiori*, of which our author has previously

9 shown himself fond (cf. ix. 14; cf. xi. 25). **Again, we had earthly fathers who disciplined us and we held them in respect; shall we not much more submit to the Father of spirits, and gain life?** There is a progression here from physical matter to the supernatural spirit which animates it. Our earthly fathers can only give us our human inheritance. God alone is the author of life, and from him alone comes the spirit which quickens our human body. If we treat our earthly parents with respect, we are under all the greater obligation to surrender ourselves without reserve to him in whose hands is the gift of present and the promise of future life.

The phrase **Father of spirits** here is strange. It can hardly be equated with 'Lord of spirits' (found in Enoch and in 2 Macc. iii. 24), for the latter signifies God's lordship over the heavenly powers, which is not intended here. Moreover the phrase seems to assert the universal fatherhood of God, since

God is called **the Father of spirits** and not just the Father of
all Christian spirits. The doctrine of universal fatherhood, however, is not found elsewhere in this Epistle (cf. comment on ii.
10) just as it is not to be found in the Pauline or Johannine
literature. The phrase must not be pressed (any more than the
similar phrase in Eph. iv. 6 should be pressed) since it is used
here simply in order to form a contrast to our **earthly fathers.**
No special theological significance should be attached to it. It
is probably derived from Nu. xvi. 22, where God is called 'God
of the spirits of all flesh'. Spirit here means human personality
not in its physical, moral or intellectual aspects but as animated
by God.

The second argument from human fatherhood takes the form
of a contrast rather than a progression. As for our human
fathers, **they disciplined us for a short time as they chose,** 10
but he for our good, that we may share his holiness.
There are of course similarities between a human parent and
our heavenly Father. They both exact discipline, and in both
cases the discipline lasts for only a short time. For children it
lasts only during their minority, and for the children of God,
only during the period of human life, which is brief compared with the immensity of eternity. The contrast lies rather
in the motives, aims and methods of correction. With human
fathers these may be good or bad, as they choose. But our
heavenly Father is constrained by his very nature to apply
correction solely that his children may profit from it. He can
also have only one end in view, the same end as he has in
creating us, that we may participate in his divine life. For this
holiness is prerequisite (cf. *v.* 14).

It would be unnatural to enjoy physical correction at the
time when it is administered. On the part of the corrector it
would imply sadism, and on the part of the corrected it would
suggest masochism. **No discipline seems pleasant at the** 11
time but painful. It cannot be fully appreciated until its results
can be experienced. Our author here reverts to his original
sporting imagery. Life itself is a kind of spiritual training
ground (cf. 1 Tim. iv. 7). **It yields to those who have been**
trained by it the peaceful harvest of righteousness. (There
is a remarkably similar phrase in James iii. 18, which raises the

question of the relationship of the two Epistles.) Only after the effort of training can the repose of victory be enjoyed. In the same kind of way it is only after the burial of the seed that the harvest can be reaped. The good life cannot be achieved without man's active co-operation with God. All this involves proper discipline. This is not of course a novel idea. Similar sentiments were attributed to Aristotle (Diogenes Laertius, 5. 1. 18) and can be found in the writings of Philo (*de Congr.* 160). But for Christians the discipline of the Lord will evoke especially the memory and the inspiration of Christ's example.

The preceding discussion of divine discipline results in a severely practical conclusion. The readers are brusquely ordered to brace themselves up. The words used are taken from the Old

12 Testament. **Stiffen your drooping hands and straighten your failing knees** contain phrases compounded from Is.

13 xxxv. 3 and Ecclus. xxv. 23. **Make straight paths for your feet**—the verse forms a hexameter in the Greek—is taken from Prov. iv. 26 (LXX). This kind of metaphorical language is used elsewhere to describe moral and spiritual exhaustion (cf. Ecclus. ii. 12; Philo, *de Congr.* 164). No doubt it has been used here because of its suitability in a passage where the imagery of the stadium has been employed. The underlying image, however, is now different, suggesting rather a route-march of the people of God. If the whole church takes a grip on itself and makes straight for its goal, those who are dragging their feet will recover instead of getting further behind than they are already. These remarks are addressed neither to the leaders of the church, nor to a minority of its members, but to all the congregation. Once again an indication is given that there are particular members of the church at fault (cf. x. 25). Responsibility for them rests on everyone. A real moral and spiritual effort by the majority can bring help and relief to individuals who are overtaken by weakness (cf. 2 Cor. ii. 6). If the author's instructions are obeyed, then it may be **that the lame limb may not be dislocated, but may rather be cured.** The Greek word ἐκτραπῇ could be translated 'turned aside' but the context demands the medical meaning of **dislocated.**

(14) Pursue peace with everyone and the holiness without which no one will see the Lord. (15) Exercise care that no one falls away from the grace of God; that no bitter root springs up and causes trouble and many are defiled by it; (16) that there is no immoral or unspiritual person like Esau, who sold his birthright for a single meal. (17) You know that when he afterwards wanted to inherit the blessing, he was rejected (for he had no opportunity of getting the decision changed) although he sought it with tears.

A further indication of trouble is now given. It seems that there may have been divisions in the church to which this letter was addressed (cf. 1 Cor. i. 10 ff.). The command to **pursue 14 peace with everyone,** adapted from Psalm xxxiv. 14, marks 'the eagerness and constancy of the pursuit' (Westcott); but it also suggests that peace was not established throughout the whole congregation. Peace here is enjoined not with all comers but between members of the church, for *v.* 15 (which in the Greek is dependent on this verse) is only concerned with matters inside the ecclesiastical community.

Two aspects of Christian character are mentioned. The first is peace, the result of harmonious relationships between fellow-Christians. The second is holiness, the fruit of a man's relationship with God. Hence the injunction to aim at **holiness without which no one will see God.** Negatively holiness may be described as the characteristic of a person who is uncontaminated by any defilement; and a sinner cannot see God (cf. 1 John iii. 6; 3 John 11). Positively described, holiness means a purity of character which has been set apart for God and consecrated by his hallowing Spirit. This leads to the vision of God (cf. Matt. v. 8).

Our author does not forget the rulers of the congregation (cf. xiii. 17); but he expects each and every member of the church to discharge his obligations of oversight (cf. iii. 13; x. 24). Church order here seems to be more primitive than that described in 1 Peter; for the word ἐπισκοποῦντες, applied here to the whole congregation, is restricted there to the elders of the church (1 Peter v. 2; cf. Acts xx. 28).

There are three dangers in particular about which the recipi-
15 ents of the letter must **exercise care**. In the first place, they are to see **that no one falls away from the grace of God. Grace** does not here signify spiritual gifts but the fundamental divine attitude of benevolence towards his elect. This divine initiative demands a human response. Failure to respond is not necessarily a deliberate insult (as in x. 29) but a falling away.

In the second place they are to be careful **that no bitter root springs up and causes trouble**. This phrase is borrowed from Deut. xxix. 18 LXX (cf. 1QH 4. 14), where there is a warning, as here, against apostasy and idolatry. Watch must be kept not against apostasy in general but for any individuals who may apostatise. (The phrase 'sinful root' is similarly applied to an individual in 1 Macc. i. 10.) Such a person is not merely bitter by his own nature but he spreads his bitterness to others, **and many are defiled by it.** As the church can come to the help and relief of an individual overtaken in weakness, so one apostate can infect the whole congregation.

There is a certain progression in these three warnings. The first was against spiritual failure, the second against spiritual corruption, and the third against profane and sensual conduct
16 resulting in outright rejection. They must ensure **that there is no immoral or unspiritual person like Esau**. Immorality and sensuality were typically pagan not Jewish vices, and the inclusion of this verse suggests Gentile elements among the church to whom this letter was sent. It is not absolutely clear in the Greek whether Esau has been introduced merely as an example of irreligion, or whether he exemplifies immorality as well. Probably the latter; for a similar collocation of these Greek words is found elsewhere (cf. Philo, *de Spec. Leg.* i. 102). πόρνος is more likely to have its literal sense here of one who is sexually immoral (cf. xiii. 4) rather than the metaphorical meaning of apostate. In later rabbinic literature Esau was regarded as sexually immoral (Gen. R. 65 on Gen. xxvi. 34; Baba Bathra 166). The tradition of Esau's depravity can be traced earlier in Palestinian (Jub. xxv. 1 ff.) and Hellenistic Judaism (Philo, *de Virt.* 208). Possibly this is one of those rare occasions when our

author draws on extra-biblical tradition; but it might be that Esau's union with Hittite women (Gen. xxvi. 34) was regarded by him as proof of Esau's immorality.

The reference to Esau's unspiritual character is further explained. It was he **who sold his birthright for a single meal.** Philo had noted that Esau was sensual by nature (*de Migr. Abr.* 153). Esau's irreligion did not consist in the fact that, in his extremity, he had no choice but to submit to his bodily instinct of hunger. For, though he was famished and faint, he made a deliberate choice. He preferred the satisfaction of a single repast to the inheritance of the divine promises (Gen. xxv. 29-34). The birthright of the first-born son normally consisted in a double portion of all that his father had (Deut. xxi. 17). But in Esau's case much more was at stake. He forfeited his right to the line of succession which had been specially ordained by God to receive his promises. Jacob had used his cunning not only to deprive Esau of his birthright, but also to deprive him of his blessing (Gen. xxvii. 27-29). **You know that when he afterwards wanted to inherit the bless-** 17 **ing, he was rejected (for he had no opportunity of getting the decision changed) although he sought it with tears.**

This verse has given much trouble to commentators on account of its ambiguities. μετάνοια can mean either 'a change of mind or decision' or 'repentance before God'. Some commentators, who take the latter meaning, believe that there is a warning here of the danger of divine rejection (cf. vi. 4 ff.), with Esau as a terrible example. According to this view Esau **was rejected** not only by Isaac but also by God, 'for he found no place for repentance'. This would mean either that Esau was given no second chance by God for repentance although he was full of remorse, or that Esau had the opportunity of repentance but did not use it. Now if a religious meaning is attached to the phrase τόπος μετανοίας, it must mean not repentance itself but opportunity for repentance (cf. Wisd. Sol. xii. 10; 4 Ezra 9. 12). Yet Esau, according to the bible, had plenty of opportunity for repentance towards God. Furthermore, if he had been finally rejected by God he would hardly have inherited the not inconsiderable blessing that belonged to the younger son (Gen. xxvii. 39 f.).

It follows therefore that a different meaning must have been intended. τόπος μετανοίας in its Latin form signified for Roman jurists 'an opportunity for changing a former decision' (Ulpian in *Digest*, 40. 7. 3). It was precisely this opportunity that Esau lacked. When the blessing of Isaac had been given to Jacob, there was no chance of getting this altered. It had been bestowed already upon Jacob, and so it could not be given to Esau. **He had no opportunity of getting the decision changed.** His rejection by his father as the first-born son still stood.

Once this meaning is accepted, further difficulties disappear. One of these concerns the meaning of the concessive clause. In the Greek text **although he sought it with tears** comes at the end of the sentence. What did Esau seek? If he sought repentance, it would have been pointless to seek this with tears, since repentance by its very nature concerns not outward show but inner change of heart. In fact Esau wanted both the blessing of the first-born and a change of decision concerning it. It was these that he sought with tears. According to the M.T. of Gen. xxvii. 38 (followed by Jub. xxvi. 33 and Josephus, *Antiq.* 1. 18. 7) Esau, when he asked for his father's blessing, lifted up his voice and wept. It is to this incident that reference is here made.

The analogy is singularly appropriate. The recipients of the Epistle must guard themselves against the danger of losing the inheritance and the blessing which God has reserved for them as his first-born among men. If they adhere to wrong priorities, they may not be for ever damned, but they will forfeit their share in the promises of God. Esau stands as a frightening example of the irreversible results of immoral or irreligious conduct on the part of the elect.

52. SINAI AND THE OLD COVENANT. xii. 18-21

(18) For you have not drawn near to what is tangible, to what was blazing with fire, to darkness, gloom and tempest (19) to the blast of a trumpet and to the sound of words. Those who heard it refused to hear any more,

(20) for they could not bear the order that was given, 'If even a beast touches the mountain, it shall be stoned'; (21) and so appalling was the sight, Moses said, 'I am terrified and trembling'.

A transition is now made to the main hortatory theme which underlies the Epistle in general and this chapter in particular. The recipients of the letter have been urged to endure faithfully to the end in the struggle of life. A further attempt is now made to keep them faithful to God and to discourage them from apostasy by reminding them of the difference between the two covenants. A contrast is made between the terrifying outward signs which accompanied the establishment of the old covenant and the spiritual, moral and immaterial nature of the society which God has brought into being through the new covenant.

In primitive religions mountains often had numinous associations, and Judaism counted several such mountains among its holy places. Mount Zion, since it was believed to be both the throne and the temple of God, was regarded as the location of the eschatological hope of all mankind (Is. ii. 2 ff.; xi. 9 ff.; xxv. 6; lxvi. 20). In the conviction that this eschatological hope was in the process of being spiritually fulfilled under the new covenant, our author uses Mount Zion here to stand for this sphere of spiritual fulfilment. Mount Sinai, however, symbolises the old covenant, although here, unlike Gal. iv. 24, it is not actually mentioned by name.

For you have not drawn near to what is tangible, to 18 what was blazing with fire, to darkness, gloom and tempest, to the blast of a trumpet and to the sound of 19 words. These natural portents, taken together, suggest a volcanic eruption; yet they all subserved God's supernatural self-revelation, described in Ex. xix. 12-19; Deut. iv. 11-14; v. 22-30. The verb προσεληλύθατε translated **drawn near** could also mean 'arrived', but it cannot mean this here, for the children of Israel did not actually go on to Mount Sinai itself but drew near and stood at its foot (Deut. iv. 11).

The phenomena surrounding the giving of the Law are described here in words largely borrowed from the biblical account. Thus, in Deut. iv. 11 (LXX) it is said that the mountain

was blazing with fire, and there was **darkness, tempest** and a great voice, and according to Ex. xix. 19 the voice **of a trumpet** gave a mighty **blast.**

In this passage there are difficulties of text and interpretation. According to D°KLP *pl* vg^{s, cl} sy^h ὄρει has been inserted after ψηλαφωμένῳ, contrasting the visible and tangible Mount Sinai with the invisible Zion of the heavenly Jerusalem. This gives the right sense, but since it is the easier reading it must be rejected as a gloss.

Without ὄρει, ψηλαφωμένῳ and κεκαυμένῳ could be regarded as both qualifying πυρί, and the phrase might be translated as in the N.E.B.: 'the palpable blazing fire'. This interpretation, however, presents grave difficulties. In the first place, while the darkness of the ninth plague is said to have been felt (Ex. x. 21), it would be inappropriate for our author to write of 'flames which may be touched'. Such a rendering would miss the whole force of the argument. Whether the fire could be felt or not is comparatively irrelevant. The point is that all the phenomena connected with Mount Sinai were visible and tangible, contrasted with the spiritual nature of Mount Zion, the city of the living God. Despite the awkward (but not impossible) Greek, the rendering must be: **you have not drawn near to what is tangible** (that is, to Mount Sinai), with its **darkness, gloom,** etc. It is better to translate **to what was blazing with fire** rather than 'to blazing fire' because of the LXX passage underlying the phrase (Deut. iv. 11).

These natural prodigies each severally signify a theophany. **Fire** was the accompaniment of a divine manifestation (Judges xiii. 20; 1 Kings xviii. 38). God dwelt in the **darkness** (1 Kings viii. 12) and had his way in the **tempest** (Nah. i. 3). **The blast of a trumpet** came to be regarded as a sign of his final manifestation (Matt. xxiv. 31; 1 Cor. xv. 42; 1 Thess. iv. 16).

It was not the physical phenomena which inspired terror so much as the sound of an intelligible voice. This was the voice of God himself, which could only be heard by man at the peril of death (Ex. xx. 19; Deut. v. 25). **Those who heard it refused to hear any more.** According to Ex. xx. 19 the people appealed to Moses to communicate with God on their behalf; and, according to Deut. v. 27, this appeal was also made by the elders

and heads of tribes. **For they could not bear the order that** 20
was given. The tense of the Greek participle here suggests that
this order continued to ring in their ears: **'If even a beast
touches the mountain, it shall be stoned'.** The order itself
included men as well as beasts (Ex. xix. 13). It was the holiness
of the mountain that had rendered it so dangerous, thus necessi-
tating the imposition of a taboo (cf. Uzzah's death through
touching the sacred Ark of God, recounted in 2 Sam. vi. 6 f.).
The whole scene must without doubt have seemed awe-
inspiring even to one who was the friend of God. According to
our author, **so appalling was the sight, Moses said, 'I am** 21
terrified and trembling'. But according to Deut. ix. 19 Moses
uttered these words on his return from the mountain when he
discovered the golden calf. It is possible that some extra-
biblical tradition is being introduced here (cf. Acts vii. 32),
but the use of the actual words of Deut. ix. 19 suggests that
there was some confusion in the mind of the author at this
point.

53. ZION AND THE NEW COVENANT. xii. 22-24

**(22) No, you have drawn near to Mount Zion, to the city
of the living God, to the heavenly Jerusalem, to myriads
of angels in festal gathering, (23) to the assembly of the
first-born who are enrolled in heaven, to the Judge who
is God of all, to the spirits of righteous men who have been
made perfect, (24) to Jesus the mediator of the new
covenant, and to the sprinkled blood which has better
things to tell than the blood of Abel.**

After his description of events on Mount Sinai, the author
contrasts Mount Zion. **No, you have drawn near to Mount** 22
**Zion, to the city of the living God, to the heavenly Jeru-
salem.** His readers have not yet actually arrived at Mount
Zion: they have drawn close (cf. *v.* 18). This translation is in
accord with the author's general viewpoint of a futurist and not
a realised eschatology. The meaning of προσεληλύθατε can only

be finally decided by the context of the word and by the theology of the Epistle. Merely linguistic considerations here are as indecisive as similar investigations about words used in the Synoptic Gospels to determine whether the Kingdom of God is said to have arrived or drawn near.

Mount Zion is traditionally the hill of Moriah where Abraham sacrificed Isaac and where the Jebusites later built a fortress which David took and renamed Zion. Here Solomon's temple was built, and here too the second Temple and Herod's temple were sited. Here God was worshipped with joy and gladness (Psalm lxv. 1) and here it was believed that the Messiah would be manifested (Psalm ii. 6).

Mount Zion is described as **the city of the living God.** 'In the spiritual reality Mount Zion represents the strong foundation of the new Order, while the City of the Living God represents the social structure in which the Order is embodied' (Westcott). God is **living** and active (cf. iii. 12; x. 31), and from Zion he exercises his rule (Psalm ix. 11; Joel iii. 17). It is because God has his seat there that it is the City with foundations (xi. 10).

But God's habitat is not the earth. He lives in heaven, and so Mount Zion must be a heavenly reality. It is **the heavenly Jerusalem.** This concept is found elsewhere in the New Testament (Gal. iv. 26; Rev. iii. 12; xxi. 2). It seems to have been accepted in current Judaism (cf. T. Dan v. 13; 'Description de la Jerusalem nouvelle' (?) *Qumran Caves*, I (1955) ed. D. Barthélemy and J. T. Milik, p. 134 f.) as well as in later rabbinic thought (Chag. 12b.). In origin the idea was probably derived from belief in a heavenly copy of the sanctuary.

Three general descriptions have now been given. There follow references to particular groups. Firstly, supernatural beings are mentioned: **myriads of angels in festal gathering,**
23 **the assembly of the first-born who are enrolled in heaven.** The punctuation here is uncertain, no less than five possibilities having been suggested! The one adopted here follows the usual rules of syntax. At this point the language and thought of the Epistle have marked affinities with some passages in Enoch, but none the less our author, according to his custom, keeps within the scriptural tradition. According to Dan. vii. 10 there

are myriads of myriads who stand before the throne of God (cf.
1 Enoch xl. 1). They throng around in joyful worship like those
who join in the celebrations of some **festal gathering.**

The next phrase must be taken as a further description of the
angelic host: **the assembly of the first-born who are enrolled
in heaven.** This phrase has been thought by some commentators to signify not the angels of heaven, but the saints who are
members of the Church Triumphant. It is true that ἐκκλησία,
here rendered **assembly,** is a technical Christian word for the
church (but it does not have this meaning in ii. 12, the only
other instance of its use in this Epistle). These commentators
have suggested that the saints could be called **the first-born** in
as much as they have received special privileges and blessings
from God. These **first-born** have been identified with the
patriarchs, or with others mentioned in the previous chapter;
the Apostles, Christians already dead, or the first converts to
the faith. It was common to speak of those who were destined
for heaven as **enrolled** (cf. Luke x. 20; Rev. xiii. 8), and critics
have supposed that the word would be more appropriately used
of men than of angels who have never left the heavens.

Nevertheless the phrase must refer to angels. It would be
quite out of keeping with our author's clarity of style and
precision of language to refer, in a list of heaven's citizens, twice
to the angels, yet to separate these by an intervening reference
to saints. On the other hand it is in keeping for him to give
two references to angels after a threefold reference to heaven.
Indeed these two references form the first of three doublets by
which heaven is described. In any case **first-born** would be an
unhappy word by which to describe the saints (especially after
the recent example of Esau the first-born); while it is appropriate to angels who were created before mankind and who could
thus be aptly so called.

The second doublet describes heaven under the aspect of
righteousness with reference to mankind; **the Judge who is
God of all** and **the spirits of righteous men who have been
made perfect.** Most commentators transpose the order of the
Greek words and render: 'God who is judge of all'. This is
to miss the force of the Greek order (which must have been
deliberate) and also the force of the argument. If the author

were to be enumerating the citizens of heaven, God could not conceivably be No. 3 in the list. But our author is not concerned here with God as God, but with the Judge (who is God) who has rewarded the spirits of righteous men. It is indicative of his inmost convictions that justice is so closely connected with the idea of God. This is in striking contrast to the Johannine tradition where God is primarily thought of as love.

Heaven contains those saints whom the Judge has considered worthy to enter. These are **the spirits of righteous men who have been made perfect.** It is not altogether clear how they can already be in heaven if they have not yet received the promise (xi. 39). It is also surprising that they should be described as **spirits** (cf. 1 Peter iii. 19); for if they have been made perfect, they might be thought to have been clothed with their resurrection body (cf. 1 Cor. xv. 45 ff.; 2 Cor. v. 4). But the word is probably used to emphasise the spiritual and immaterial nature of the new order of existence: and the cognate phrase 'souls of the righteous' is found in the Old Testament (Wisd. Sol. iii. 1).

These men were not righteous through their own deserts. They have been faithful to God, and God has favoured them with the reward of righteousness (cf. xii. 11). Our author has understood Hab. ii. 4 in its usual Jewish and not in its special Pauline sense (cf. x. 38 f.); and the Pauline language of justification through faith is foreign to him. For our author the just are those who in virtue of their faithful lives pass the scrutiny of the Judge and instead of an adverse sentence gain the reward of life. In one sense they have already been made perfect through Jesus' taking of his humanity into heaven; and, in another sense, they cannot be made fully perfect until the society of heaven is complete (cf. xi. 40).

Any description of heaven must include Jesus, and the third 24 doublet describes his work of salvation: **Jesus the mediator of the new covenant** and **the sprinkled blood which has better things to tell than the blood of Abel.** Moses, the mediator of the old covenant, stood trembling at the foot of Mount Sinai but Jesus who is **the mediator of the new covenant** (cf. viii. 6; ix. 15) is in Mount Zion of the heavenly Jerusalem. The reference to **sprinkled blood** recalls the inaugurating sacrifice of the old covenant (Ex. xxiv; cf. He. ix. 19) and signifies the finished work of Jesus' sacrifice. The use of the name **Jesus** emphasises here, as elsewhere in the Epistle, the humanity of the glorified Christ. His blood **speaks better things than the blood of Abel** in as much as Abel's blood cried for vengeance while Jesus' blood speaks reconciliation. Abel was regarded by the Jews as the proto-martyr (cf. xi. 4 for our author's view of his piety); and a martyr's blood was believed to have atoning efficacy (4 Macc. vi. 28; xvii. 21 f.). There is no suggestion here, however, that Jesus' blood is more efficacious than Abel's in its intercessory power. It speaks quite differently of **better things,** that is, things concerning the new covenant (cf. xi. 40).

54. THE FEAR OF THE LORD. xii. 25-29

(25) See that you do not refuse to hear him who is speaking. For if they did not escape when they had refused to hear the voice of their divine instructor on earth, how much less shall we escape if we turn our backs on him who speaks from heaven? (26) God's voice shook the earth then, but he has promised, saying, 'Once more I will shake not earth alone but heaven as well'. (27) The words 'Once more' indicate the removal of the things that are shaken, that is, created things, that the unshaken things may remain. (28) Therefore, because we are receiving an unshakable kingdom, let us hold on to God's grace, and so worship God acceptably, with reverence and awe; (29) for our God is a consuming fire.

The last section ended with a reference both to Jesus as the mediator of the new covenant and to his sprinkled blood which speaks better things than the blood of Abel. This sentence starts abruptly without a participle to connect it with the last; but the connection is made by picking up the verb λαλεῖν, to speak. **See that you do not refuse to hear him who is speaking.** 25 This must be understood by reference to the preceding sentence.

233

It is not God who is speaking by his Son (i. 2), but Jesus who speaks from heaven.

The author explains the reasons for his urgency. The only way to safety is through Jesus as the mediator of the new covenant. **For if they did not escape when they had refused to hear their divine instructor on earth, how much less shall we escape if we turn our backs on him who speaks from heaven?** The order of the Greek words here (according to the best reading) makes it more natural to translate 'when they had refused on earth to hear their divine instructor'; but the sense requires the translation given above.

There have been many interpretations of this passage. According to some, God spoke on earth under the old covenant by angels and prophets, but under the new covenant through Christ from heaven. Others interpret the passage to mean that the pre-existent Christ spoke under the old covenant by earthly means, but the glorified Christ under the new covenant speaks from heaven. Others see a contrast not between the two mediators of the covenants, but between the two spheres of revelation in which each mediates.

The context, however, and the plain meaning of the Greek, require a contrast between Moses and Jesus. For God spoke to the Israelites not on earth but from heaven (Ex. xx. 22; Deut. iv. 36). It was Moses who was their divine instructor on earth (Acts vii. 38). It was Moses whom they refused to hear (cf. x. 28). The Israelites' refusal to listen to God's voice on the mountain can hardly have been intended here (cf. *v.* 19), for this refusal met with divine approval (cf. Deut. v. 28). It was rather their refusal to listen to Moses in the desert which caused the Israelites to die before they could enter into the promised land (cf. iii. 7).

Since Jesus is far greater than Moses (cf. iii. 3), and since the covenant which he inaugurated is far better than the old covenant (cf. viii. 6), to turn away from the better things that Jesus speaks is far more serious. To turn one's back is, in fact, to apostatise (2 Tim. iv. 4; Titus i. 14). Although the circumstances under which the old covenant was established were frightening enough, they are as nothing compared with the results of apostasy from the new covenant.

God himself by his own words and actions has pointed to the difference between the two. **God's voice shook the earth** 26 **then.** Mount Sinai quaked at the promulgation of the law (Ex. xix. 18; Psalm lxviii. 8). An earthquake was regarded as an apocalyptic sign of God's presence and power (cf. Is. vi. 4; Psalm xviii. 7). But a far greater portent than this had been ordained for the future. **He has promised, saying, 'Once more I will shake not earth alone, but heaven as well'.** This quotation is adapted from Hag. ii. 6 (LXX).

In the Hebrew text the oracle runs: 'Yet once, it is a little while and I will shake the heavens and the earth . . .'. The purpose behind this shaking is declared to be the filling of the second temple with desirable things so that it may be more glorious than the first. The LXX version, however, suggests not so much a promise of divine assistance for temple building as an apocalyptic sign of consummation. It is this meaning that our author attaches to the verse.

The shaking of the heavens as well as the earth was part of what Christian expectation took over from Jewish apocalyptic hope (cf. T. Levi iii. 9; Luke xxi. 26). Heaven and earth were both expected to pass away at the consummation of all things (cf. Mark xiii. 31; 2 Peter iii. 10; cf. Matt. v. 18). Since this eschatological hope was regarded as in some sense fulfilled in the death and resurrection of Jesus, these apocalyptic signs were associated with these events. Thus at Jesus' death the heavens grew dark (Matt. xxvii. 45) and the earth was shaken (Matt. xxvii. 51). It is not, however, to these portents that reference is made here, but rather to the apocalyptic hope of consummation itself.

The words 'Once more' indicate the removal of the 27 **things that are shaken, that is, of created things.** In our author's judgement the Holy Spirit had divinely inspired the scriptures to point to this future, single, final and universal catastrophe. The created universe itself had not yet been removed. 'That which is antiquated and ageing has nearly disappeared' (viii. 13); but the material world was still in existence when our author wrote, even if it was in process of disappearing (cf. 1 Cor. vii. 31; 1 John ii. 17).

The purpose underlying this future disintegration of the

universe is **that the unshaken things may remain.** This is
expressed rather differently elsewhere in scripture as the hope
of a new heaven and a new earth (Is. lxv. 17; 2 Peter iii. 13; Rev.
xxi. 1). The unchangeable and unassailable character of the
new covenant will be revealed at this final dénouement. It is
ironical that Philo applies the same word **unshaken** to the very
commandments of Moses which our author regards as destined
to vanish away with the old covenant (*de Vita Moys.* 2. 14).

A moral conclusion is now drawn from this apocalyptic hope.
28 **Therefore, because we are receiving an unshakable
kingdom, let us hold on to God's grace.** The present tense
of παραλαμβάνοντες suggests that the readers are in process of
receiving, not that they have already received the kingdom
(cf. comment on xii. 22). If the kingdom had actually been
received, there would have been no need of this final exhortation. For the kingdom is the Kingdom of God, described earlier
in verses 22-24. This phrase, common in the Synoptic Gospels,
is rare in the Epistles, and when it is found it usually refers, as
here, to the final destiny of the elect.

The words ἔχωμεν χάριν, rendered here **let us hold on to
God's grace,** usually signify the giving of thanks when the
person thanked is mentioned. In this Epistle, however, χάρις
never signifies gratitude but always **God's grace.** Great as
the Christian duty of thanksgiving may be, it is not mentioned
elsewhere in this Epistle, nor is it particularly appropriate here.
For the recipients of the letter have been urged to stand fast,
and to match God's grace with their own faithfulness (cf. iv. 16;
xii. 15). Our author is here reaching the end of his Epistle (apart
from the particular instructions of the final chapter). He is
therefore coming to the climax of his whole argument. He is
deducing his final moral exhortation from the last doctrinal
exegesis of scripture of this chapter. It is wholly in keeping
with the whole tenor of his letter to end this section with an
exhortation to **hold on to God's grace** (cf. Acts xiii. 43).

The whole Epistle has had a liturgical undertone. The angels
of heaven are ministering spirits (i. 14). The redeeming work
of Christ has been expounded as a cultic act, and the exalted
Lord ministers in the heavenly sanctuary (viii. 2). The sacrifice
of Christ has enabled man to worship the living God (ix. 14).

And so by holding on to the grace of God the recipients of the Epistle will be enabled to **worship God acceptably.** This seems to involve neither the intimacy of love nor the tenderness of human affection. God is conceived as transcendant and austere. He should be worshipped **with reverence and awe.**

It is in keeping with our author's vision of God that the final theological statement in his Epistle's main section should be a citation from the Old Testament of an uncompromising and intimidating nature. In Deut. iv. 24 it is said that **our God is a** 29 **consuming fire.** This fire is not the kindling of love, nor the flames of purgation nor even illumination. It is the holy fire of anger and resentment, for, as Deut. iv. 24 continues, God is a jealous God. There is no attempt here to allegorise this meaning, such as Philo undertook (*de Dec.* 49). Our author's final word to his readers here is not about the attraction of divine love but about the fearfulness of holy wrath.

55. CHRISTIAN ATTITUDES. xiii. 1-6

(1) Let love among fellow-Christians continue. (2) Do not forget hospitality, for through it some have entertained angels unawares. (3) Remember those in prison, as though you were imprisoned with them; remember those who are suffering, for you too have bodies. (4) Let marriage be honoured in every way, and the bed kept undefiled, for God will judge fornicators and adulterers. (5) Let your life be free from the love of money, being content with what you have, for he has said, 'I will never leave nor forsake you'. (6) Therefore we say with confidence, 'The Lord is my helper, I will not be afraid; what can man do to me?'

Chapter xiii reads in some ways like an appendix to the main work. If the previous chapters have a rhetorical style more appropriate to a homily than to a letter, this final chapter with its terse list of duties and responsibilities is more like the other epistles of the New Testament. So marked is the difference of

style and content between this chapter and the rest of the
Epistle that chapter xiii (or part of it) has been thought to have
been added by an editor who was changing an earlier anonymous
homily into an epistle addressed to a particular church. It has
even been suggested that chapter xiii was originally part of the
'severe letter' of 2 Cor. x-xiii.[1] This is because of the numerous
correspondences between this chapter and the Corinthian
letters.

If the vocabulary, linguistic usage and literary construction
of chapter xiii are examined, and if its thought and argument
are analysed, it will appear extremely improbable either that Paul
could ever have written it, or that it is constructed out of earlier
chapters of the Epistle. The whole of the Epistle to the Hebrews
comes from the same hand. The connections with the Corinthian letters show the milieu for which it was written, not its
Pauline authorship. The distinctive style and content of chapter
xiii are sufficiently explained by the author's adaptation of his
original homily to the needs of an epistle.

The author briefly enumerates basic Christian social duties.

1 **Let love among fellow-Christians continue.** φιλαδελφία
means primarily love for a brother or sister. The word had
already in the Jewish world gained an extended meaning so as
to include fraternal love between fellow-Jews (4 Macc. xiii. 33).
The Christian Church had transferred the duty of loving one's
neighbour (Lev. xix. 18) from the national to the specifically
religious group. Since Christians regarded one another as
brothers and sisters in Christ, φιλαδελφία happily expressed this
mutual love (cf. Ro. xii. 10; 1 Peter i. 22). The word also fits our
author's conception of the church as the household of God. This
mutual love between Christians lay at the heart of Christian
ethics (Ro. xiii. 9). The recipients of this Epistle had shown
evidence of loving service in the past, and still continued to do
so in the present (vi. 10). Yet a hint has already been dropped
that encouragement is needed to persevere (x. 25). The need
for such love to continue is again stressed here.

One particular aspect of mutual love among Christians was
the practice of hospitality (cf. Ro. xii. 13). In the ancient world

[1] Cf. D. Jones, 'Authorship of Hebrews xiii', *Expository Times*, xlvi
(1935), 562-567.

the duty of offering hospitality to strangers had the force of binding obligation. In the case of Christians who were probably poor and possibly under suspicion, hospitality fulfilled a special need. Once again there is a suggestion that the recipients of the Epistle needed encouragement. **Do not forget hospitality, 2 for through it some have entertained angels unawares.** People who had come to the aid of those in need will find on Judgement Day that they have, without realising it, served the Son of Man (Matt. xxv. 31-46). Our author, however, does not suggest to his readers that by practising hospitality they may be entertaining Christ himself. Possibly an allusion to this would have seemed like a reference to the pagan conception of God dwelling among men (cf. Acts xiv. 11 f.). In any case our author does not conceive of the risen Lord as dwelling with men (cf. Matt. xxviii. 20) but as seated in heaven until his final return to this world (Acts iii. 21). The possibility of entertaining angels unawares is not put forward as a reason for practising hospitality, but as a possible result. This actually happened to Abraham and Sarah (Gen. xviii), Lot (Gen. xix), Manoah (Judges xiii) and Tobit (Tobit v).

Remember those in prison, as though you were im- 3 prisoned with them; remember those who are suffering, for you too have bodies. The prisoners' lot could be relieved by visiting (Matt. xxv. 44), or by prayer (Col. iv. 3) or by gifts (2 Tim. i. 16). Such actions are the expression not merely of natural sympathy but also of brotherly love. Those who were free should realise that but for the grace of God they too might have been imprisoned. In the Christian family the fate of one is the concern of all (cf. 1 Cor. xii. 26). The literal translation of our text would be 'for you too are in the body'. This recalls similar Pauline usage (2 Cor. v. 6; xii. 2); but it would be wrong to see here a reference to common membership of the Body of Christ, since this does not form part of our author's ecclesiology.

The next injunction concerns sexual behaviour. **Let marri- 4 age be honoured in every way, and the bed kept undefiled, for God will judge fornicators and adulterers.** The Greek sentence has no verb. In view of the context, it is best to understand it in a jussive rather than a declaratory sense. It is also best to take ἐν πᾶσι as a neuter plural to mean **in every way** rather than 'by everyone'. Our author is not, of course, limiting the honour in which all should hold the married state; on the contrary, he is saying that it should be honoured under every circumstance, however adverse it may be. It is just possible that some kind of ascetic beliefs were current in the church to which he was writing (cf. 1 Cor. vii. 36-38; 1 Tim. iv. 3); but the context suggests not so much a warning against sexual abstention as the doom of those who practise sexual promiscuity. This in turn suggests that there were gentile Christians among the congregation to whom the Epistle was sent (cf. xii. 16). **The bed** is used here as a euphemism for sexual intercourse. By demanding that it be kept **undefiled** our author is referring in sacrificial terms to married chastity (cf. Eph. v. 26). Unlike Paul, he gives no positive reasons for the church's teaching on marriage (cf. 1 Cor. vi. 16; Eph. v. 25 f.), but the negative aspect is strongly stressed: **God will judge fornicators and adulterers.** Although the word translated **fornicators** can signify those who indulge in any kind of sexual immorality, there is probably here a condemnation of both pre-marital and extra-marital relationships. It was common in the primitive church to issue these dire warnings about the dreadful consequences of sexual immorality (cf. 1 Cor. vi. 9; Eph. v. 5).

5 The earlier injunctions were concerned with social virtues; now a more personal matter is broached which has none the less social consequences. **Let your life be free from the love of money, being content with what you have.** Paul, like our author, also connects warnings against greed with warnings against immorality (cf. 1 Cor. vi. 9 f.; Eph. v. 3). There are many condemnations of the love of money in the gospels (cf. Mark iv. 19), in the Acts (cf. Acts v. 1 ff.) and in the epistles (1 Cor. vi. 8; 1 Tim. vi. 10; James v. 1 ff.). In pagan as well as in Jewish circles it was a commonplace in the ancient world to extol an attitude of contentment with present possessions. With this teaching the primitive church concurred (cf. Matt. vi. 34; 2 Cor. ix. 8; 1 Tim. vi. 6). Christians were to be content with their present lot because of their certitude about God's presence among them. **For he has said, 'I will never leave nor forsake you'.** This is an adaptation of words found in Deut.

xxxi. 6 and Josh. i. 5. Philo had earlier cited these very words, like our author, in the belief that he too was quoting scripture (*de Conf. Ling.* 166). This suggests, if not the dependence of our author on Philo, at least a very close connection between them both.

The knowledge of God's help gives an assurance of personal security such that a person feels invincible against the attacks of his fellow-men. **Therefore we say with confidence, 'The 6 Lord is my helper, I will not be afraid; what can man do to me?'** These words are quoted almost exactly from Psalm cxviii. 6.

56. WARNING AGAINST FALSE TEACHING.
xiii. 7-16

(7) Remember your leaders; they spoke God's message to you. Consider the outcome of their lives and imitate their faith. (8) Jesus Christ is the same yesterday, today and for ever. (9) Do not be carried away by various kinds of strange teachings; for it is good for the soul to be strengthened by grace and not by prescribed foods; those who have lived by them have not been benefited. (10) We have an altar from which those who serve the Tent have no right to eat. (11) The bodies of the animals whose blood is brought into the sanctuary by the high priest as an offering for sin are burnt outside the camp. (12) Therefore Jesus also suffered outside the gate to consecrate the people by his own blood. (13) So then let us go out to him outside the camp bearing his reproach. (14) For we have here no lasting City, but we seek for one which is to come. (15) Through him therefore let us offer to God continually a sacrifice of praise, that is, the fruit of lips that confess his name. (16) Do not forget to do good and to share; these are the sacrifices with which God is pleased.

Our author is anxious to guard his readers against false teaching. He turns first to the example of Christian leaders.

7 **Remember your leaders: they spoke God's message to you.** The language here suggests a primitive form of church order in which the leaders of the community (cf. Acts xv. 25) were those who first told them about the good news of Christ. Such men are not called here by the more formal title of 'overseers' (cf. Acts xx. 28) or 'elders' (Acts xv. 6). One may perhaps imagine a community such as the church in Corinth, with originally Paul and Aquila as its leaders; and, after they had left, with Crispus and Titus Justus among the remaining principal men (cf. Acts xviii. 7). Our author bids his readers to **consider the outcome of their lives.** The Greek word ἔκβασις could signify here 'close' or 'conclusion' of life, but it does not have this meaning elsewhere in the New Testament (1 Cor. x. 13). Certainly these leaders must have been in trouble as a result of their Christian leadership; but it is not clear that they had died as martyrs. They are mentioned here because they are a source of inspiration. As Paul ordered the Corinthians to imitate him (1 Cor. iv. 16; xi. 1), so our writer orders his readers to **imitate their faith.**

Mention of the leaders of the community naturally leads to Jesus himself. Although the leaders may have left or passed 8 on, Jesus Christ remains for ever. **Jesus Christ is the same yesterday, today and for ever.** The terse aphoristic form of this saying (for which a verb has to be supplied) suggests a semi-credal liturgical formula (cf. Ro. x. 9; 1 Cor. xii. 3). The Greek words of the text might bear the meaning: 'Jesus is the same Christ'; but this rendering is improbable since there is no suggestion that anyone was preaching a different Christ (cf. Gal. i. 6). **Yesterday** does not refer specifically either to the Son's pre-existence or to the period of his incarnation. **Yesterday, today and for ever** is a graphic way of alluding to past, present and future in order to affirm the unchanging nature of Christ.

In contrast to the immutability of the Son is a new-fangled doctrine against which the recipients of the Epistle are now 9 warned. **Do not be carried away by various kinds of strange teachings.** These **teachings** are **strange** to our author, and it seems that he did not have first-hand knowledge of them. Because of the way in which he argues against them later in this passage, it would seem that he regards them as Jewish in origin. On the other hand his puzzlement is indicated by the phrase **strange teachings,** for Jewish teaching can hardly have been strange to him in view of the great knowledge of the old dispensation which he shows throughout the Epistle.

Our author explains the reasons for his warnings. **It is good for the soul to be strengthened by grace and not by prescribed foods. Grace** here is not a particular gift or means of grace, but, according to our author's customary usage, the gracious action of God upon the soul. βρώματα means simply **foods,** and **prescribed** is not in the Greek. It has had to be supplied in the English translation to make it clear that the author's contrast is not between grace and food as such, but between God's inward action upon the soul and strange teaching about external rites. Our author is not opposing ascetic teaching (cf. 1 Tim. iv. 3; Col. ii. 16, 21 f.), since his warning is not against abstention from food but against the idea that the soul can be strengthened by foods. βρώματα, translated here **foods,** is never used in the LXX of Jewish sacrifices except to distinguish pure from impure food (Lev. xi. 43). It is not easy to see what Jewish sacrificial food the recipients of the Epistle could have been consuming: for our author is dealing with a specific danger, so that he must have had some food particularly in mind. Yet sacrificial offerings could only have been consumed within the Temple precincts (or, in the case of the paschal lamb, within the confines of Jerusalem). There can hardly be a reference here to the fellowship meals (σύνδειπνα) of the Jewish Diaspora (Josephus, *Antiq.* 14.10.8). As for Jewish food laws (as distinct from sacrificial foods) no one thought that 'kosher' food strengthened the soul. Their fear was rather lest 'non-kosher' food should bring about spiritual weakness (cf. Ro. xiv. 20 ff.).

It seems probable that, while our author thought that the trouble was concerned with Jewish rites, in fact the question at issue concerned pagan sacrifices. βρῶμα was used by Paul to refer to pagan offerings in his letter to the Corinthians. Writing about meat offered to idols, he reached a conclusion strikingly similar to that of our author: 'Certainly food (βρῶμα) will not bring us into God's presence' (1 Cor. viii. 8). The recipients of our

Epistle seem to have been tempted to partake in pagan rites. Paul, in his same letter to the Corinthians, had to give a severe warning about this very matter (1 Cor. x. 20). Paul proved his point about pagan rites by reference to Jewish sacrifice (1 Cor. x. 18). Our author not merely makes his point by reference to the Jewish cultus, but he seems also to have assumed that the rites themselves were Jewish (cf. ix. 10).

This seems to be confirmed by the following clause. By writing **those who have lived by them have not been benefited** our author is probably referring to Jews who had kept the sacrificial cultus. No doubt many Jews in the Diaspora would have echoed these sentiments (cf. Sibylline Oracles, iv. 27 f.). Our author, however, has a specifically Christian reason why 10 Christians should have nothing to do with sacrificial food. **We have an altar from which those who serve the Tent have no right to eat.** The levitical priesthood served the Tent (no doubt there is irony in describing them as serving the Tent and not serving God in the Tent), but the meaning of the phrase should probably be extended to include here all those who worshipped under the old covenant.

The priests were enjoined to share in the food of all sacrificial victims (cf. Lev. vi. 26; x. 14 f.; Nu. xviii. 9 ff., etc.). Paul actually describes this as sharing in the **altar** (1 Cor. ix. 13, x. 18). But the one sacrifice which could not be shared was the sin-offering of which the blood was brought into the Tent of Meeting; and this of course included the sin-offering of the Day of Atonement. These particular sacrificial offerings were to be burnt with fire, and no one was to eat any part of them (Lev. vi. 30).

Already Jesus has been shown to be the fulfilment of all that the sin-offering of the Day of Atonement stood for (cf. ix. 11-14). It therefore follows that the levitical priesthood has no right to share in his body. To share in this sacrifice is the privilege not of Jews but of Christians. Thus when our writer proudly writes: **We have an altar,** he is referring not to the altar itself but to the victim upon it. No allegorical interpretation of this altar is intended (contrast Philo, *Leg. All.* 1. 50). Calvary is meant, not some heavenly altar of the true sanctuary. For in our author's view the heavenly sanctuary does not have sacrificial furniture and furnishings: it is a symbol for heaven itself (cf. ix. 24). It may be noted that previously the argument had been concerned with the disannulling of the levitical priesthood (vii. 18) because Jesus' high priesthood had made it irrelevant (cf. vii. 27 ff.). Now, however, Jesus is not considered as high priest but as victim (cf. x. 9).

The reference to the holocaust of the sin-offering is explained in phrases taken from Lev. xvi. 27: **The bodies of the animals** 11 **whose blood is brought into the sanctuary by the high priest as an offering for sin are burnt outside the camp.** This scriptural rubric is fulfilled in the sacrifice of Jesus. **There-** 12 **fore Jesus also suffered outside the gate to consecrate the people by his own blood.** Jesus' death has previously been described in terms of consecration (x. 10) for the people of God (ii. 17). The word **suffered** (instead of a simple reference to Jesus' death) is characteristic of our author's emphasis on the humanity of Jesus (cf. ii. 9 ff.). Criminals were customarily put to death outside the city gate in order to avoid the ritual pollution of the city. Jesus' crucifixion was no exception (John xix. 20). Although our author is not the only New Testament writer to see significance in its location (cf. Matt. xxi. 39), he is the only one to see the place of Jesus' death as a fulfilment of the law concerning the sin-offering.

The argument here seems to have become slightly confused. Our author has set out to show that Christians do not need extraneous sacrificial food, since they share in the spiritual benefits of the sacrifice of Christ, and in these benefits the Jewish priesthood have no share at all. But he has already shown earlier that the levitical priesthood has nothing whatsoever to do with the sacrifice of the new covenant. The disannulling of their rights has stemmed primarily from the nature of the new covenant, not from the form of its sacrifice. Our author, strictly speaking, had no need to adduce the law of the sin-offering to show that the spiritual benefits of Jesus' sacrifice rendered otiose any other sacrificial rites.

A practical lesson is now drawn from the location of Jesus' death. It is a lesson which does not seem to be connected with the strange teachings concerning sacrificial foods which formed the point of departure for this whole passage. It concerns rather

the relations of Christians with Judaism in general. No doubt the particular case has led to the general question of the relation-
13 ship of Christianity to Judaism. **So then let us go out to him outside the camp bearing his reproach.** Whoever lets go the goat for the scapegoat on the Day of Atonement shall 'bathe his flesh in water and afterwards come into the camp' (Lev. xvi. 26); but Christians are to remain 'outside the camp' in the unclean world. The actual reproach of Jesus himself is not placed upon Christians, but theirs will be the same kind of reproach as his (cf. xi. 26; Psalm lxix. 9). They may even, like Jesus carrying his Cross, literally have to bear its weight.

Christians are here exhorted to cut themselves off from Judaism. Where Jesus died, there they should be. Although they have been redeemed by Jesus from the curse of the law, they should take their stand at the very place where he became a curse for them (cf. Gal. iii. 10). In thus cutting themselves off from Jewry, they will **go out** into the unknown, as Abraham went out to his unknown inheritance (xi. 8) and as Moses went out into the unknown wilderness (cf. iii. 16). To **go outside the camp** is to witness to the transitoriness and impermanence
14 of this world. **For here we have no lasting City but we seek for one which is to come** (cf. xi. 10; xii. 22). This does not mean that the Christian altar situated 'outside the camp' is to be identified with the **City which is to come.** On the contrary, the thought of Jesus' death outside the earthly city of Jerusalem has put our author in mind of our journey to the eternal City of the heavenly Jerusalem. He is not thinking here of the fall of the earthly Jerusalem, either in prospect or in retrospect. This simply does not enter into his argument at all.

A further lesson is drawn from the thought of Jesus as a sin-offering. His sacrifice was final and complete. Although Christians must bear his reproach, they cannot repeat his sacrifice. Indeed there is no further sacrifice for sin, since Jesus has him-
15 self effected this (cf. x. 18). **Through him therefore let us offer to God continually a sacrifice of praise, that is, the fruit of lips that confess his name.** The law of Moses prescribes the sacrifice of thanksgiving (Lev. vii. 12); but this is a repeatable sacrifice which has been abolished by the new covenant (cf. vii. 27). The sacrifice of Christians must be one

that can be made **continually**. It must be made **through him,**
that is, offered in response to and made possible by the sacrifice
of Jesus. It follows then that the only sacrifice that Christians
must offer is a spiritual sacrifice (cf. 1 Peter ii. 5). Philo too had
taught that a thank-offering must be an inward sacrifice (*de
Plant.* 126). Our author spiritualises the 'sacrifice of thanksgiving' by means of the LXX mistranslation of Hos. xiv. 3,
according to which **the fruit of lips** is to be offered to God
(cf. Psalm l. 14, 23). (This is a mistranslation because the best
Hebrew text here has 'the fruit of bullocks'. The phrase **that
confess his name** is an addition with biblical overtones (cf.
Psalm liv. 8). Our author's use of scriptural texts here is open to
question; and it is strange that he has ignored the one kind of
spiritual sacrifice that is mentioned in the scriptures, the sacrifice of a broken spirit (Psalm li. 17).

Our author explains that, although a spiritual explanation
of the sacrifice of thanksgiving has been given, it has very
practical implications which are in danger of being overlooked
(cf. xiii. 2). **Do not forget to do good and to share: these** 16
are the sacrifices with which God is pleased. Gratitude
to God will involve beneficence to others. Since Christians
share together in the benefits of Christ's sacrifice, they must
show their gratitude by sharing with others what God has
given to them. The noun κοινωνία, translated here **share,** is
employed in the New Testament for Christians' common par-
ticipation in the Holy Spirit, and hence it became used for
contributions which gave practical expression to this spiritual
fellowship (Ro. xv. 26; 2 Cor. viii. 4; ix. 13; cf. Acts ii. 44 f.).

Having begun by condemning strange teachings about food,
our author ends by giving a spiritual interpretation of the
sacrifice that Christians themselves are bound to offer. It is very
tempting indeed to see this whole passage as a condemnation of
new eucharistic doctrine which has been introduced into the
church to which this Epistle is addressed. It is conceivable that
this church had a rite of breaking the bread in Christ's name,
but that no sacrificial meaning had as yet been given to it. Our
author might have opposed the introduction of a doctrine of the
eucharistic sacrifice on the grounds that it detracted from the
spiritual nature of the new covenant and because it obscured

the inward action of God through Christ upon the human soul. Christians cannot be thought to partake of the sacrifice of the altar, because Jesus offered himself as a sin-offering and no one can share in the body of such a sacrificial victim. Christians must share in Jesus' reproach, not in his body. It is not by consecrated food but by the benefits of Christ's sacrifice that Christians can reach their heavenly destination. The only sacrifice which Christians can offer is not the offering of the gifts at the Eucharist, but a spiritual sacrifice of praise that finds expression in good works and the common life of the community.

This explanation, although very tempting, must be rejected. It could hardly be said of a new Christian doctrine that those who have lived by it have not been profited; for if it were new, how could our author have known that it had proved unprofitable? The transference from the first person plural **we have an altar** to the third person plural **those who serve the Tent** in *v.* 10 suggests two different sets of people, Christians and Jews. It seems improbable that our author would have dismissed something as important as new eucharistic doctrine in two or three sentences at the end of his Epistle.

On the other hand, if the passage is not anti-eucharistic, neither is it pro-eucharistic. Our author is simply not thinking of the Eucharist at all (cf. comment on vii. 3). He does not state that it is contrary to the spiritual sacrifice of Christians; nor does he state whether Christians can or cannot partake of the perfect sin-offering. He simply contents himself with saying that Jews cannot partake of it. It is later associations, not the words of the text itself, which have led commentators to see in this passage a reference to the Eucharist.

57. RESPECT FOR AUTHORITY. xiii. 17-19

(17) Be obedient to your leaders and submit to them; for they are vigilant on your behalf, as men who will render an account. Let them do this with joy and not with grief; for that would not be profitable for you. (18) Continue to

**pray for us; for we are sure that we have a clear con-
science, since we want to behave rightly in all circumstances. (19) I entreat you the more earnestly to do this,
that I may be restored to you the sooner.**

The readers have already been exhorted to imitate the faith
of their leaders (xiii. 7): now they are ordered to **be obedient** 17
to them. They are not merely to carry out their commands, but
also to **submit to them** as persons. This is no exhortation to
blind obedience; for the leaders are conscientious and trustworthy. Like soldiers on guard all night, or rather, like shepherds who never cease their care for their flocks, **they are
vigilant on your behalf.** ('They are vigilant for your souls'
would be a literal but incorrect rendering here.) This vigilance
is grounded in the realisation that they are **men who will
render an account,** like the steward in the gospel parable
(Matt. xxv. 19). Although our author has impressed on his
readers the lay ministry of Christian oversight (cf. xii. 15), yet
he apportions special responsibilities to the community's
leaders. **Let them do this with joy and not with grief,** he
urges. This grief would not be due to their own shortcomings,
but to the disobedience of their charges. With a touch of irony
our author understates the consequences of such disobedience:
that would not be profitable for you. He thus continues the
metaphor of a profit and loss account which he has introduced
earlier in the verse.

The next command concerns the author himself. **Continue** 18
to pray for us. Like Paul, he asks for the prayers of his readers
(cf. Col. iv. 3; 1 Thess. v. 25). There is a suggestion that our
author's intentions may have been misunderstood, or at least
open to misunderstanding, for he adds to his request a personal
assurance about himself: **we are sure that we have a clear
conscience, since we wish to behave rightly in all circumstances.** Possibly our author fears that he may be reproached
for his advocacy of a break with Judaism (in which case **in all
circumstances** should be rendered 'to all men'). But more
probably there is a reference here to his future plans. Paul,
writing to the Corinthians, also asked for the prayers of his
readers and protested that he had a clear conscience (2 Cor. i.

11 f.; cf. 1 Cor. iv. 1-5); for he had been hoping to visit the
church at Corinth, and was concerned to show that his change
of plans did not imply a change of heart. Probably our author
19 had the same concern, for he adds: **I entreat you the more
earnestly to do this, that I may be restored to you the
sooner.** The Greek word ἀποκατασταθῶ, translated here
restored, could refer to recovery from sickness or to release
from prison; but in the context it seems to refer to a return visit
by our author to his readers. The language implies that he was
no stranger to them. The meaning of the Greek could be that
our author hopes that he may visit them soon as a result of his
readers' prayers; but more probably the meaning is that he hopes
in any case to come soon, and he expects their prayers to speed
his coming.

58. CONCLUDING PRAYER. xiii. 20-21

**(20) May the God of peace, who brought up from the dead
the great Shepherd of the sheep, our Lord Jesus, with the
blood of the eternal covenant, (21) equip you with all that
is good to do his will. May he do in us through Jesus Christ
what is pleasing to him, to whom be glory for ever and
ever. Amen.**

The closing verses of this Epistle follow normal usage, with
a prayer, a word of encouragement and an exchange of greetings.
Correspondences here with the Pauline corpus are due to
natural similarities of form and subject-matter rather than to
literary dependence.

After asking his readers to pray for him, our author next
prays for them. A closing prayer and doxology are found at the
conclusion of other New Testament epistles (1 Peter v. 11; cf.
1 Thess. v. 23). The particular prayer here is in the classic
structure of a collect, and it has a marked liturgical character.
Our author may have been using a prayer current in his church,
or he may himself have originally composed the prayer for
liturgical use. The fact that the prayer and doxology have points

of contrast with the rest of chapter xiii does not mean that they did not originally form part of the same chapter. There are no good grounds for attributing any part of the letter to anyone but the author of the whole Epistle.

The God of peace is a phrase commonly used by Paul at the **20** conclusion of his letters, and it is particularly apt here, in view of the dissensions and dangers of apostasy among the readers of the Epistle. Jesus is seen here as the greater Moses; for the phrase **who brought up from the dead the great Shepherd of the sheep** is modelled on the words of Is. lxiii. 11 (LXX): 'Where is he that brought up from the sea the shepherd of the sheep?', where the shepherd designates Moses. This is the only reference to the resurrection in the whole Epistle, a fact which suggests that our author may not have been the original author of this prayer. **Our Lord Jesus** is not the commonest way of referring to Christ, but it is a phrase found elsewhere in the New Testament (cf. 2 Cor. viii. 9). He has been raised **with the blood of the eternal covenant.** This phrase is based on Zech. ix. 11. 'The raising of Jesus was indissolubly united with the establishment of the Covenant made by his blood and effective in virtue of it' (Westcott). The new **covenant** is superior to Moses' in as much as it is **eternal** (Jer. xxxii. 40).

The description of Jesus as a shepherd is found elsewhere in the New Testament. It is derived from the Old Testament, where shepherd was a symbol for the national ruler (Ez. xxxiv. 2). It was also used of the coming Messiah (Ez. xxxiv. 23 f.). As has been noted above, Isaiah spoke of Moses as a shepherd. Jesus is a **great shepherd** in the same way as he is a great priest (cf. x. 21); that is, he is superior to all other shepherds including Moses. Jesus is reported to have applied the title of shepherd to himself (Mark xiv. 27; cf. Mark vi. 34), and according to the Fourth Evangelist he described himself as 'the good shepherd' (John x. 14). According to the author of 1 Peter, he is not merely a shepherd (1 Peter ii. 25), but also the chief shepherd (1 Peter v. 4).

Our author prays that God, who has established the new covenant, **may equip you with all that is good to do his 21 will.** The Greek verb καταρτίσαι, translated **equip,** can mean to perfect, to make good or to amend. There is a flavour of

all these meanings here. Our author here prays not merely for
a right intention on the part of his readers, but also for right
action. Throughout this Epistle there is a severely practical note.
God's grace is implored so that God's will may be done. Our
right action is dependent on the prevenient grace of God. **May
he do in us through Jesus Christ what is pleasing to him.**
God's grace must go before and follow us if we are to be continually given to all good works. In the Greek the juxtaposition
of the two words ποιῆσαι and ποιῶν nicely brings out God's
action in our souls leading to our action in his name.

There follows a doxology: **to whom be glory for ever and
ever. Amen.** The structure of the Greek permits this doxology
to be ascribed to Christ (cf. 2 Tim. iv. 18; 2 Peter iii. 18; Rev.
i. 6), but more probably it is addressed to **the God of peace,**
who is the subject of the whole prayer. It is more in keeping
with the thought of this Epistle and the usage of the primitive
church to take it in this latter sense (cf. 1 Peter iv. 11).

59. FINAL GREETINGS. xiii. 22-25

**(22) I entreat you, brothers, to bear patiently with this
word of exhortation; in fact I have written briefly to you.
(23) I want you to know that our brother Timothy has been
released; if he comes soon enough, I will see you with
him. (24) Greet all your leaders and all God's people.
Those who are from Italy greet you. (25) Grace be with
you all.**

Our author senses that his Epistle may not be warmly
22 welcomed. He tries to allay criticism before it can be voiced. **I
entreat you, brothers, to bear patiently with this word
of exhortation.** It is not the letter's contents but its length
about which he feels some anxiety. **In fact I have written
briefly to you,** he explains, and he is not the only New Testament writer to proffer this explanation (cf. 1 Peter v. 12). The
matters of which he has treated have been very considerable,
and they have been hard to explain (cf. v. 11). The concentrated

style and the compressed contents of the letter may have made
it seem lengthy; but in fact it could all be read aloud in an hour.
A piece of news is now added: and it may be put at the end of
the letter because our author has only recently known of it. **I 23
want you to know that our brother Timothy has been
released.** Only one Timothy is known in the New Testament;
and there is no reason to believe that a different Timothy is
meant here. Paul took Timothy as his companion when he passed
through Lystra on his second missionary journey (Acts xvi. 1-3).
Timothy crossed into Asia and into Macedonia with Paul and
later joined him in Corinth (Acts xviii. 5). With Paul he was
joint-author of 2 Corinthians, the Epistles to the Colossians and
to the Philippians, and 1 and 2 Thessalonians. When Paul was
living in Ephesus Timothy was with him, and Paul dispatched
him to the Corinthians as his deputy (1 Cor. iv. 17; xvi. 10),
before he wrote 1 Corinthians. The word ἀπολελυμένον, translated **released,** means 'set free'. Timothy may have discharged
some obligation, or been set free from some accusation, or even
started on a journey. The circumstances are unknown; but it
seems most probable from the context that Timothy had been
released from imprisonment. He seems to have been known to
the readers of the Epistle as well as to its author. The reasons
for Timothy's detention seem different from those which had
delayed the journey of our author. **If he comes soon enough,
I will see you with him.** This may mean that Timothy is
expected to make his way direct to the recipients of this letter,
and that, if he arrives in time, our author will see him there;
but more probably it means that, if Timothy reaches our author
in time, they will make their journey together.[1]

The final greetings follow. **Greet all your leaders and all 24
God's people.** This does not mean that the Epistle has been
sent only to one section of the congregation. On the contrary, it
suggests that there is already incipient party strife within the
church. Already its members have been told to obey their
leaders: now they are charged not to adhere only to some of
their leaders or of the congregation, but to greet them all.

[1] Professor Lo Bue (*op. cit.* p. 56) makes the attractive suggestion that the
passage could be rendered: 'You know about our brother Timothy, who has
been despatched. If he comes soon, he and I will see you together.' This
would certainly fit well into our historical reconstruction.

A further greeting is added. **Those who are from Italy greet you.** This might imply that the letter has been written from Italy, and that the author has included the greetings of Italians. Alternatively it might mean that the letter has been written to a church situated in Italy, and that some Italians, who were living abroad in the same place as our author, had asked that their greetings be included. There is, however, a third possibility. It might be that a group of Italians was known both to the recipients of the letter and to our author. For example, Aquila and Prisca were Jews who had left Rome when Jews were banished by Claudius (Acts xviii. 2). They had gone to Corinth and, having become Christians, later went with Paul to Ephesus (Acts xviii. 19). From Ephesus they sent special greetings via Paul to the church at Corinth (1 Cor. xvi. 19). They are mentioned in 2 Tim. iv. 19. They are the only people in the New Testament described as **from Italy** (Acts xviii. 2). If this Epistle was written from Ephesus to Corinth, then **those who are from Italy** could be identified with Aquila and Prisca and the church in their house.

New Testament epistles conventionally end with an invocation for grace to be given to the readers. Usually Paul prays for the grace of Christ. Our author, however, understands by **grace**
25 the gracious action of God himself. **Grace be with you all** is also found in Titus iii. 15. The addition of Amen, found in A D *pl* lat sy, is a liturgical gloss.

INDEX OF BIBLICAL REFERENCES

OLD TESTAMENT

INDEX OF BIBLICAL REFERENCES

APOCRYPHA

INDEX OF BIBLICAL REFERENCES

NEW TESTAMENT

INDEX OF BIBLICAL REFERENCES

INDEX OF BIBLICAL REFERENCES

INDEX OF NON-BIBLICAL REFERENCES

INDEX OF AUTHORS

INDEX OF GREEK WORDS AND PHRASES DISCUSSED